York County Virginia

LAND RECORDS

1713–1729

Abstracted and Edited by
Mary Marshall Brewer

HERITAGE BOOKS
2019

HERITAGE BOOKS

AN IMPRINT OF HERITAGE BOOKS, INC.

Books, CDs, and more—Worldwide

For our listing of thousands of titles see our website
at
www.HeritageBooks.com

Published 2019 by
HERITAGE BOOKS, INC.
Publishing Division
5810 Ruatan Street
Berwyn Heights, Md. 20740

International Standard Book Number
Paperbound: 978-1-68034-950-4

CONTENTS

INTRODUCTION

This book contains abstracts of deeds and bonds, Liber 3, covering the period, 1713-1729.

The original page number is given at the end of major entry.

Punctuation has been added in numerous instances for clarity.

Earlier works

Between 1938 and 1949 Beverley Fleet created 34 volumes of Virginia Colonial Abstracts covering the earliest vital records of birth, marriage and death; tax lists; court orders; militia lists; wills; and deeds. These volumes were merged into three volumes by and published by Genealogical Publishing Co., Baltimore. Volume three has records of York, Charles City, Henrico, Lower Norfolk and Washington counties.

Abstracts by Benjamin B. Weisiger III have been published by New Papyrus Publishing Co., Inc., Athens Georgia. These include York County Virginia Records 1665-1672; York County Virginia Records 1672-1676, and York County Virginia Records, 1672-1676.

John Frederick Dorman has abstracted and published 7 volumes of York County Deeds, Orders, Wills, for the period 1687-1697.

Work is proceeding to complete the abstraction of York County Deeds, Wills, Court Orders, etc. up to 1783 and Land Records (deeds, bonds, etc.) to 1777.

F. Edward Wright
Lewes, Delaware
2006

ABBREVIATIONS and TERMS

Some of the abbreviations are those made by the original clerk and others are by the abstractor.

adj. - adjoining
afsd - aforesaid
agt - against
atty - attorney
co. - county
complt(s) - complaintant(s)
dau. - daughter
decd - deceased
def - defendant
DShf. - Deputy Sheriff
entrd - entered
esqr - esquire
in account with - estate was administered by
gent. - gentleman
pd - pounds
pg - page
plt(s) - plaintiff(s)
pn - pennies
pt/o - part of
Quarter - usually a slave quarter at a different location than the home
    plantation
Returned - submitted to the authority (York Co. Court)
sl - shillings
wit - witness or witnesses

YORK COUNTY, VIRGINIA
DEEDS AND BONDS
No. 3
1713-1729

15 May 1713. Deed of Lease. John Clayton & Wil Robertson feofees or
trustees for the land appropriated for the building & erecting the City of
Williamsburgh for five shillings farm letten to Francis Sharpe of York Co two
lotts of ground lying on the n side of Duke of Gloucester's Street in the City of
Williamsburgh designed in the plot of the sd city by the figures 57 & 58 ... .
Wit: Michl Archer, C. Jackson. Ackn 15 Jun 1713 by Jno Clayton gent & ackn
21 Sep 1713 by Wm Robertson gent & admitted to record. Attest: Phi Lightfoot
clerk. (Pg 1)

16 May 1713. Deed of Release. John Clayton & Wil Robertson feofees or
trustees for the land appropriated for the building & erecting the City of
Williamsburgh for 30 shillings released to Francis Sharpe of York Co two lotts
number 57 & 58 in the City of Williamsburgh ... [same as above] ... if the sd
Francis Sharpe shall not within 24 months begin to build & finish upon each lott
of the sd granted premises one good dwelling house then it shall & may be
lawfull to & for the sd feofees or trustees to enter & the same to have again as of
their former estate ... . Ackn 15 Jun 1713 by Jno Clayton gent & ackn 21 Sep
1713 by Wm Robertson gent & admitted to record. Attest: Phi Lightfoot clerk.
(Pg 1)

21 Sep 1713. Deed. Edward Athy of James City Co for £45 sold to Jno
Doswell Junr of Charles Parish, York Co a tr of land in Charles Parish granted
by patent to be 73 a. of land adj Jno Tomer, Capt Chisman, the Mill Path, Jno
Doswell the elder, Jno Clark & York Road, all which granted premises were by
patent dated 6 Jun 1699 taken up by the sd Jno Doswell the elder & Robert
Sheild & afterwards that part thereof belonging to the sd Robt Sheild was sold
by the sd Shield to the sd Doswell the elder & since that sd whole tr was purch
by the afsd Edwd Athy of the sd Jno Doswell the elder ... . Wit: Wm
Armistead, John Moss, Wm Gordon. Ackn 21 Sep 1713 & admitted to record.
Attest: Phi Lightfoot clerk. (Pg 3)

21 Sep 1713. Bond. I Edwd Athy of James City Parish am firmly bound unto
Jno Doswell the younger of Charles Parish, York Co planter for £90 ... the
condition of this obligation is such that whereas the afsd Edwd Athy for £45
hath sold unto the sd Jno Doswell the younger all his 73 a. tr of land [see above]
... whereas the sd Edwd Athy liveth at a great distance from York Co Court
House & Mary the w/o the sd Edwd Athy cannot come down to the sd court to
ackn her consent to the sale of the sd lands & to give up her right of dower in the

same although thereunto freely willing, if therefore the afsd Edwd Athy do & shall well & truly warrant & forever defend the sd tr of land & shall obey, abide, observe, perform, fullfill & keep all the covenants, contracts, articles & agreements mentioned in the indentures then this obligation to be void ... . Wit: Wm Armistead, John Moss, Wm Gordon. Ackn 20 Sep 1713 & admitted to record. Attest: Phi Lightfoot clerk. (Pg 4)

16 May 1713. Deed. Richard Page of Bruton Parish, York Co carpenter for £7 sold to Claude Rouviere & Eliza Chermeson executors of the will of Joseph Chermeson decd & late of parish afsd for the use & benefit of the heirs of the sd Chermeson all that parcel of land which the sd Richard formerly sold to the sd Joseph Chermeson decd but never sealed or executed any conveyance for the same in the lifetime of the sd Joseph, therefore the sd Richard for the consideration afsd doth sell unto the executors for the sole use & behoof of the children & heirs of the sd Chermeson a 25 a. parcel of land lying near & contiguous to the land which the sd Chermeson dwelled on at & before the time of his death, some part thereof lying in York Co & part thereof in James City Co bounded by the road which divides the cos of York & James City & is pt/o the lands formerly of Richard Page father of the sd Richard & fell & became due to the sd Richard as son & heir at law to the sd Richard the father & is bounded by land late of the sd Chermeson, the Broad Road into James City Co, James Browne, line formerly of the sd Richard Page, land formerly of Richd Jones & Jno Tayler ... . Wit: Rebecca Curtis, Eliza Scrimshaw, Hen Holdcraft.8 May 1713 livery & seisen of the sd lands & premises was made & delivered by the sd Richd Page to the sd executors in the presence of Henry Holdcraft & Richd Bloxom & is ackn by me Richard Page. Ackn 16 Nov 1713 & admitted to record. Attest: Phi Lightfoot clerk. (Pg 5)

18 Dec 1713. Deed of Lease. Francis Tyler of James City Parish & Co, VA gent for 5 shillings farm letten unto William Davis of Bruton Parish, York Co a 38 a. tr of land in Bruton Parish bounded by Capt James Archer, Ralph Graves & Major Jno Custis ... for the term of one year ... . Wit: James Hubard, Robt Hyde, Hen Holdcraft. Ackn 21 Dec 1713 & admitted to record. Attest: Phi Lightfoot clerk. (Pg 6)

19 Dec 1713. Deed. Francis Tyler of James City Co, VA gent for £30 released to William Davis of Bruton Parish, York Co husbandman a 38 a. tr of land ... [*same as above*] ... . Wit: James Hubard, Robt Hyde, Hen Holdcraft. Ackn 21 Dec 1713 by Fran Tyler & on 15 Feb 1713 Philip Lightfoot by vertue of a power of atty from Rebecca Tyler relinquished her right of dower & admitted to record. Attest: Phi Lightfoot clerk. (Pg 7)

19 Dec 1713. Bond. I Francis Tyler of James City Parish & Co am firmly bound unto Wm Davis of Bruton Parish, York Co husbandman for £60 ... the condition of this obligation is such that if the afsd Francis Tyler do well & truly perform, obey, fullfill & keep all the articles, clauses, covenants, grants & agreements mentioned in one indenture of release [*see above*] then this obligation to be void ... . Wit: James Hubard, Robt Hyde, Hen Holdcraft. Ackn 21 Dec 1713 & admitted to record. Attest: Phi Lightfoot clerk. (Pg 9)

15 Jan 1713. Deed of Lease. Jno Adduston Rogers of Charles Parish, York Co planter for 5 shillings farm lett unto Nicholas Phillips of York Hampton Parish, York Co merchant a 270 a. tr of land in Charles Parish which sd land was the land late of Henry Andrews from whom the sd land was found to escheat & by patent granted to the sd Jno Adduston Rogers by the Honble Alexander Spotswood her Majestys Lt Governour dated 17 Dec 1710 being bounded by Bennets Cr, Kerby's line, Callowhill's line & Rogers Dwelling house, including 200 a. the residue being bounded by the brs of Bennetts Cr, as by the plot thereof taken & surveyed by Major Wm Buckner 10 Apr 1710 ... for the term of one year ... . Wit: Jno Chisman, Benjamin Moss. Ackn 18 Jan 1713 & admitted to record. Attest: Phi Lightfoot clerk. (Pg 9)

16 Jan 1713. Deed of Release. John Adduston Rogers of Charles Parish, York Co planter for £150 released to Nicholas Phillips of York Hampton Parish, York Co a 270 a. tr of land ... [*same as above*] ... . Wit: Jno Chisman, Benjamin Moss. Ackn 18 Jan 1713 & admitted to record. Attest: Phi Lightfoot clerk. (Pg 10)

14 Jan 1713. Deed of Lease. John Martin of York Hampton Parish, York Co marriner for 5 shillings farm letten to Cole Digges of same place merchant all his lott or ½ a. of land in York Town containing 10 poles in length & 8 in breadth, being pt/o the Portland bounded by land lately purch by the Churchwardens of David Condon, opposite to the land of Charles Cox, the Main Street & land of Edward Powers, which lott is distinguished by the number 42 together with his warehouse under the bank called Martins Store, the sd lott was purch by Tho Pate of the trustees for the Portland in York Co by deed dated 11 Aug 1699 & by the sd Tho Pate & Eliza his wife by deed dated 4 Apr 1703 conveyed to Joan Lawson who sold the same land to the sd Jno Martin by deed dated 17 Sep 1705 ... for the term of one year ... . Wit: None. Ackn 18 Jan 1713 by John Martin & on the mocon of Jno Clayton the sd Digges's atty is admitted to record. Attest: Phi Lightfoot clerk. (Pg 12)

15 Jan 1713. Deed of Release. John Martin of York Hampton Parish, York Co marriner for £90 released to Cole Digges of same place merchant a lott in York Town number 42 ... [*same as above*] ... . Wit: None. Ackn 18 Jan 1713 by

4

John Martin & on the mocon of Jno Clayton the sd Digges's atty is admitted to record. Attest: Phi Lightfoot clerk. (Pg 13)

15 Jan 1713. Bond. I John Martin of York Hampton Parish, York Co marriner am firmly bound unto Cole Digges of same place merchant for £180 ... the condition of this obligation is such that if the afsd Jno Martin shall well & truly observe, perform, fullfill, accomplish & keep all the covenants, grants, articles, clauses, conditions & agreements mentioned in a pair of indentures of lease & release [*see above*] then this obligation to be void ... . Wit: None. Ackn 18 Jan 1713 by Jno Martin & on the mocon of Jno Clayton the sd Digges's atty is admitted to record. Attest: Phi Lightfoot clerk. (Pg 14)

14 May 1714. Deed of Lease. Jno Robinson of Charles Parish, York Co gent & Frances his wife for 5 shillings leased to Edmund Curtis of same place gent all the third pt/o of a plantation & tr of land called Jumps in Charles Parish containing 41 a. now or late in the occupation of the sd Edmund Curtis abutting upon the river, Hickman's Cr & Robins Cr ... the land descended to Frances w/o the sd John Robinson by inheritance as one of the daus & coheirs of Armiger Wade late of the parish & co afsd decd ... for the term of one year ... . Wit: John Marshall, Jno Cooke, James Shelton. Ackn 17 May 1714 & admitted to record. Attest: Phi Lightfoot clerk. (Pg 15)

15 May 1713. Deed of Release. Jno Robinson of Charles Parish, York Co gent & Frances his wife for £27 released to Edmund Curtis of same place gent a 41 a. tr of land ... [*same as above*] ... . Wit: Jno Marshall, Jno Cook, James Shelton. Ackn 17 May 1714 by Jno Robinson also appeared Frances w/o the sd Jno who being first privately examined relinquished her right of dower & admitted to record. Attest: Phi Lightfoot clerk. (Pg 15)

15 --- 1714. Bond. I John Robinson of Charles Parish, York Co am firmly bound unto Edmund Curtis of same place for £56 ... the condition of this obligation is such that if the afsd Jno Robinson shall well & truly observe, perform, fullfill & keep the covenants, articles, contracts, clauses & agreements mentioned in indentures of grant, release & confirmation [*see above*] then this obligation to be void ... . Wit: Jno Marshall, Jno Cooke, James Shelton. Ackn 17 May 1714 & admitted to record. Attest: Phi Lightfoot clerk. (Pg 17)

2 Mar 1713. Deed of Lease. Jno Clayton & Wil Robertson feofees or trustees for the land appropriated for building & erecting the City of Williamsburgh for 5 shillings leased to Benjamin Harrison of Charles City Co gent a lott of ground in the sd City of Wmsburgh designed in the plot of the sd city by the figure 35 ... during the term of one year paying the yearly rent of one grain of Indian corn on

10 Oct if demanded ... . Wit: None. Ackn 21 Jun 1714 & admitted to record. Attest: Phi Lightfoot clerk. (Pg 17)

3 Mar 1713. Deed of Release. Jno Clayton & Wil Robertson feofees or trustees for the land appropriated for building & erecting the City of Williamsburgh for 15 shillings released to Benjamin Harrison of Charles City Co gent a lott of ground in the sd City of Wmsburgh designed in the plot of the sd city by the figure 35 ... if the sd Benjamin Harrison shall not within 24 months begin to build & finish upon each lott of the sd granted premises one good dwelling house then it shall & may be lawfull to & for the sd feofees or trustees to enter & the same to have again as of their former estate ... . Wit: None. Ackn 21 Jun 1714 & admitted to record. Attest: Phi Lightfoot clerk. (Pg 18)

27 May 1713. Deed. Jno Sarjanton of York Co chirurgeon & Winifred his wife for £25 sold to Danl Blewet of sd co peruke maker a lott of land now lying in the City of Wmsburgh in York Co as also the messuage or house now standing thereon now in the tenure & occupation of the sd Jno Sarjanton & Winifred his wife ... . Wit: Michl Archer, John Guy Rey, Jean Pasteur. Ackn 15 Jun 1713 by Jno Guy Rey by vertue of a power of atty from Jno Sarjanton & also Winifred the w/o the sd Jno Sarjanton relinquished her right of dower & admitted to record. Attest: Phi Lightfoot clerk. (Pg 18)

14 Jan 1713. Deed of Lease. Jno Clayton & Wil Robertson feofees or trustees for the land appropriated for building & erecting the City of Williamsburgh for 5 shillings farm letten unto John Anderson of co afsd gent a lott of ground in the City of Wmsburgh designed in the plot of the sd city by the figure 40 ... for one year paying the yearly rent of one grain of Indian corn on 10 Oct if demanded ... . Wit: None. Ackn 21 Jun 1714 & admitted to record. Attest: Phi Lightfoot clerk. (Pg 20)

15 Jan 1713. Deed of Release. Jno Clayton & Wil Robertson feofees or trustees for the land appropriated for building & erecting the City of Williamsburgh for 15 shillings released unto John Anderson of co afsd gent a lott of ground in the City of Wmsburgh designed in the plot of the sd city by the figure 4 ... if the sd John Anderson shall not within 24 months begin to build & finish upon each lott of the sd granted premises one good dwelling house then it shall & may be lawfull to & for the sd feofees or trustees to enter & the same to have again as of their former estate ... . Wit: None. Ackn 21 Jun 1714 & admitted to record. Attest: Phi Lightfoot clerk. (Pg 20)

19 Jun 1714. Deed. Jno Bates of Bruton Parish (alias Beverton), York Co for 4,600 lbs of sweet sented tobacco & cask sold to Alexander Gary of same place planter a 25 a. parcel of land upon the head of Skimino Mill Swamp adj Robert

Ivory, the sd land being now in possession of the sd Gary & is pt/o 111 a. sold to the sd Bates by Wm Jordan by deed dated 20 Jan 1705 ... . Wit: John Higgins, Bartho Farthing, Thomas Gary. Ackn 14 Jun ---- & admitted to record. Attest: Phi Lightfoot clerk. (Pg 21)

15 Jul 1714. Deed of Lease. John Coman son & heir at law of William Coman late of Bruton Parish, York Co decd for 5 shillings leased to Jacob Goddin of same place a plantation & 45 a. tr of land in the parish afsd being the tr of land which descended to him as being heir at law to his sd decd father Wm Coman bounded by Maiden Swamp & land of David Stoner, being pt/o a dividend of land formerly granted to Nicho Sebrell by patent dated 24 Feb 1663 & afterward by the will of the sd Nicho he devised the sd land between his two sons Nicho & Antho Sebrell, & by the sd Nicho & Antho by a joint consent was divided between them according to the sd will as per division under their hands & seals dated 24 Jun 1672, & this part hereby mentioned to be granted belonged to Antho Sebrell & was by him sold & conveyed to Saml Eburne clerk & by him sold to Jno Eaton cordwainer by deed dated 23 Jan 1695/6 & afterwards sold & conveyed by the sd Eaton to Wm Coman father of the sd Jno by deed of sale dated 14 Jul 1696 ... for the term of one year ... . Wit: Tho Brodhust, Wm Kerle, Henry Holdcraft. Ackn 19 Jul 1784 & admitted to record. Attest: Phi Lightfoot clerk. (Pg 21)

16 Jul 1714. Deed of Release. John Coman son & heir at law of William Coman late of Bruton Parish, York Co decd for £20 released to Jacob Goddin of same place a plantation & 45 a. tr of land in the parish afsd ... [*same as above*] ... . Wit: Thomas Brodhust, William Kerle, Henry Holdcraft. Ackn 19 Jul 1714 by Jno Coman & also appeared Jane w/o the sd Jno who being first privately examined relinquished her right of dower & admitted to record. Attest: Phi Lightfoot clerk. (Pg 23)

18 Jun 1714. Deed of Lease. John Wills of Mulberry Island Parish, Warwick Co & Elizabeth his wife for 5 shillings farm lett unto Jno Cook of York Hampton Parish, York Co their lott or ½ a. of land in York Town containing 10 poles in length & 8 poles in breadth being pt/o the Port Land bounding on Broad Street & abutting upon the land of Edward Powers & the Court House lotts & is known by the number 30 as also one storehouse or warehouse being in York Town upon the bank or shoar of York River & abutting upon the storehouse of Thomas Nelson & the storehouse of Cole Digges ... for the term of one year ... . Wit: Wm Sheldon, Michl Dewick. Ackn 19 Jul 1714 & admitted to record. Attest: Phi Lightfoot clerk. (Pg 24)

19 Jun 1714. Deed of Release. John Wills of Mulberry Island Parish, Warwick Co & Elizabeth his wife for £55 released to Jno Cook of York Hampton Parish,

York Co their lott or ½ a. of land in York Town number 30 ... [*same as above*] ... . Wit: Wm Sheldon, Michl Dewick. Ackn 19 Jul 1714 by John Wills & admitted to record. Attest: Phi Lightfoot clerk. (Pg 25)

19 Jun 1714. Bond. I John Wills of Mulberry Island Parish, Warwick Co am firmly bound unto Jno Cook of York Hampton Parish, York Co for £200 ... the condition of this obligation is such that if the afsd Jno Wills & Eliza his wife do well & truly obey, observe, perform, accomplish, fullfill & keep all the covenants, grants, articles & agreements mentioned in one indenture of grant & release [*see above*] then this obligation to be void ... . Wit: Wm Sheldon, Michl Dewick. Ackn 19 Jul 1714 by John Wills & admitted to record. Attest: Phi Lightfoot clerk. (Pg 26)

21 Sep 1713. Deed. Edward Athy of James City Co for £45 sold to Jno Doswell Junr of Charles Parish, York Co planter a tr of land in Charles Parish granted by patent to be 73 a. of land adj Jno Tomer, Capt Chisman, the Mill Path, John Doswell the elder, Jno Clark & York Road, all which granted premises were by patent dated 6 Jun 1699 taken up by the sd Jno Doswell the elder & Robert Sheild & afterwards that part belonging to the sd Robt Sheild was sold by the sd Sheild to the sd Doswell the elder & since the whole tr was purch by the afsd Edwd Athy of the sd Jno Doswell the elder ... . Wit: Wm Armistead, Jno Moss, Wm Gordon. 20 Sep 1714 Mary the w/o Edwd Athy came into court being first privately examined & relinquished her right of dower to Jno Doswell Junr & on his motion is admitted to record. Attest: Phi Lightfoot clerk. (Pg 27)

11 Nov 1714. Deed of Lease. Jno Clayton & Wil Robertson feofees or trustees for the land appropriated for building & erecting the City of Williamsburgh for 5 shillings farm letten unto William Robertson of York Co eight lotts of ground in the sd City of Wmsburgh designed in the platt of the sd city by the figures 232, 233, 234, 235, 236, 237, 207 & 208 ... during the term of one year paying the yearly rent of one grain of Indian corn on 10 Oct if demanded ... . Wit: None. Ackn 15 Nov 1714 & admitted to record. Attest: Phi Lightfoot clerk. (Pg 28)

12 Nov 1714. Deed of Release. Jno Clayton & Wil Robertson feofees or trustees for the land appropriated for building & erecting the City of Williamsburgh for £6 released to William Robertson of York Co eight lotts of ground in the sd City of Wmsburgh designed in the platt of the sd city by the figures 232, 233, 234, 235, 236, 237, 207 & 208 ... [*same as above*] ... if the sd William Robertson shall not within 24 months begin to build & finish upon each lott of the sd granted premises one good dwelling house then it shall & may be lawfull to & for the sd feofees or trustees to enter & the same to have again as of

their former estate ... . Wit: None. Ackn 15 Nov 1714 & admitted to record.
Attest: Phi Lightfoot clerk. (Pg 29)

2 Apr 1713. Deed of Lease. Jno Clayton & Wil Robertson feofees or trustees
for the land appropriated for building & erecting the City of Williamsburgh for 5
shillings farm letten unto Christopher Jackson of York Co six lotts of ground in
the sd City of Wmsburgh designed in the plot of the city by the figures 267, 268,
172, 271, 12 & 43 ... for the term of one year paying the yearly rent of one grain
of Indian corn on 10 Oct if demanded ... . Wit: C.C. Thacker, Michl Archer.
Ackn 15 Nov 1714 & admitted to record. Attest: Phi Lightfoot clerk. (Pg 30)

3 Apr 1713. Deed of Release. Jno Clayton & Wil Robertson feofees or trustees
for the land appropriated for building & erecting the City of Williamsburgh for
£4:10 released unto Christopher Jackson of York Co six lotts of ground in the sd
City of Wmsburgh designed in the plot of the city by the figures 267, 268, 172,
271, 12 & 43 ... [same as above] ... if the sd Christopher Jackson shall not
within 24 months begin to build & finish upon each lott of the sd granted
premises one good dwelling house then it shall & may be lawfull to & for the sd
feofees or trustees to enter & the same to have again as of their former estate ... .
Wit: C.C. Thacker, Michl Archer. Ackn 15 Nov 1714 & admitted to record.
Attest: Phi Lightfoot clerk. (Pg 30)

7 Oct 1714. Deed of Lease. Jno Clayton & Wil Robertson feofees or trustees
for the land appropriated for building & erecting the City of Williamsburgh for 5
shillings farm letten unto Francis Sharp of York Co a lott of ground at Queen
Marys Port designed in the plot of the sd Port by the figure 7 ... for the term of
one year paying the yearly rent of one grain of Indian corn if demanded ... .
Wit: None. Ackn 15 Nov 1714 & admitted to record. Attest: Phi Lightfoot
clerk. (Pg 31)

8 Oct 1714. Deed of Release. Jno Clayton & Wil Robertson feofees or trustees
for the land appropriated for building & erecting the City of Williamsburgh for
15 shillings released unto Francis Sharp of York Co a lott of ground at Queen
Marys Port designed in the plot of the sd Port by the figure 7 ... [same as above]
... if the sd Francis Sharp shall not within 24 months begin to build & finish
upon each lott of the sd granted premises one good dwelling house then it shall
& may be lawfull to & for the sd feofees or trustees to enter & the same to have
again as of their former estate ... . Wit: None. Ackn 15 Nov 1714 & admitted
to record. Attest: Phi Lightfoot clerk. (Pg 32)

30 Jun 1714. Deed of Lease. James Bates of Bruton Parish, York Co merchant
for 5 shillings leased to James Morris carpenter of same place a tr of land in
Bruton Parish on the n side of the upper pt/o Queens Cr nearly opposite of the

Capitol Landing being that parcell or remainder of land which the sd James Bates purch of Jno Hall & Sarah his wife (who was the only surviving sister of & heir at law to Edwd Davis late of the sd co decd) by deeds of lease & release dated 25 & 27 Mar 1710 being pt/o a tr of land formerly belonging to Ashwell Batten late of York Co decd who was grandfather to the sd Edwd Davis & Sarah Hall, the sd Jno Hall & Sarah his wife had right, title & claim unto the sd tr of land which descended to the sd Sarah by & from her brother Edward decd at the time & before their executing the sd recited deeds to the sd James Bates ... for the term of one year .... Wit: Tho Warde, Jno Bates, Wm Warbarton. Ackn 15 Nov 1714 & admitted to record. Attest: Phi Lightfoot clerk. (Pg 33)

30 Jun 1714. Deed of Release. James Bates of Bruton Parish, York Co merchant for £20 released to James Morris carpenter of same place a tr of land in Bruton Parish ... [*same as above*] .... Wit: Tho Warde, Jno Bates, Wm Warbarton. Ackn 15 Nov 1714 & admitted to record. Attest: Phi Lightfoot clerk. (Pg 34)

12 Nov 1714. Deed of Lease. Jno Lewis of Charles Parish, York Co for 50 shillings farm letten unto James Bennett of same place a 50 a. tr of land which sd land was mortgaged by Jno Stevens to David Lewis grandfather of the sd Jno Lewis for 99 years to be renewed for other 99 years paying to the heirs of the sd Jno Stevens (if any) 10 shillings in money or one cow calf & which sd tr of land is bounded by James Sclater, Mary Hayward widow & land which the sd Jno Lewis hath now sold to the sd James Bennett ... during the remainder of the term of 99 years paying yearly unto the Jno Lewis the rent of one grain of Indian corn on the feast of St. Michael ye Archangel if demanded .... Wit: Joseph Stacy, John Tomer Junr, James Shelton. Ackn 15 Nov 1714 & admitted to record. Attest: Phi Lightfoot clerk. (Pg 36)

11 Nov 1714. Deed of Lease. Jno Lewis of Charles Parish, York Co for 5 shillings farm lett unto James Bennett of same place a 55 a. tr of land in Charles Parish bounded by the severall lands of James Sclater, Mary Hayward widow & the lands which David Lewis father of the sd Jno Lewis held by lease & purch of Jno Stevens decd ... for the term of one year .... Wit: Joseph Stacy, John Tomer Junr, James Shelton. Ackn 15 Nov 1714 & admitted to record. Attest: Phi Lightfoot clerk. (Pg 37)

12 Nov 1714. Deed of Release. Jno Lewis of Charles Parish, York Co for £10 released unto James Bennett of same place a 55 a. tr of land in Charles Parish ... [*same as above*] ... (excepting a right of dower due to Anne Eaton mother of the sd Jno Lewis) .... Wit: Joseph Stacy, John Tomer Junr, James Shelton. Ackn 15 Nov 1714 & recorded. Attest: Phi Lightfoot clerk. (Pg 37)

12 Nov 1714. Bond. I Jno Lewis of Charles Parish, York Co am firmly bound unto James Bennett of same place for £60 ... the condition of this obligation is such that if the afsd Jno Lewis shall well & truly obey, observe, perform, fullfill & keep all the covenants, articles, contracts, premises & agreements mentioned in an indenture of grant, release & confirmation [see above] then this obligation to be void ... . Wit: Joseph Stacy, John Tomer Junr, James Shelton. Ackn 13 Nov 1714 & admitted to record. Attest: Phi Lightfoot clerk. (Pg 38)

29 Nov 1714. Deed of Lease. George Baskervyle of Bruton Parish, York Co for 5 shillings leased to Ralph Graves of same place a 350 a. tr of land in Bruton Parish with a dwelling thereon being the tr of land formerly of Jno Baskervyle father to the sd George, by him purch of Jno Horsington to whom the 350 a. of land was granted by patent dated 18 Mar 1662, bounded by 300 a. pt/o the parish formerly called Marston Parish, the Main Swamp, St. Andrews Cr, land of Thomas Pinkethman & the Rockahock Path, the first mentioned 50 a. the residue on the Main Br of St. Andrews Cr bounded by the sd Horsington ... for the term of one year paying the yearly rent of on graine of Indian corn if demanded ... . Wit: Tho Crips, Henr Holdcraft, Phil Jackson, Edwd Nelson. Ackn 20 Dec 1714 & admitted to record. Attest: Phi Lightfoot clerk. (Pg 39)

30 Nov 1714. Deed of Release. Geo Baskervyle of Bruton Parish, York Co yeoman for £200 released to Ralph Graves of same place yeoman a 350 a. tr of land ... [same as above] ... . Wit: Tho Crips, Hen Holdcraft, Phil Jackson, Edwd Nelson. Ackn 20 Dec 1714 by Geo Baskervyle & also appeared Eliza w/o the sd Geo who being first privately examined relinquished her right of dower & admitted to record. Attest: Phi Lightfoot clerk. (Pg 40)

13 Nov 1714. Bond. I George Baskervyle of Bruton Parish, York Co yeoman am firmly bound unto Ralph Graves of same place yeoman for £500 ... the condition of this obligation is such that whereas the afsd George Baskervyle by deeds of lease & release [see above] sold to the afsd Ralph Graves a 350 a. tr of land, if the sd George Baskervyle shall well & truly observe, perform, obey, fullfill & keep all the articles, covenants, clauses, grants & agreements mentioned in the sd indentures then this obligation to be void ... . Wit: Tho Crips, Hen Holdcraft, Phil Jackson. Ackn 20 Dec 1714 & admitted to record. Attest: Phi Lightfoot clerk. (Pg 41)

29 Nov 1714. Deed of Lease. Ralph Graves of Bruton Parish, York Co yeoman for 5 shillings leased to George Baskervyle of same place yeoman an 825 a. tr of land being pt/o a greater tr of land called Boar Quarter in Charles Parish formerly purch by the sd Ralph Graves of Edmd Jenings esqr being ½ of the sd tr called Boar Quarter which in all did contain 1650 a. & was surveyed & divided by Major Wm Buckner surveyor 25 Apr 1712, the 825 a. of land is

11

bounded by Boar Quarter Cr & Pocoson River, including Batchelors Island, Tobacco Swamp & Tobacco Ridge ...for the term of one year ... . Wit: Tho Crips, Hen Holdcraft, Phil Jackson, Edwd Nelson. Ackn 20 Dec 1714 & admitted to record. Attest: Phi Lightfoot clerk. (Pg 42)

30 Nov 1714. Deed of Release. Ralph Graves of Bruton Parish, York Co yeoman for £200 released to George Baskervyle of same place yeoman an 825 a. tr of land ... [same as above] ... . Wit: Tho Crips, Hen Holdcraft, Phil Jackson, Edwd Nelson. Ackn 20 Dec 1714 by Ralph Graves & also appeared Mary the w/o the sd Ralph who being first privately examined relinquished her right of dower & admitted to record. Attest: Phi Lightfoot clerk. (Pg 43)

30 Nov 1714. Bond. I Ralph Graves of Bruton Parish, York Co am firmly bound unto Geo Baskervyle of same place for £500 ... the condition of this obligation is such that whereas the afsd Ralph Graves hath sold to the sd Geo Baskervyle one plantation & 825 a. of land by deeds of lease & release [see above], now if the sd Ralph Graves shall well & truly observe, obey, perform, fullfill & keep all the articles, covenants, clauses, grants & agreements mentioned in the sd indenture then this obligation to be void ... . Wit: Hen Holdcraft, Tho Crips, Phil Jackson. Ackn 20 Dec 1714 & admitted to record. Attest: Phi Lightfoot clerk. (Pg 45)

17 Dec 1714. Deed of Lease. Jno Hillyard & Frances his wife late dau of Joseph White of York Co decd for 5 shillings leased to Ralph Graves of same co a 130 a. tr of land being all that tr of land which was devised to the sd Frances by the will of her sd father Joseph White decd dated 27 Feb 1705/6 & is bounded by Forked Swamp, Col Jenings' mill dam, the Main Mill Road, Capt Mathew's land, land of Thomas Crips & the Mill Dam ... for the term of one year ... . Wit: Francis Sharp, Geo Baskervyle, Saml Sweny. Ackn 20 Dec 1714 by Jno Hillyard & Frances his wife & admitted to record. Attest: Phi Lightfoot clerk. (Pg 45)

18 Dec 1714. Deed of Release. Jno Hillyard & Frances his wife late dau of Joseph White of York Co decd for £50 released to Ralph Graves of same co a 130 a. tr of land ... . Wit: Francis Sharp, Geo Baskervyle, Saml Sweny. Ackn 20 Dec 1714 by Jno Hillyard & also appeared Frances the w/o the sd John who being first privately examined relinquished her right of dower & admitted to record. Attest: Phi Lightfoot clerk. (Pg 46)

18 Dec 1714. Bond. I Jno Hillyard of St. Johns Parish, King William Co, VA am firmly bound unto Ralph Graves of Bruton Parish, York Co for £100 ... the condition of this obligation is such that whereas the afsd Jno Hillyard & Frances his wife dau & devisee of Joseph White late of York Co decd have sold to the sd

Ralph Graves a 130 a. dividend of land by deeds of lease & release [*see above*], now if the sd Jno Hillyard & Frances his wife shall well & truly obey, observe, perform, fullfill & keep all the grants, covenants, articles, clauses & agreements mentioned in the sd indenture then this obligation to be void ... . Wit: Francis Sharp, Geo Baskervyle, Saml Sweny. Ackn 20 Dec 1714 by Jno Hillyard & admitted to record. Attest: Phi Lightfoot clerk. (Pg 48)

6 Jan 1714/15. Deed of Lease. Jno Cook of York Town, York Co for 5 shillings farm letten unto Edwd Powers of same place a lott or ½ a. of land in York Town containing 10 poles in length & 8 poles in breadth being pt/o the Port Land bounded by the Main Street, Esther Powell, the Court House lott & opposite to the land of the sd Edwd Powers which sd lott is known by the number 30 & was purch by the sd Jno Cook of Jno Wills by deeds dated 18 & 19 Jun 1714 ... for the term of one year ... . Wit: Edward Wade, John Young, Michl Dewick. Ackn 17 Jan 1714 & admitted to record. Attest: Phi Lightfoot clerk. (Pg 49)

7 Jan 1714/15. Deed of Release. Jno Cook of York Town, York Co for £40 released unto Edwd Powers of same place a lott or ½ a. of land in York Town ... [*same as above*] ... . (Pg 50)

7 Jan 1714/15. Bond. I Jno Cook of York Town, York Co am firmly bound unto Edwd Powers of same place for £100 ... the condition of this obligation is such that if the afsd Jno Cook shall well & truly observe, obey, perform, fullfill, accomplish & keep all the covenants, grants, articles, clauses & agreements mentioned in one pair of indentures [*see above*] then this obligation to be void ... . Wit: Edward Wade, John Young, Michl Dewick. Ackn 17 Jan 1714 & admitted to record. Attest: Phi Lightfoot clerk. (Pg 51)

14 Jan 1714/15. Deed of Lease. Jno Cook of York Town, York Co for 5 shillings farm lett unto Edwd Powers of same place all his now dwelling house upon the bank or shoar of York River (late the house of Jno Wills & purch by the sd Jno Cook of the sd Jno Wills by deeds dated 18 & 19 Jun 1714) ... for the term of one year ... . Wit: Edwd Wade, John Young, Michl Dewick. Ackn 17 Jan 1714 & admitted to record. Attest: Phi Lightfoot clerk. (Pg 52)

15 Jan 1714/15. Deed of Release. Jno Cook of York Town, York Co for £15 released unto Edwd Powers of same place all his now dwelling house upon the bank or shoar of York River ... [*same as above*] ... it is agreed by & between the partys that the true intent & meaning of these presents is that if the sd Jno Cook shall well & truly pay unto the sd Jno Wills of Mulberry Island Parish, Warwick Co £55 in such manner & at such times as are specified & expressed in one certain indenture of release made between Jno Wills & Eliza his wife & the sd Jno Cook then this granted premises & every part thereof shall revert unto &

be again the proper estate of the sd Jno Cook & Mary his wife & this present indenture of release to be void ... . Edward Wade, John Young, Michl Dewick. Ackn 17 Jan 1714 by Jno Cook & Mary his wife also the sd Mary relinquished her right of dower. Attest: Phi Lightfoot clerk. (Pg 52)

15 Jan 1714/15. Bond. I Jno Cook of York Town, York Co am firmly bound unto Edwd Powers of same place for £40 ... the condition of this obligation is such that if the afsd Jno Cook shall well & truly obey, observe, perform, fullfill & keep all the covenants, grants, articles, clauses & agreements mentioned in certain indentures of lease & release [*see above*] then this obligation to be void ... . Wit: Edward Wade, John Young, Michl Dewick. Ackn 17 Jan 1714 & admitted to record. Attest: Phi Lightfoot clerk. (Pg 54)

12 Jan 1714. Deed of Lease. Mary Bass of York Hampton Parish, York Co widow for 5 shillings farm letten unto Joseph Walker of co afsd a 192 a. tr of land in York Hampton Parish bounded by a path that leads to the house of Tho Buck & a br of a cr formerly called Wests Cr, which tr of land was by the will of Tho Whitehead given & devised unto the sd Mary Bass ... for the term of one year ... . Wit: None. Ackn 17 Jan 1714 & admitted to record. Attest: Phi Lightfoot clerk. (Pg 54)

13 Jan 1714. Deed of Release. Mary Bass of York Hampton Parish, York Co widow for £92 released unto Joseph Walker merchant of co afsd a 192 a. tr of land in York Hampton Parish ... [*same as above*] ... . Wit: None. Ackn 17 Jan 1714 & admitted to record. Attest: Phi Lightfoot clerk. (Pg 55)

13 Jan 1714. Bond. I Mary Bass of York Co widow am firmly bound unto Joseph Walker of co afsd gent for £200 ... the condition of this obligation is such that if the afsd Mary Bass shall well & truly obey, observe, perform, fullfill & keep all the articles, clauses, covenants, grants, conditions & agreements mentioned in certain indentures of lease & release [*see above*] then this obligation to be void ... . Wit: None. Ackn 17 Jan 1714 & admitted to record. Attest: Phi Lightfoot clerk. (Pg 56)

13 Oct 1714. Deed of Lease. Chichley Corbin Thacker & John Clayton feofees or trustees for the land appropriated for building & erecting the City of Wmsburgh for 5 shillings farm letten unto Jean Pasteur of James City Co a lott of ground in the sd City of Wmsburgh designed in the plot of the sd city by the figure 271 ... during the term of one year paying the yearly rent of one grain of Indian corn on 10 Oct if demanded ... . Wit: John Brooke, David Cuningham, Susanna Allen. Ackn 17 Jan 1714 by Jno Clayton esqr & proved to be the act & deed of Chichley Corbin Thacker gent & admitted to record. Attest: Phi Lightfoot clerk. (Pg 57)

20 Oct 1714. Deed of Release. Chichley Corbin Thacker & John Clayton feofees or trustees for the land appropriated for building & erecting the City of Wmsburgh for 15 shillings released unto Jean Pasteur of James City Co a lott of ground in the sd City of Wmsburgh designed in the plot of the sd city by the figure 271 ... [same as above] ... if the sd Jean Pasteur shall not within 24 months begin to build & finish upon each lott of the sd granted premises one good dwelling house then it shall & may be lawfull to & for the sd feofees or trustees to enter & the same to have again as of their former estate .... Wit: John Brooke, David Cuningham, Susanna Allen. Ackn 17 Jan 1714 by Jno Clayton esqr & proved to be the act & deed of Chichley Corbin Thacker gent & admitted to record. Attest: Phi Lightfoot clerk. (Pg 57)

12 Feb 1714. Deed. Jno Harrison of Bruton Parish, York Co planter for £52:10 sold to Florence Macarte of same place tayler a 60 a. tr of land in the parish afsd bounded by the road that goes to Oaken Neck Bridge, Tho Wade, Tho Steer decd, a br of Oaken Swamp & Widow Jones .... Wit: James Queen, Susanna Queen, Alex Bonyman. Ackn 21 Feb 1714 by Jno Harrison as also appeared Mary the w/o the sd Jno who relinquished her right of dower & admitted to record. Attest: Phi Lightfoot clerk. (Pg 58)

12 Feb 1714. Bond. I Jno Harrison of Bruton Parish, York Co am firmly bound unto Florence Macarte of same place for £105 ... the condition of this obligation is such that whereas the afsd Jno Harrison hath sold unto the sd Florence Macarte one 60 a. tr of land by deed [see above], now if the sd Jno Harrison shall well & truly observe, perform, obey, fullfill & keep all the covenants, articles, clauses, grants & agreements mentioned in the sd indenture then this obligation to be void .... Wit: James Queen, Susanna Queen, Alex Bonyman. Ackn 21 Feb 1714 & admitted to record. Attest: Phi Lightfoot clerk. (Pg 60)

15 Mar 1714/15. Deed of Gift. Jno Rogers of York Hampton Parish, York Co for natural love & affection have given to my loving son Jno Adduston Rogers of Charles Parish, co afsd three Negroes (viz) one man named Tom, one man named Barnaby & one girl named Betty with her increase together with all my personall estate that I now enjoy (all my lawfull debts, funerall expenses & the like to be thereout honestly paid & discharged) as also have given by these presents unto the sd Jno Adduston Rogers all my right, title & interest that I have or may have to any lands or Negroes in VA or elsewhere which are now in the hands & possession of other men unjustly detailed, I the sd Jno Rogers still reserving unto myself what crops my two Negroes Tom & Barnaby shall make upon my plantation or elsewhere for my maintenance, I the sd Jno Rogers paying what debts I shall or may contract in the same time during my life, with this proviso & upon this consideration that my sd son Jno Adduston Rogers do keep & maintain me his father during my naturall life with good & wholesome

meat & drink, warm & decent apparel & lodging, a good fire in cold weather, necessary suitable & convenient to my old age & at seasonable times a cup of good liquor to drink with a friend & after my decease to bury my body decently in a Christian buriall but in case my son Jno Adduston Rogers should happen to dye before me, than all the gifts & grants in this writing I do give unto my loving dau in law Jane Rogers w/o my son Jno Adduston Rogers, provided that the sd Jane Rogers take the same care of me & make such provision for me as is in this present deed of gift, but if she should marry before my decease, I do for all her extraordinary diligence & care I hope she will take of me in this my old age to the value of 35 to be paid her out of my estate & the residue & remainder thereof to return to me the sd Jno Rogers ... . Wit: John Clarke, John Franklin, Richd Sclater. Ackn 21 Mar 1714 by Jno Pond by vertue of a power of atty from Jno Rogers & on his mocon is admitted to record. Attest: Phi Lightfoot clerk. (Pg 61)

12 Feb 1714. Deed. Wm Buckner & Lawr Smith gent trustees to the Portland of York Town in York Co for 180 lbs of tobacco sold to Nathl Hook a lott or ½ a. of land in York Town being pt/o the Portland number 70 as by the plot on the records of the co doth appear, the sd lott containing 10 poles in length & 8 in breadth ... provided that the sd Nathl Hook shall & do within 12 months build & finish on the sd lott one good house to contain at least 20' wherein if he fail then this present grant to be void in law ... . Wit: None. Ackn 21 Mar 1714 & admitted to record. Attest: Phi Lightfoot clerk. (Pg 62)

21 Mar 1714. Deed. Nathl Burwell of Gloster Co for £300 sold to James Burwell of York Co a 300 a. tr of land in York Hampton Parish bounded by a br of Kings Cr (which divides the sd James Burwell's Neck from the land that was formerly Stanup's), the Old Field, Stockers Neck Cr, the Main Road that leads from the sd James Burwell's house to Wmsburgh, opposite the place where Capt Tayler formerly lived, the Neck Gate near the Widow Cosby's plantation & Mr. Hyde ... to the sd James Burwell & the mail heirs of his body lawfully begotten forever & to no other use, intent or purpose whatsoever ... . Wit: Edwd Powers, Edward Wade, Miles Cary. Ackn 21 Mar 1714 & admitted to record. Attest: Phi Lightfoot clerk. (Pg 63)

25 Mar 1714. Bond. I Nathl Burwell of Gloster Co am firmly bound to James Burwell of York Co for £600 ... the condition of this obligation is such that if the afsd Nathl Burwell shall well & truly observe, perform, fullfill, accomplish & keep all the covenants, grants, articles, clauses & agreements mentioned in one indenture of release [see above] then this obligation to be void ... . Wit: Edwd Powers, Edward Wade, Miles Cary, Ackn 21 Mar 1714 & admitted to record. Attest: Phi Lightfoot clerk. (Pg 64)

21 Mar 1714. Deed. James Burwell of York Co for £120 sold to Nathl Burwell of Gloster Co a 120 a. tr of land in York Hampton Parish bounded by the road that leads from the sd James Burwell to Wmsburgh, opposite to that old house Cherry Orchards where Capt Taylor formerly lived & Stockers Neck Cr … . Wit: Edwd Powers, Edward Wade, Miles Cary. Ackn 21 Mar 1714 & admitted to record. Attest: Phi Lightfoot clerk. (Pg 64)

21 Mar 1714. Bond. I James Burwell of York Co am firmly bound unto Nathl Burwell of Gloster Co for £500 … the condition of this obligation is such that if the afsd James Burwell shall well & truly observe, perform, fullfill, accomplish & keep all the covenants, grants, articles, clauses & agreements mentioned in one indenture of release [*see above*] then this obligation to be void … . Wit: Edwd Powers, Edward Wade, Miles Cary. Ackn 21 Mar 1714 & admitted to record. Attest: Phi Lightfoot clerk. (Pg 66)

13 May 1715. Deed of Lease. John Clayton, Will Robertson feofees or trustees for the land appropriated for the building & erecting the City of Wmsburgh for 5 shillings farm letten unto Jno Holloway of York Co gent nine lotts of ground in the sd City of Wmsburgh designed in the plot of the sd city by the figures 218, 220, 221, 222, 223, 224, 225, 226 & 227 … for the term of one year paying the rent of one grain of Indian corn on 10 Oct if demanded … . Wit: None. Ackn 16 May 1715 & admitted to record. Attest: Phi Lightfoot clerk. (Pg 66)

14 May 1715. Deed of Release. John Clayton, Will Robertson feofees or trustees for the land appropriated for the building & erecting the City of Wmsburgh for £6:15 released unto Jno Holloway of York Co gent nine lotts of ground in the sd City of Wmsburgh designed in the plot of the sd city by the figures 218, 220, 221, 222, 223, 224, 225, 226 & 227 … [*same as above*] … if the sd Jno Holloway shall not within 24 months begin to build & finish upon each lott of the sd granted premises one good dwelling house then it shall & may be lawfull to & for the sd feofees or trustees to enter & the same to have again as of their former estate … . Wit: None. Ackn 16 May 1715 & admitted to record. Attest: Phi Lightfoot clerk. (Pg 67)

13 May 1715. Deed of Lease. Christopher Jackson of James City Co for 5 shillings leased to Tho Ravenscraft of same co a lott or parcel of land in the City of Wmsburgh adj a lott purch of Michl Archer in the sd city by the sd Tho Ravenscraft, designed in the plot of the sd city by the number 268 … for the term of one year paying the rent of one ear of Indian corn on the last day of the sd year if demanded … . Wit: James Burwell, Edward Powers. Ackn 16 May 1715 & admitted to record. Attest: Phi Lightfoot clerk. (Pg 68)

14 May 1715. Deed of Release. Christopher Jackson of James City Co for £7 released to Tho Ravenscraft of same co a lott or parcel of land in the City of Wmsburgh number 268 ... [*same as above*] ... . Wit: James Burwell, Edw Powers. Ackn 16 May 1715 & admitted to record. Attest: Phi Lightfoot clerk. (Pg 69)

13 May 1715. Deed of Lease. Richd Platt of James City Co, VA & Judith his wife for 5 shillings farm lett unto Jno Doswell Junr of Charles Parish, York Co a plantation & 100 a. tr of land in Charles Parish adj Capt Tho Chisman, land late of Tho Woodfield decd, Jno Doswell the elder & Jno Chisman ... for the term of one year ... . Wit: Michl Dewick, Jno Adduston Rogers, James Shelton. Ackn 16 May 1715 by Richd Platt & Judith his wife & admitted to record. Attest: Phi Lightfoot clerk. (Pg 70)

14 May 1715. Deed of Release. Richd Platt of James City Co, VA & Judith his wife for £60 released unto Jno Doswell the younger of Charles Parish, York Co a plantation & 100 a. tr of land in Charles Parish ... [*same as above*] ... . Wit: Michl Dewick, Jno Adduston Rogers, James Shelton. Ackn 16 May 1715 by Richd Platt & Judith his wife (also the sd Judith being first privately examined) relinquished her right of dower & admitted to record. Attest: Phi Lightfoot clerk. (Pg 71)

14 May 1715. Bond. I Richd Platt of James City Co, VA am firmly bound unto Jno Doswell the younger of Charles Parish, York Co for £120 ... the condition of this obligation is such that if the afsd Richard Platt shall well & truly obey, observe, perform, fullfill & keep all the covenants, articles, contracts, clauses & agreement mentioned in indentures of grant, release & confirmation [*see above*] then this obligation to be void ... . Wit: Michl Dewick, Jno Adduston Rogers, James Shelton. Ackn 16 May 1715 & admitted to record. Attest: Phi Lightfoot clerk. (Pg 71)

17 Feb 1714. Deed. Ralph Graves of Bruton Parish, York Co for £80 sold to William Jones of same place a 120 a. tr of land lying in the Indian Field in the parish afsd & is pt/o a greater tr of land belonging to the sd Graves & bounded by Major Custis, the Old School House, Flax Hole Swamp, Capt Archer, Archers Road & Wm Davis ... . Wit: J. Thornton, Wm Allerast, Jno Brodnax, Anne Granger. 17 Feb 1714 full & peaceable possession & seizin of all the land was delivered by the sd Ralph Graves to the sd Wm Jones in the presence of Richd Hester & Edwd Nelson. Wit: J. Thornton, Jonathan Drewit. Ackn 16 May 1715 by Ralph Graves & at the same time appeared Mary w/o the sd Ralph who being first privately examined relinquished her right of dower. Attest: Phi Lightfoot clerk. (Pg 73)

17 Feb 1714. Bond. I Ralph Graves of Bruton Parish, York Co am firmly bound unto William Jones of same place for £200 ... the condition of this obligation is such that if the afsd Ralph Graves shall well & truly observe, perform, fullfill, accomplish & keep all the covenants, grants, articles, clauses & agreements in one indenture [*see above*] then this obligation to be void ... . Wit: J. Thornton, Wm Allerast, Jno Brodnax, Anne Granger. Ackn 16 May 1715 & admitted to record. Attest: Phi Lightfoot clerk. (Pg 74)

10 Jun 1715. Deed of Lease. Edwd Powers of the Town & Co of York for 5 shillings farm letten unto Tho Nelson of same place gent all his lott or ½ a. of land in York Town containing 10 poles in length & 8 poles in breadth being pt/o the Portland designed in the plot of the sd town by the number 50 bounded by Wm Rogers, Jno Marshall, sd Tho Nelson & the street opposite to the land of the sd Edwd Powers, which lot was purch by the sd Edward Powers of the feofees or trustees for the Portland by deed dated 19 Feb 1710 ... for the term of one year ... . Wit: Michl Dewick, Phi Lightfoot. Ackn 20 Jun 1715 & admitted to record. Attest: Phi Lightfoot clerk. (Pg 75)

11 Jun 1715. Deed of Release. Edwd Powers of the Town & Co of York for £10 released unto Tho Nelson of same place gent all his lott or ½ a. of land in York Town number 50 ... [*same as above*] ... . Wit: Michl Dewick, Phi Lightfoot. Ackn 20 Jun 1715 & admitted to record. Attest: Phi Lightfoot clerk. (Pg 76)

16 May 1715. Deed of Gift. Henry Hayward & Eliza his wife of Charles Parish, York Co for naturall affection have given to our well beloved cousin Edward Tabb son of Edwd Tabb of same place all our right, title & interest to a 100 a. tr of land in Charles Parish being pt/o a tr of land called Pinny Neck lately devised to the sd Edwd Tabb by the will of Isabell Toplady widow of the parish afsd decd dated 1 Feb 1714 & now in the tenure & occupation of Edwd Tabb father to the sd Edwd Tabb ... . Wit: Tho Nutting, Willm Tabb. Ackn 20 Jun 1715 by Henry Hayward & also appeared Eliza w/o the sd Henry who relinquished her right of dower & admitted to record. Attest: Phi Lightfoot clerk. (Pg 77)

2 Jul 1714. Indenture Quadripartite between Wm Gordon, Char Cox, Jno Andrews & Nicho Phillips of York Town, York Co, wit that the sd Wm Gordon, Charles Cox, Jno Andrews & Nicho Phillips for & in consideration of the fidelity, trust, confidence & good opinion which every one of them always had & yet hath & reposeth in every three of them have joyned themselves copartners in digging & stoning a well to be placed in the lott of Wm Gordon one of the copartners on the s side of the sd lott adj to the Main Street of the sd town, which lott is known in the plot of the sd town by a figure 9, & the sd Wm

Gordon, Charles Cox, Jno Andrews & Nicho Phillips have joyntly & mutually agreed together & with each other in manner following, that is to say, that the sd Wm Gordon being now seized as of fee of the afsd lott in York Town now in the tenure & occupation of the sd Wm Gordon doth for & in consideration of the convenience of the sd well give, grant, sell & release unto the sd Char Cox, Jno Andrews & Nicho Phillips so much & such pt/o the sd lott on which the sd well is to be digged containing 10' square in such pt/o the sd lott as is before mentioned & under the limitations & reservations hereafter named, viz, that he the sd Wm Gordon besides the gift & demise of the sd pt/o his lott shall contribute & be chargeable with 20 shillings over & above the preportionable charge of digging & stoning the sd well wherewith the sd Wm Gordon, Char Cox, Jno Andrews & Nicho Phillips & each of them shall be chargeable with the same which sd pt/o the lott & well when finished shall equally be & appertain to the sd Wm Gordon, Char Cox, Jno Andrews & Nicho Phillips to the use & behoof of them & all & every of them forever … . Wit: Michl Dewick, Edward Wright, Charles Calthorp. Ackn 20 Jun 1715by Wm Gordon & admitted to record. Attest: Phi Lightfoot clerk. (Pg 78)

18 Jul 1715. Deed of Gift. Tho Wootton & Priscilla his wife of York Hampton Parish, York Co for naturall love & affection have given unto our well beloved son Tho Wooton of same place a 111 a. tr of land in Charles Parish adj to the land of Henry Hayward surveyed by Col Lawr Smith surveyor of co afsd as by the survey dated 13 Dec 1681, & known by the name of Oaken Swamp & now in the tenure & occupation of the sd Tho Wootton & Priscilla his wife … . Wit: Michl Dewick, Edwd Tabb. Ackn 18 Jul 1715 & Tho Wooton & also appeared Priscilla the w/o the sd Tho & relinquished her right of dower & admitted to record. Attest: Phi Lightfoot clerk. (Pg 79)

18 Jul 1715. Deed. Wm Buckner & Lawr Smith gent trustees to the Port Land of York Town in York Co for 360 lbs of tobacco sold to Geo Allen chyrurgeon two lotts or ½ acres of land in York Town being pt/o the Port Land known by the numbers 67 & 71 as by the plot on the records of the co doth appear the sd lotts each containing 10 poles in length & 8 in breadth … provided that the sd Geo Allen shall & do within 12 months build & finish on each of the sd lotts one good house to contain at least 20' wherein if he fail, then this present grant to be void in law … . Ackn 18 Jul 1715 & admitted to record. Attest: Phi Lightfoot clerk. (Pg 80)

13 May 1715. Deed. Matthew Ballard of York Hampton Parish, York Co gent for £30 sold to Philip Lightfoot of same place gent all his lott or ½ a. of land in the Town of York bounded by York River, the street opposite to the land of Warren Cary & land of Joseph Walker, known in the plot of the sd town by the number 16 together with the houses, barns, stables & gardens … which sd

granted premises were granted to Tho Ballard father of the sd Matthew (as one of the trustees for the Port Land for & in consideration of his trouble & charge in the sd office) by the order of York Court dated 25 Nov 1692, & after his decease came & descended to the sd Matthew as son & heir at law of the sd Thomas ... . Wit: Wm Barbar, Christo Jackson, Michl Dewick. Ackn 15 Aug 1715 by Matthew Ballard & at the same time appeared Anne w/o the sd Matthew who being first privately examined relinquished her right of dower & admitted to record. Attest: Phi Lightfoot clerk. (Pg 81)

13 May 1715. Bond. I Matthew Ballard of York Hampton Parish, York Co am firmly bound unto Philip Lightfoot of same place for £60 ... the condition of this obligation is such that if the afsd Matthew Ballard shall well & truly observe, perform, fullfill, accomplish & keep all the covenants, grants, articles, clauses & agreements mentioned in one indenture of sale [see above] then this obligation to be void ... . Wit: Wm Barbar, Christo Jackson, Michl Dewick. Ackn 15 Aug 1715 & admitted to record. Attest: Phi Lightfoot clerk. (Pg 82)

17 Jun 1715. Deed. Between Wm Buckner & Lawr Smith gent trustees to the Port Land of York Town in York Co of the one part & Philip Lightfoot of York Co of the other part, wit that the sd Wm Buckner & Lawr Smith for & in consideration that whereas Lt Col Tho Ballard late of York Co (one of the then feofees for the Port Land afsd) decd dyed seized & possessed of one lott or ½ a. of land number 16 by vertue of an order of York Court dated 25 Nov 1692 specifying the sd lott or ½ a. of land to be granted & confirmed by the sd court to the sd Lt Col Tho Ballard in consideration of his extraordinary care & trouble in discharge of this office & place of feofee in trust as afsd (& for which sd lot there was never yet any deed granted by the feofees or trustees for the Port Land afsd, the sd lott being by the sd Lt Col Tho Ballard built upon according to the directions of the Act of Assembly, the sd lott containing 10 poles in length & 8 poles in breadth descending to Matthew Ballard son & heir at law of the sd Lt. Col Tho Ballard decd & purch of the sd Matthew by the sd Phi Lightfoot by deed [see above], have sold & confirmed unto the sd Phi Lightfoot all that afsd lott or ½ a. of land in York Town ... . Ackn 15 Aug 1715 & admitted to record. Attest: Phi Lightfoot clerk. (Pg 83)

30 Jul 1715. Deed of Gift. Hester Power of York Town, York Co widow for love, goodwill & affection have given to my loving friend Wm Davis of same place cooper all that one lott or ½ a. of land in York Town (being pt/o the Port Land designed in the plot of the sd town by the number 29 as by the plot on the records of the co more fully may appear) together with all houses, buildings, gardens & advantages containing 70' in breadth & 120' in length adj to the land of Edward Powers, Wm Tunley, the remaining pt/o the sd lott now in the tenure

& occupation of me the sd Hester Powell & the street opposite to the lott whereon the Church now standeth ... . Wit: Peter Vaudery, Michl Dewick. Ackn 19 Sep 1715 & admitted to record. Attest: Phi Lightfoot clerk. (Pg 83)

14 Sep 1715. Deed of Lease. Wm Jones of Bruton Parish, York Co planter for 5 shillings leased to Wm Davis of same place planter a 56 a. parcel of land lying in the sd parish at a place called Indian Field upon the brs of a swamp issueing out of Queens Cr being the plantation & pt/o the land purch by the sd Wm Jones of Ralph Graves of same parish & is adj Graveners Spring Br, Graveners Spring & the path that leads towards Capt Timson's ... for the term of one year ... . Wit: Jonath Drewit, Jno Hubard, Robert Clark. Ackn 19 Sep 1715 & admitted to record. Attest: Phi Lightfoot clerk. (Pg 84)

15 Sep 1715. Deed of Release. Wm Jones of Bruton Parish, York Co planter for £56 released to Wm Davis of same place planter a 56 a. parcel of land purch by the sd Wm Jones of Ralph Graves of same parish ... [same as above] ... being pt/o a greater tr formerly belonging to Ralph Graves father of the sd Ralph Graves formerly of York Co decd ... . Wit: Jonath Drewit, Jno Hubard, Robert Clark. Ackn 19 Sep 1715 & admitted to record. Attest: Phi Lightfoot clerk. (Pg 85)

15 Sep 1715. Bond. I Wm Jones of Bruton Parish, York Co am firmly bound unto Wm Davis of same place planter for £112 ... the condition of this obligation is such that whereas the afsd Wm Jones hath granted & sold unto the afsd Wm Davis one plantation & 56 a. of land by way of deeds of lease & release [see above], now if the afsd Wm Jones shall well & truly observe, perform, fullfill & keep all the articles, covenants, clauses, grants & agreements mention in the sd deed of release then this obligation to be void ... . Wit: Jonath Drewit, Jno Hubard, Robert Clark. Ackn 19 Sep 1715 & admitted to record. Attest: Phi Lightfoot clerk. (Pg 87)

14 Oct 1715. Deed of Lease. John Clayton & Wil Robertson feofees or trustees for the land appropriated for the building & erecting the City of Wmsburgh for 5 shillings leased to Jno Holloway of York Co gent a lott of ground lying at Queens Port in the City of Wmsburgh containing 53 square poles adj Lott Number 32 ... during the term of one year paying the yearly rent of one grain of Indian corn on 10 Oct if demanded ... . Wit: None. Ackn 21 Nov 1715 & admitted to record. Attest: Phi Lightfoot clerk. (Pg 87)

15 Oct 1715. Deed of Release. John Clayton & Wil Robertson feofees or trustees for the land appropriated for the building & erecting the City of Wmsburgh for 10 shillings released to Major Jno Holloway of York Co gent a lott of ground lying at Queens Port in the City of Wmsburgh ... [same as above]

... if the sd Jno Holloway shall not within 24 months begin to build & finish upon each lott of the sd granted premises one good dwelling house then it shall & may be lawfull to & for the sd feofees or trustees to enter & the same to have again as of their former estate ... . Wit: None. Ackn 21 Nov 1715 & admitted to record. Attest: Phi Lightfoot clerk. (Pg 88)

17 Nov 1715. Deed of Lease. John Clayton & Wil Robertson feofees or trustees for the land appropriated for the building & erecting the City of Wmsburgh for 5 shillings leased to Francis Tyler of York Co one lott of ground in the sd City of Wmsburgh designed in the plot of the sd city by the figure 262 ... . Wit: None. Ackn 21 Nov 1715 & admitted to record. Attest: Phi Lightfoot clerk. (Pg 89)

18 Nov 1715. Deed of Release. John Clayton & Wil Robertson feofees or trustees for the land appropriated for the building & erecting the City of Wmsburgh for 15 shillings released to Francis Tyler of York Co one lott of ground in the sd City of Wmsburgh designed in the plot of the sd city by the figure 262 ... [*same as above*] ... if the sd Francis Tyler shall not within 24 months begin to build & finish upon each lott of the sd granted premises one good dwelling house then it shall & may be lawfull to & for the sd feofees or trustees to enter & the same to have again as of their former estate ... . Wit: None. Ackn 21 Nov 1715 & admitted to record. Attest: Phi Lightfoot clerk. (Pg 90)

16 Sep 1715. Deed of Lease. John Clayton & Wil Robertson feofees or trustees for the land appropriated for the building & erecting the City of Wmsburgh for 5 shillings farm letten unto Jno Marott of York Co one lott of ground in the City of Wmsburgh designed in the plot of the sd city by the figure 802 ... for the term of one year paying yearly rent of one grain of Indian corn on 10 Oct if demanded ... . Wit: None. Ackn 21 Nov 1715 & admitted to record. Attest: Phi Lightfoot clerk. (Pg 91)

17 Sep 1715. Deed of Release. John Clayton & Wil Robertson feofees or trustees for the land appropriated for the buil2ding & erecting the City of Wmsburgh for 15 shillings released unto Jno Marott of York Co one lott of ground in the City of Wmsburgh designed in the plot of the sd city by the figure 802 ... [*same as above*] ... if the sd Jno Marott shall not within 24 months begin to build & finish upon each lott of the sd granted premises one good dwelling house then it shall & may be lawfull to & for the sd feofees or trustees to enter & the same to have again as of their former estate ... . Wit: None. Ackn 21 Nov 1715 & admitted to record. Attest: Phi Lightfoot clerk. (Pg 91)

15 Dec 1715. Deed of Lease. Jno Drewry of Charles Parish, York Co wheel wright & Mary his wife for 5 shillings leased to Wm Row of same place planter a messuage & 50 a. of land in Charles Parish whereon the sd Jno Drewry & Mary his wife now lives bounded by Elias Love, sd Wm Row, Charles River & land belonging to the heirs of Capt Willis Wilson decd, which sd 50 a. of land was given to the sd Jno Drewry by his father Jno Drewry Senr decd as by deed of gift dated 15 Dec 1711 ... during the term of one year ... . Wit: Tho Hinde Senr, Tho Roberts Junr, Henry Taylor. Ackn 19 Dec 1715 by Jno Drewry & Mary his wife & admitted to record. Attest: Phi Lightfoot clerk. (Pg 93)

16 Dec 1715. Deed of Release. Jno Drewry of Charles Parish, York Co wheel wright & Mary his wife for 5 shillings released to Wm Row of same place planter a messuage & 50 a. of land ... [same as above] ... . Wit: Tho Hinde Senr, Tho Roberts Junr, Henry Taylor. Ackn 19 Dec 1715 by Jno Drewry & also appeared Mary the w/o the sd Jno who being first privately examined relinquished her right of dower & admitted to record. Attest: Phi Lightfoot clerk. (Pg 93)

16 Dec 1715. Bond. I Jno Drewry of Charles Parish, York Co wheel wright am firmly bound unto Wm Row of same place planter for £100 ... the condition of this obligation is such that if the afsd Jno Drewry shall well & truly keep, perform, observe & fullfill all the clauses, articles, covenants, grants & agreements mentioned in one indenture of release [see above] then this obligation to be void ... . Wit: Tho Hinde Senr, Tho Roberts Junr, Henry Taylor. Ackn 19 Dec 1715 & admitted to record. Attest: Phi Lightfoot clerk. (Pg 95)

19 Dec 1715. Deed. Wm Robertson of James City Co gent for 30 shillings sold to Philip Ludwell of same co esqr two lotts or ½ acres of ground in the City of Wmsburgh being on the n side of the Market Place denoted in the plan of the sd city by the figures 233 & 234 ... . Wit: Will Keith. Ackn 16 Jan 1715 & admitted to record. Attest: Phi Lightfoot clerk. (Pg 95)

16 Dec 1715. Deed. Jno Pasteur of the City of Wmsburgh in York Co for £70 sold to Henry Holdcraft of Blisland Parish, New Kent Co all his plantation & 150 a. of land in the upper pt/o York Co on the s side of the Main Swamp of Skimino Cr bounded by the land formerly of Daniel Wild (now the land of the sd Holdcraft), br of Skimino Swamp & the Main Swamp Runn, being formerly the land of Matthew Hubbard of York Co decd & after his death descended to his son Matthew Hubbard of James City Co & by him sold to George Martin late of York Co decd who by his will dated 9 Feb 1702 devised all the sd land & plantation to his then wife Winifred Martin in fee simple who afterwards was married to Jno Sarjanton & together with her sd husband by deeds of lease &

release dated 15 Aug 1712 was sold to the sd Jno Pasteur ... . Wit: Robt Woodcock, John Price, Richd Kennon, Wm Lester. Memorandum that full & peaceable possession & seizing of the within mentioned granted messuage land & plantation was deliver'd by the within named Jno Pasteur unto the within named Henry Holdcraft in the presence of us, Sarah Anderson widow & John Ashley. Ackn 16 Jan 1715 by Jno Pasteur & also appeared Mary the w/o the sd Jno who being first privately examin'd voluntarily relinquished her right of dower & admitted to record. Attest: Phi Lightfoot clerk. (Pg 96)

16 Dec 1715. Bond. I Jno Pasteur of the City of Wmsburgh in York Co am firmly bound unto Henry Holdcraft of Blisland Parish, New Kent Co for £140 ... the condition of this obligation is such that whereas the sd Jno Pasteur hath sold unto the afsd Henry Holdcraft a plantation & 150 a. tr of land by one deed of sale [see above] now if the sd Jno Pasteur shall well & truly observe, obey, perform, fullfill & keep all the covenants, articles, clauses, grants & agreements according to the true intent & meaning of the sd indenture then this obligation to be void ... . Wit: Robt Woodcock, Wm Lester, John Price. Ackn 16 Jan 1715 & admitted to record. Attest: Phi Lightfoot clerk. (Pg 98)

17 Feb 1715. Deed of Lease. Susanna Allen of the City of Wmsburgh in York Co inholder for 5 shillings leased to James Bates of Bruton Parish, York Co merchant all her lott or ½ a. of land in the sd City of Wmsburgh on the n side of Duke of Gloucester's Street bounded by the lott late of Richd Wharton esqr decd, Nicholson's Street & lott of Tho Jones ... for the term of one year ... . Wit: Jacob Godwin, John Clarke, Hen Holdcraft. Ackn 20 Feb 1715 & admitted to record. Attest: Phi Lightfoot clerk. (Pg 99)

18 Feb 1715. Deed of Release. Susanna Allen of the City of Wmsburgh in York Co inholder for £150 released to James Bates of Bruton Parish, York Co merchant all her lott or ½ a. of land in the sd City of Wmsburgh ... [same as above] ... . Wit: John Clarke, Hen Holdcraft, Jacob Godwin. Ackn 20 Feb 1715 & admitted to record. Attest: Phi Lightfoot clerk. (Pg 100)

16 Mar 1715. Deed of Lease. Benja Read (Reade) of Petsoe Parish, Glouster Co for 5 shillings farm letten unto Tho Nelson of York Hampton Parish, York Co gent a 215 a. tr of land in York Hampton Parish bounded by the br of York Town Cr, land late of Robert Reade, the swamp dividing this land from the land late of David Condon & land late of Wm Buckner, which sd dividend of land is pt/o a greater tr devised by the will of Nicho Martien to his dau Eliza w/o Geo Read esqr as by the same will dated 1 Mar 1656, & afterwards came & descended to the sd Benja Reade as son & heir at law of Francis Reade (son of the afsd Geo Reade esqr & Eliza his wife) by the death of Geo Reade to whom ½ of the greater tr afsd was devised by the will of the sd Geo Read esqr dated 29

Sep 1670 ... for the term of one year paying the rent of one ear of Indian corn on 20 Dec yearly if demanded ... . Wit: Tho Nutting, Peter Goodwin, Wm Sheldon. Ackn 19 Mar 1715 & admitted to record. Attest: Phi Lightfoot clerk. (Pg 102)

17 Mar 1715. Deed of Release. Benja Read (Reade) of Petsoe Parish, Glouster Co for £115 released unto Tho Nelson of York Hampton Parish, York Co gent a 215 a. tr of land in York Hampton Parish ... [same as above] ... . Wit: Tho Nutting, Peter Goodwin, Wm Sheldon. Ackn 19 Mar 1715 & admitted to record. Attest: Phi Lightfoot clerk. (Pg 103)

17 Mar 1715. Bond. I Benja Read (Reade) of Petsoe Parish, Glocester Co am firmly bound unto Tho Nelson of York Hampton Parish, York Co gent for £230 ... the condition of this obligation is such that if the afsd Benja Read shall well & truly observe, perform, fullfill, accomplish & keep al the covenants, grants, articles, clauses, conditions & agreements mentioned in one pair of indentures of lease & release [see above] then this obligation to be void ... . Wit: Tho Nutting, Peter Goodwin, Wm Sheldon. Ackn 19 Mar 1715 & admitted to record. Attest: Phi Lightfoot clerk. (Pg 104)

27 Jan 1715. Deed of Lease. Ralph Graves of Bruton Parish, York Co for 5 shillings leased to Richd Easter of same place a plantation & 100 a. parcel of land in the parish afsd being now in the tenure & occupation of the sd Richd & is pt/o the sd Graves's Indian Field tr of land near where the old Church stood, bounded by sd Graves's land, land of Major Jno Custice, Wm Jackson, land lately sold by the sd Graves to Wm Jones, the old School House, Tho Crips, the Spring Br & land which the sd Ralph lately sold to Edmund Jenings esqr ... for the term of one year paying the rent of one ear of Indian corn if demanded ... . Wit: Hen Holdcraft, John Harris, Wm Jackson, Simon Jeffreys. Ackn 19 Mar 1715 & admitted to record. Attest: Phi Lightfoot clerk. (Pg 105)

28 Jan 1715. Deed of Release. Ralph Graves of Bruton Parish, York Co for £30 released to Richd Easter of same place a plantation & 100 a. parcel of land ... [same as above] ... . Wit: Henry Holdcraft, John Harris, Wm Jackson, Simon Jeffreys. Ackn 19 Mar 1715 by Ralph Graves & at the same time appeared Mary the w/o the sd Ralph who being first privately examined relinquished her right of dower & admitted to record. Attest: Phi Lightfoot clerk. (Pg 106)

28 Jan 1715. Bond. I Ralph Graves of Bruton Parish, York Co am firmly bound unto Richard Easter of same place for £60 ... the condition of this obligation is such that whereas the afsd Ralph Graves hath sold & conveyed to the sd Richd Easter a plantacon & 100 a. parcel of land by way of deeds of lease & release [see above] now if the sd Ralph Graves shall well & truly observe, perform,

26

obey, fullfill & keep all the articles, covenants, clauses, grants & agreements
mentioned in the sd indenture of release then this bond to be void ... . Wit: Hen
Holdcraft, John Harris, Wm Jackson, Simon Jeffreys. Ackn 19 Mar 1715 &
admitted to record. Attest: Phi Lightfoot clerk. (Pg 108)

16 Mar 1715. Deed of Lease. John Clayton & Wil Robertson feofees or trustees
for the land appropriate for the building & erecting the City of Williamsburgh
for 5 shillings farm letten unto William Timson of York Co gent three lotts of
ground in the sd City of Wmsburgh designed in the plot of the sd city by the
figures 323, 46 & 47 ... for the term of one year paying the yearly rent of one
grain of Indian corn on 10 Oct if demanded ... . Wit: None. Ackn 19 Mar 1715
& admitted to record. Attest: Phi Lightfoot clerk. (Pg 109)

17 Mar 1715. Deed of Release. John Clayton & Wil Robertson feofees or
trustees for the land appropriate for the building & erecting the City of
Williamsburgh for 45 shillings released unto William Timson of York Co gent
three lotts of ground in the sd City of Wmsburgh designed in the plot of the sd
city by the figures 323, 46 & 47 ... [same as above] ... if the sd William Timson
shall not within 24 months begin to build & finish upon each lott of the sd
granted premises one good dwelling house then it shall & may be lawfull to &
for the sd feofees or trustees to enter & the same to have again as of their former
estate ... . Wit: None. Ackn 19 Mar 1715 & admitted to record. Attest: Phi
Lightfoot clerk. (Pg 109)

16 Mar 1715/6. Deed of Lease. Jno Welsh (Welch) of Charles Parish, York Co
& Elizabeth his wife for 5 shillings farm letten unto Jno Doswell Junr of same
place a 30 a. parcel of land in Charles Parish adj Edmd Sweny, a line into Dead
Maires Brook, Edwd Worley, Jno Welsh & Jno Doswell Senr ... for the term of
one year ... . Wit: David Holloway, Jacob Lohman, Richard Slater. Ackn 19
Mar 1715 by Jno Welsh & Eliza his wife & admitted to record. Attest: Phi
Lightfoot clerk. (Pg 111)

17 Mar 1715/6. Deed of Release. Jno Welsh (Welch) of Charles Parish, York
Co & Elizabeth his wife for £22 released unto Jno Doswell Junr of same place a
30 a. parcel of land in Charles Parish ... [same as above] ... . Wit: David
Holloway, Jacob Lohman, Richd Slater. Ackn 19 Mar 1715 by Jno Welsh &
Eliza his wife & the sd Eliza being first privately examined relinquished her
right of dower & admitted to record. Attest: Phi Lightfoot clerk. (Pg 112)

17 Mar 1715/16. Bond. We Jno Welsh (Welch) & Eliza my wife of Charles
Parish, York Co are firmly bound unto John Doswell Junr of same place for £44
... the condition of this obligation is such that if the afsd Jno Welsh shall well &
truly obey, observe, perform, fullfill & keep all the covenants, articles, contracts,

clauses & agreements mentioned in a certain indenture of grant, release & confirmation [*see above*] then this obligation to be void ... . Wit: David Holloway, Jacob Lohman, Richard Slater. Ackn 19 Mar 1715 by Jno Welsh & Eliza his wife & admitted to record. Attest: Phi Lightfoot clerk. (Pg 113)

16 Feb 1716. Deed of Lease. Edwd Worldly (Worley) of Charles Parish, York Co planter for a parcel of money & tobacco & covenants & agreements hereafter in & by these presents mentioned farm letten unto James Callowhill of same place planter all that plantacon that was formerly Francis Clark adj Jno Welsh, Jno James & Geo James for the full time of 21 years paying ready down now the sum of £20 & the sum of 1100 lbs of good sweet sented tobo payable as the law directs & to pay unto the sd Edwd Worldly & his heirs during this present demise yearly one ear of Indian corn & also the sd James Callowhill doth covenant & agree to & with the sd Edwd Worldly to leave in good & sufficient repair at the expiration of this present demise one dwelling house of 28' long & 16' wide & one tobo house of 30' long & 20' wide together to plant in this present demise 100 winter apple trees upon the above demised premises ... . Wit: Joseph Stacy, Edmund Sweny. Ackn 21 May 1716 by Edwd Worley & at the same time also appeared Mary w/o the sd Edward who being first privately examined relinquished her right of dower & admitted to record. Attest: Phi Lightfoot clerk. (Pg 114)

16 Feb 1715/16. Bond. I Edwd Worldly (Worley) of Charles Parish, York Co planter am firmly holden unto James Callowhill of same place for £50 ... the condition of this obligation is such that if the afsd Edwd Worldly shall well & truly observe, perform, fullfill, accomplish & keep all the covenants, grants, articles, conditions, clauses & agreements mentioned in an indenture of lease [*see above*] then this obligation to be void ... . Wit: Joseph Stacy, Edmund Sweny. Ackn 21 May 1716 & admitted to record. Attest: Phi Lightfoot clerk. (Pg 115)

23 Apr 1716. Deed of Lease. George Baskervyle of Charles Parish, York Co for 5 shillings farm letten unto Wm Wise Junr of same place a 100 a. tr of land in Charles Parish (being pt/o a greater tr or dividend of land called Boar Quarter heretofore sold to the sd George by Ralph Graves of Bruton Parish, York Co by deed dated 30 Nov 1714) bounded by Charles Thurman, Jno Lyall, land late of Francis Callowhill & James Parsons ... for the term of one year paying the yearly rent of one grain of Indian corn on the last day of the sd year if demanded ... . Wit: Wm Sheldon, Wm Gordon, Edwd Worley. Ackn 21 May 1716 & admitted to record. Attest: Phi Lightfoot clerk. (Pg 116)

24 Apr 1716. Deed of Release. George Baskervyle of Charles Parish, York Co for £30 released unto Wm Wise Junr of same place a 100 a. tr of land in Charles

Parish ... [*same as above*] ... . Wit: Wm Sheldon, Wm Gordon, Edwd Worley. Ackn 21 May 1716 by Geo Baskervyle & at the same time appeared Eliza w/o the sd George who being first privately examined relinquished her right of dower & admitted to record. Attest: Phi Lightfoot clerk. (Pg 116)

24 Apr 1716. Bond. I Geo Baskervyle of Charles Parish, York Co am firmly bound unto Wm Wise Junr of same place for £60 ... the condition of this obligation is such that if the afsd Geo Baskervyle shall well & truly observe, perform, fullfill, accomplish & keep all the covenants, grants, articles, clauses, conditions & agreements mentioned in one pair of indentures of lease & release [*see above*] then this obligation to be void ... . Wit: Wm Sheldon, Wm Gordon, Edwd Worley. Ackn 21 May 1716 & admitted to record. Attest: Phi Lightfoot clerk. (Pg 118)

22 May 1716. Deed of Lease. Richd Bland of Pr George Co for the rents & covenants hereafter named & also for divers other good causes & considerations farm letten unto the Honble Col Nathl Harrison of Surry Co two lotts or ½ acres of land on which the sd Bland did lately live in the City of Wmsburgh on the s side of Duke of Gloucester Street in the sd city designed in the plot thereof by the numbers 20 & 21 with all houses, gardens, orchards & other advantages thereunto belonging ... for & during the full term of two years paying the yearly rent of one ear of Indian corn if demanded ... . Wit: M. Ingles, Benja Weldon, Tho Mitchell, Fran Tyler, James Shield, Jno Blair, Joseph Davenporte. Proved 18 Jun 1716 & admitted to record. Attest: Phi Lightfoot clerk. (Pg 118)

23 May 1716. Deed of Release. Richd Bland of Pr George Co for £100 released to the Honble Col Nathl Harrison of Surry Co two lotts or ½ acres of land in the City of Wmsburgh on which he lately lived ... [*same as above*] ... . Wit: M. Ingles, Benja Weldon, Fras Tyler, Tho Mitchell, James Shield, Jno Blair, Joseph Davenporte. Proved 18 Jun 1716 & admitted to record. Attest: Phi Lightfoot clerk. (Pg 119)

11 Jun 1716. Deed. Jno Anderson of York Co for £24 sold to Tho Allen of same co shoemaker all that lott or ½ a. of ground in the City of Wmsburgh denoted in the plan of the sd city by the figure 40 formerly granted by the feoffees or trustees of the sd city to the present grantor, with all houses, buildings, yards & gardens ... . Wit: Joseph Day, Richd Brand, Francis Sharp. Ackn 18 Jun 1716 & also appeared Anne w/o the sd Jno who being first privately examined relinquished her dower & admitted to record. Attest: Phi Lightfoot clerk. (Pg 120)

11 Jun 1716. Bond. I Jno Anderson of York Co am firmly bound unto Tho Allen of same co shoemaker for £25 ... the condition of this obligation is such

that if the afsd Jno Anderson shall well & truly observe, perform, fullfill & keep all the covenants, grants, articles, clauses, conditions & agreements mentioned in one certain indenture of sale [*see above*] then this obligation to be void ... . Wit: Joseph Day, Richd Brand, Francis Sharp. Ackn 18 Jun 1716 & admitted to record. Attest: Phi Lightfoot clerk. (Pg 121)

15 Jul 1716. Deed of Lease. Robt Jackson of York Co planter & Sarah his wife for 5 shillings leased to Nathl Burwell of Gloster Co gent all that 150 a. tr of land in York Hampton Parish adj Beaverdam Swamp, Mr. Ring's land, land of sd Jackson, the road that leads from Wmsburgh to James Burwell, land the sd Jackson formerly sold to the sd Burwell & the head of King Cr below the Beaverdam Bridge ... for the term of one year paying the rent of one ear of Indian (corn) on the last day of the sd year if demanded ... . Wit: Edwd Powers, Char Cozby, Ezekiel Gilbert. Ackn 16 Jul 1716 by Robt Jackson & Sarah his wife & admitted to record. Attest: Michl Dewick dep clerk. (Pg 121)

16 Jul 1716. Deed of Release. Robt Jackson of York Co planter & Sarah his wife for £35 released to Nathl Burwell of Gloster Co gent all that 150 a. tr of land in York Hampton Parish ... [*same as above*] ... . Wit: Edwd Powers, Char Cozby, Ezekiel Gilbert. Ackn 16 Jul 1716 by Robt Jackson & Sarah his wife & admitted to record. Attest: Michl Dewick dep clerk. (Pg 122)

16 Jul 1716. Bond. I Robt Jackson of York Co planter am firmly bound unto Nathl Burwell of Gloucester Co, VA gent for £150 ... the condition of this obligation is such that if the afsd Robt Jackson shall well & truly observe, perform, fullfill, accomplish & keep all the covenants, grants, articles, clauses & agreements mention in one indenture of release [*see above*] then this obligation to be void ... . Wit: Edwd Powers, Char Cozby, Ezekiel Gilbert. Ackn 16 Jul 1716 & admitted to record. Attest: Michl Dewick dep clerk. (Pg 125)

14 Jul 1716. Deed of Lease. John Clayton & Hugh Norvell feofees or trustees for the land appropriated for building & erecting the City of Wmsburgh for 5 shillings farm letten unto Archibald Blair of James City Co gent four lotts of ground in the sd City of Wmsburgh designed in the plot of the city by the figures 170, 171, 172 & 173 ... for the term of one year paying the yearly rent of one grain of Indian corn on 10 Oct if demanded ... . Wit: None. Ackn 16 Jul 1716 & admitted to record. Attest Michl Dewick dep clerk. (Pg 126)

15 Jul 1716. Deed of Release. John Clayton & Hugh Norvell feofees or trustees for the land appropriated for building & erecting the City of Wmsburgh for £3 released unto Archibald Blair of James City Co gent four lotts of ground in the sd City of Wmsburgh designed in the plot of the city by the figures 170, 171, 172 & 173 ... [*same as above*] ... if the sd Archibald Blair shall not within the

space of 24 months build & finish upon each lott one good dwelling house then
it shall & may be lawfull to & for the sd feofees or trustees into the granted
premises & every part thereof to enter & the same to have again as of their
former estate to have, hold & enjoy in like manner as they might otherwise have
done if these presents had never been made ... . Wit: None. Ackn 16 Jul 1716
& admitted to record. Attest: Michl Dewick dep clerk. (Pg 126)

2 Aug 1708. Deed of Lease. Mongo Ingles & Chishley Corbin Thacker feofees
or trustees for the land appropriated for the building & erecting the City of
Wmsburgh for 5 shillings lett unto Richd Bland of Pr George Co two lotts of
land in the sd City of Wmsburgh designed in the plot of the sd city by the
numbers 53 & 54 ... . Wit: Tho Jones, Wil Robertson. Ackn 16 Jul 1716 &
admitted to record. Attest: Michl Dewick dep clerk. (Pg 128)

3 Aug 1716. Deed of Release. Mongo Ingles & Chishley Corbin Thacker
feofees or trustees for the land appropriated for the building & erecting the City
of Wmsburgh for 30 shillings unto Richd Bland of Pr George Co two lotts of
land in the sd City of Wmsburgh designed in the plot of the sd city by the
numbers 53 & 54 ... [same as above] ... if the sd Richd Bland shall not within
the space of 24 months build & finish upon each lott one good dwelling house
then it shall & may be lawfull to & for the sd feofees or trustees into the granted
premises & every part thereof to enter & the same to have again as of their
former estate to have, hold & enjoy in like manner as they might otherwise have
done if these presents had never been made ... . Wit: Tho Jones, Wil
Robertson. Ackn 16 Jul 1716 & admitted to record. Attest: Michl Dewick dep
clerk. (Pg 128)

20 Aug 1716. Quit Claim. Micajah Perry & Richd Perry of London merchants
together with Thomas Lane since decd at a Genl Court held at the Capitol 2 Nov
1709 did recover judgmt agt Joseph Mountfort heir of Tho Mountfort for £2,000
to be levied & paid among other things out of one plantation containing 200 a. of
land purch of Jno & Susanna Duke lying in York Co, now these presents wit that
the sd Micajah Perry & Richd Perry for £40 release & quitt claim to the sd Jos
Mountfort all their estate, right, title, interest, claim & demand whatsoever to
200 a. of land & the sd Micajah Perry & Richd Perry do by these presents
covenant & agree to & with the sd Joseph Mountfort that notwithstanding any
act comitted or done by them the sd Micajah Perry & Richd Perry or by either of
them or by the sd Tho Lane that the sd Thomas Mountfort may have, hold,
possess & enjoy the 200 a. of land freely & clearly acquitted & discharged from
the sd judgment & all & every other the claim & demand of them the sd Micajah
Perry & Richd Perry & of the sd Tho Lane decd ... . Ackn 20 Aug 1716 by Jno
Clayton esqr atty of Micajah & Richd Perry of London & on his motion is
admitted to record. Attest: Michl Dewick clerk. (Pg 130)

28 Jun 1716. Deed. Joseph Mountfort of York Hampton Parish, York Co for £80 sold to Philip Lightfoot of same place gent a lott or ½ a. of land in York Town containing 10 poles in length & 8 poles in breadth bounded by the land of Cole Digges, land whereon the Church now standeth, the street opposite to the land of Edwd Powers & the Main Street opposite to the land of the sd Edwd Powers, which sd land & premises were formerly granted by Tho Ballard gent decd & Wm Buckner gent decd feofees in trust of the Port Land in York Town afsd to Eliza Summerwell (afterwards Eliza Powers late decd) by deed dated 21 May 1707 & by the death of the sd Eliza Powers came & descended to the sd Joseph Mountfort as heir at law of the sd Eliza (which sd granted premises are now in the tenure & occupation of Mary Smith) ... . Wit: Fran Lightfoot, James Burwell, Michl Dewick, Charles Cox, Jno Gibbons. Ackn 20 Aug 1716 by Joseph Mountfort & on the mocon of Jno Clayton esqr (his atty) admitted to record. Attest: Michl Dewick clerk. (Pg 130)

28 Jun 1716. Bond. I Joseph Mountfort of York Hampton Parish, York Co am firmly bound unto Philip Lightfoot of same place gent for £160 ... the condition of this obligation is such that if the afsd Joseph Mountfort shall well & truly observe, perform, fullfill, accomplish & keep all the covenants, grants, articles, clauses, conditions & agreements mentioned in one indenture of sale [see above] then this obligation to be void ... . Wit: Fran Lightfoot, James Burwell, Michl Dewick, Charles Cox, Jno Gibbons. Ackn 20 Aug 1716 by Joseph Mountfort & on the mocon of Jno Clayton esqr (his atty) admitted to record. Attest: Michl Dewick clerk. (Pg 132)

20 Aug 1716. Deed. Tho Nelson & Lawr Smith gent trustees to the Port Land of York Town in York Co for 180 lbs of tobacco sold to Nathl Hooke of York Co carpenter a lott or ½ a. of land in York Town being pt/o the Port Land known by the number 70 as by the plot on the records of the sd co doth appear, the sd lott containing 10 poles in length & 8 in breadth ... provided that the sd Nathl Hooke shall within 12 months build & finish on the sd lott one good house to contain at least 20' wherein if he fail then this present grant to be void in law ... . Ackn 20 Aug 1716 & admitted to record. Attest: Michl Dewick clerk. (Pg 133)

14 Sep 1716. Deeds of Lease and release. James Sclater of Charles Parish, York Co & Mary his wife for 5 shillings farm letten unto Benjamin Clifton of same place all their lott or ½ a. of land in York Town being pt/o the Port Land known by the number 25 containing 10 poles in length & 8 in breadth as by the records of the sd co may appear, together with all houses & buildings, which sd demised premises were by patent dated 8 Jan 1706 granted to Danl Taylor gent & his heirs & assigns forever & afterwards on 25 Jun 1707 assigned over by the sd Danl Taylor & Mary his wife to the afsd James Sclater as by the sd patent

more fully may appear ... for the term of one year ... . Wit: Jno Andrews, Tho Ray, Chrismas Ray. Ackn 17 Sep 1716 by James Sclater & Mary his wife & admitted to record. Attest: Michl Dewick clerk. (Pg 133-6)

15 Sep 1716. Deed of Release. James Sclater of Charles Parish, York Co & Mary his wife for £26 released unto Benjamin Clifton of same place all their lott or ½ a. of land in York Town being pt/o the Port Land known by the number 25 ... [same as above] ... . Wit: Jno Andrews, Tho Ray, Chrismas Ray. Ackn 17 Sep 1716 by James Sclater & also the sd Mary being first privately examined relinquished her right of dower & admitted to record. Attest: Michl Dewick clerk. (Pg 134)

15 Sep 1716. Bond. I James Sclater of Charles Parish, York Co clerk am firmly bound unto Benjamin Clifton of same place for £62 ... the condition of this obligation is such that if the afsd James Sclater shall well & truly obey, observe, perform, fullfill & keep all the covenants, articles, clauses, contracts & agreements mentioned in certain indentures of grant, release & confirmation [see above] then this obligation to be void ... . Wit: Wm Row, Wm Wise Junr. Ackn 17 Sep 1716 & admitted to record. Attest: Michl Dewick clerk. (Pg 136)

16 Feb 1715. Deed of Lease. Saml Cooper, Isles Cooper & Eliza his wife of Charles Parish, York Co for £50 leased to Wm Sheldon of York Hampton Parish, York Co all our right & title of that messuage & 275 a. tr of land in York Hampton Parish formerly in the possession of Tho Isles & the sd Tho Isles dying without will leaving two daus whose names were Katherine & Eliza & the sd Eliza leaving the sd Isles Cooper heir apparent at law, the sd land being bounded by Chisman's Cr, Black Cr, land of Adduston Rogers & Jno Read ... for the term of one year ... . Wit: Tho Roberts, Tho Edmunds, Richd Slater, John Chapman. Ackn 19 Nov 1716 by the parties & admitted to record. (Pg 137)

18 Feb 1815/16. Deed of Release. Saml Cooper, Isles Cooper & Eliza his wife of Charles Parish, York Co for £50 leased to Wm Sheldon of York Hampton Parish, York Co all our right & title of that messuage & 275 a. tr of land in York Hampton Parish ... [same as above] ... . Wit: Tho Roberts, Tho Edmunds, Richd Slater, John Chapman. Ackn 19 Nov 1716 by the parties & admitted to record. Attest: Michl Dewick clerk. (Pg 137)

17 Feb 1715/6. Bond. We Saml Cooper & Isles Cooper of Charles Parish, York Co are firmly bound to Wm Sheldon of York Hampton Parish, York Co for £100 ... the condition of this obligation is such that if the afsd Saml Cooper & Isles Cooper do well & truly observe, perform, fullfill & keep all the covenants, grants, articles & agreements mentioned in a pair of indentures of sail [see above] then this obligation to be void ... . Wit: Thos Roberts, Tho Edmunds,

Richd Slater, John Chapman. Ackn 19 Nov 1716 by Saml Cooper & Isle Cooper & admitted to record. Attest: Michl Dewick clerk. (Pg 139)

19 Nov 1716. Deed. Lawr Smith & Tho Nelson gent trustees to the Port Land of York Town in York Co for 180 lbs of tobacco sold to Saml Cooper of York Co a lott or ½ a. of land in York Town being pt/o the Port Land known by the number 75 as by the plot on the records of the sd co doth appear, the sd lott containing 10 poles in length & 8 in breadth ... provided that the sd Saml Cooper shall within 12 months build & finish on the sd lott one good house to contain at least 20' wherein if he fail then this present grant to be void in law ... . Ackn 19 Nov 1716 & admitted to record. Attest: Michl Dewick clerk. (Pg 140)

17 Sep 1716. Deed. Lawr Smith & Tho Nelson gent trustees for the Port Land of York Town in York Co for 180 lbs of tobacco sold to Jno Lewis of Gloucester Co esqr one lott or ½ a. of land in York Town being pt/o the Port Land known by the number 28 as by the plot of the sd town on the records of the sd co doth appear the sd lott containing 10 poles in length & 8 poles in breadth bounded by the street opposite to the land late in the tenure & occupation of Jno Marshall, land of Warren Cary, York River & land of Hester Powell (which sd lott was formerly granted to Simon Stacy by the trustees for the sd Port Land in 1691 & a deed for the same admitted to record & hath hitherto been deemed to be conveyed to Mrs. Mildred Warner though the sd deed or other conveyance be not found on the sd record, & the sd lott known to have been heretofore built upon according to the direction of the Act of Assembly) ... . Wit: Wm Smith, Jno Gibbons. Ackn 17 Dec 1716 & admitted to record. Attest: Michl Dewick clerk. (Pg 141)

15 Feb 1716. Deed of Lease. Wm Starke of York Hampton Parish, York Co for 5 shillings farm letten unto Wm Fuller of same place a 112 a. tr of land appearing by a survey thereof taken by Col Jno Soam dated 14 May 1694 bounded by Spring Br, land of Mr. Hansford, the Cow Path, Tho Weston, Mr. Roberts & the Cart Path, which tr of land was purch by Richd Stark (father of the sd Wm Stark) late of York Co decd (as by deed dated 4 Sep 1689) of David Condon of York Co decd & by the death of the sd Richd Stark came & descended to the sd Wm Stark (party to these presents) as son & heir at law of the sd Richd Stark decd ... for one year paying the yearly rent of one ear of Indian corn on 10 Dec if demanded ... . Wit: Michl Dewick, Char Hansford, Walter Butler. Ackn 18 Feb 1716 & admitted to record. Attest: Phi Lightfoot clerk. (Pg 142)

16 Feb 1816. Deed of Release. Wm Starke of York Hampton Parish, York Co for £50 released unto Wm Fuller of same place a 112 a. tr of land ... [*same as*

above] ... . Wit: Michl Dewick, Char Hansford, Walter Butler. Ackn 18 Feb 1716 & admitted to record. Attest: Phi Lightfoot clerk. (Pg 143)

16 Feb 1716. Bond. I Wm Stark of York Hampton Parish, York Co am firmly bound unto Wm Fuller of same place for £112 ... the condition of this obligation is such that if the afsd Wm Stark shall well & truly observe, perform, fullfill, accomplish & keep all the covenants, grants, articles, clauses, conditions & agreements mentioned in one pair of indentures of lease & release [*see above*] then this obligation to be void ... . Wit: Michl Dewick, Char Hansford, Walter Butler. Ackn 18 Feb 1716 & admitted to record. Attest: Phi Lightfoot clerk. (Pg 145)

15 Feb 1716. Deed of Lease. Wm Starke of York Hampton Parish, York Co for 5 shillings farm letten unto Wm Fuller of same place a 162 a. tr of land part in York Co & part in Warwick Co as appears by a survey thereof taken by Col Jno Underhill then surveyor dated 10 May 1667 bounded by the land of Robert Hubard, Tho Hansford, Mr. Petters & the White Marsh, which sd tr of land was formerly sold & conveyed by Wm Townsend to Alexander Young (as by deed dated 6 Jul 1686) & afterwards sold by the sd Alexander Young to Richard Stark father of the sd Wm Stark (by deed dated 4 Sep 1688) & afterwards by the death of the sd Richard came & descended to the sd Wm Stark as son & heir at law of the sd Richd decd ...for the term of one year paying the yearly rent of one ear of Indian corn on 10 Dec if demanded ... . Wit: Michl Dewick, Char Hansford, Walter Butler. Ackn 18 Feb 1716 & admitted to record. Attest: Phi Lightfoot clerk. (Pg 145)

15 Feb 1716. Deed of Release. Wm Starke of York Hampton Parish, York Co for £74 released unto Wm Fuller of same place a 162 a. tr of land ... [*same as above*] ... . Wit: Michl Dewick, Char Hansford, Walter Butler. Ackn 18 Feb 1716 & admitted to record. Attest: Phi Lightfoot clerk. (Pg 146)

16 Feb 1716. Bond. I Wm Stark of York Hampton Parish, York Co am firmly bound unto Wm Fuller of same place for £158 ... the condition of this obligation is such that if the afsd Wm Stark do & shall well & truly observe, perform, fullfill, accomplish & keep all the covenants, grants, articles, clauses, conditions & agreements mentioned in one pair of indentures of lease & release [*see above*] then this obligation to be void ... . Wit: Michl Dewick, Char Hansford, Walter Butler. Ackn 18 Feb 1716 & admitted to record. Attest: Phi Lightfoot clerk. (Pg 148)

5 Feb 1716. Deed of Lease. John Clayton & Hugh Norvel feofees or trustees for the land appropriated for the building & erecting the City of Wmsburgh for 5 shillings farm letten unto Samuel Cobbs of York Co two lotts of ground in the sd

City of Wmsburgh designed in the plot of the sd city by the figures 161 & 162
... for one year paying the yearly rent of one grain of Indian corn on 10 Oct if
demanded .... Wit: None. Ackn 18 Feb 1716 & admitted to record. Attest:
Phi Lightfoot clerk. (Pg 149)

6 Feb 1716. Deed of Release. John Clayton & Hugh Norvel feofees or trustees
for the land appropriated for the building & erecting the City of Wmsburgh for
30 shillings released unto Samuel Cobbs of York Co two lotts of ground in the
sd City of Wmsburgh designed in the plot of the sd city by the figures 161 & 162
... [same as above] ... if the sd Samuel Cobbs shall not within the space of 24
months build & finish upon each lott one good dwelling house then it shall &
may be lawfull to & for the sd feofees or trustees into the granted premises &
every part thereof to enter & the same to have again as of their former estate to
have, hold & enjoy in like manner as they might otherwise have done if these
presents had never been made .... Wit: None. Ackn 18 Feb 1716 & admitted
to record. Attest: Phi Lightfoot clerk. (Pg 150)

15 Feb 1716/17. Deed of Gift. Saml Cooper of York Hampton Parish, York Co
for natural love & affection have given unto my son & dau Lewis & Sarah St.
Leger & their children one lott No. 75 with the buildings thereunto belonging in
the Town of York in York Hampton afsd in manner following (that is to say)
unto my son & dau Lewis & Sarah St. Leger with the whole profits & benefits of
the sd lott for their own proper use until my grandson Abraham St. Leger shall
come to the age of 21 & then my sd grandson Abraham St. Leger shall have the
½ of the sd lott to settle, build or what benefits he shall think fitt for his own
proper use & behoof without molesting or disturbing my sd son & dau Lewis &
Sarah St. Leger in the tenement or other conveniences of the other half of the sd
lott during the naturall lives of my sd son & dau Lewis & Sarah St. Leger &
after the decease of both my sd son & dau then the whole lott shall be for the use
& benefit of my grandson Abraham St. Leger & his male heirs, but if the sd
Abraham St. Leger should dye without any male heir then it shall be for the use
of the eldest female of the sd Abraham St. Leger ... but if my grandson should
dye without heir male or female & my dau Sarah St. Leger should have more
male children either by this present husband or another husband then the sd lott
shall be for the use & benefit of the eldest male child & his male heirs, but if
there should be none of the afsd heirs surviving then the sd lott & benefits shall
be for the use of my grandau Mary St. Leger & her male heirs for want of such
to her eldest female heir .... Wit: Jno Mattocke, Wm Hilsman, Benja Lawson,
Hanah Hilsman. Ackn 18 Feb 1716 & admitted to record. Attest: Phi Lightfoot
clerk. (Pg 151)

21 Jan 1716. Deed. Lawr Smith & Tho Nelson gent trustees for the Port Land
of York Town in York Co for 180 lbs of tobacco sold to Tho Haynes Junr of

36

Mulberry Island Parish, Warwick Co gent a lott or ½ a. of land in York Town being pt/o the Port Land known by the number 62 as by the plot on the records of the sd co doth appear the sd lott containing 10 poles in length & 8 poles in breadth ... provided that the sd Tho Haynes Junr shall & do within 12 months build & finish on the sd lott one good house to contain at least 20' wherein if he fail then this present grant to be void in law ... . Wit: None. Ackn 18 Mar 1716 & admitted to record. Attest: Phi Lightfoot clerk. (Pg 152)

15 Mar 1716. Deed of Lease. Geo Baskervyle of Charles Parish, York Co for 5 shillings farm letten unto Wm Wise Junr of same place a 200 a. tr of land in Charles Parish together with the marsh thereto adjoining being pt/o a greater tr of land called Boar Quarter heretofore sold & conveyed to the sd Geo by Ralph Graves of Bruton Parish, York Co by deed dated 30 Nov 1714 bounded by Charles Thurman & land of Col Edmd Jenings now in the tenure & occupation of Jno Lyall ... for the term of one year paying the yearly rent of one ear of Indian corn on the last day of the sd year if demanded ... . Wit: Tho Roberts Junr, Elestrange Calthorpe, Saml Roberts. Ackn 18 Mar 1716 & admitted to record. Attest: Phi Lightfoot clerk. (Pg 153)

16 Mar 1716. Deed of Release. Geo Baskervyle of Charles Parish, York Co for £35 released unto Wm Wise Junr of same place a 200 a. tr of land in Charles Parish ... [same as above] ... . Wit: Tho Roberts Junr, Elestrange Calthorpe, Saml Roberts. Ackn 18 Mar 1716 by Geo Baskervyle & also appeared Elizabeth w/o the sd Geo who being first privately examined relinquished her right of dower & admitted to record. Attest: Phi Lightfoot clerk. (Pg 154)

16 Mar 1716. Bond. I Geo Baskervyle of Charles Parish, York Co am firmly bound unto Wm Wise Junr of same place for £70 ... the condition of this obligation is such that if the afsd Geo Baskervyle shall well & truly observe, perform, fullfill, accomplish & keep all the covenants, grants, articles, clauses, conditions & agreements mentioned in one pair of indentures of lease & release [see above] then this obligation to be void ... . Wit: Tho Roberts Junr, Elistrange Calthorpe, Saml Roberts. Ackn 18 Mar 1716 & admitted to record. Attest: Phi Lightfoot clerk. (Pg 156)

13 Mar 1716. Deed of Lease. Wm Wise Junr of Charles Parish, York Co for 5 shillings farm lett unto Wm Blackstone of same place a 100 a. tr of land in Charles Parish which sd tr of land is pt/o a greater tr of land called Boar Quarter heretofore sold by Ralph Graves of Bruton Parish, York Co to Geo Baskervyle & afterwards sold & conveyed by the sd Geo Baskervyle to the sd Wm Wise 23 & 24 Apr last past bounded by Charles Thurman, Jno Lyall, sd Baskervyle, land late of Francis Callowhill & land of James Parsons & also 100 a. of marsh adj ... for the term of one year paying the yearly rent of one ear of Indian corn on the

last day of the sd year if demanded ... . Wit: Tho Roberts Junr, Wm Barbar, Geo Baskervyle. Ackn 18 Mar 1716 & admitted to record. Attest: Phi Lightfoot clerk. (Pg 156)

14 Mar 1716. Deed of Release. Wm Wise Junr of Charles Parish, York Co for £20 released unto Wm Blackstone of same place a 100 a. tr of land in Charles Parish & 100 a. of marsh ... [same as above] ... . Wit: Tho Roberts Junr, Wm Barbar, Geo Baskervyle. Ackn 18 Mar 1716 & admitted to record. Attest: Phi Lightfoot clerk. (Pg 156)

14 Mar 1716/7. Bond. I Wm Wise Junr of Charles Parish, York Co am firmly bound unto Wm Blackstone of same place for £60 ... the condition of this obligation is such that if the afsd Wm Wise Junr do & shall well & truly observe, perform, fullfill, accomplish & keep all the covenants, grants, articles, clauses, conditions & agreements mentioned in one pair of indentures of lease & release [see above] then this obligation to be void ... . Wit: Tho Roberts Junr, Wm Barbar, Geo Baskervyle. Ackn 18 Mar 1716 & admitted to record. (Pg 159)

1 Mar 1716. Deed of Lease. Charles Calthorpe of Charles Parish, York Co for 5 shillings farm lett unto Wm Wise Junr of same place a 165 a. tr of land in Charles Parish adj land late belonging to James Calthorpe decd ... for the term of one year paying the yearly rent of one ear of Indian (corn) on 10 Oct if demanded ... . Wit: Tho Roberts Junr, Saml Roberts. Ackn 18 Mar 1716 & admitted to record. Attest: Phi Lightfoot clerk. (Pg 159)

2 Mar 1716. Deed of Release. Charles Calthorpe of Charles Parish, York Co for £90 released unto Wm Wise Junr of same place a 165 a. tr of land in Charles Parish ... [same as above] ... which sd tr of land was given & granted to the sd Charles Calthorp by patent under the hand of Francis Nicholson esqr Lt Govr of VA dated 20 Oct 1691 ... . Wit: Tho Roberts Junr, Saml Roberts. Ackn 18 Mar 1716 & admitted to record. Attest: Phi Lightfoot clerk. (Pg 160)

2 Mar 1716. Bond. I Charles Calthorp of Charles Parish, York Co am firmly bound unto Wm Wise Junr of same place for £180 ... the condition of this obligation is such that if the afsd Charles Calthorp do & shall well & truly observe, perform, fullfill, accomplish & keep all the covenants, grants, articles, clauses, conditions & agreements mentioned in one pair of indentures of lease & release [see above] then this obligation to be void ... . Wit: Tho Roberts Junr, Saml Roberts, Geo Baskervyle. Ackn 18 Mar 1716 & admitted to record. Attest: Phi Lightfoot clerk. (Pg 163)

16 May 1717. Deed of Lease. John Clayton & Wil Robertson feofees or trustees for the land appropriated for the building & erecting the City of Wmsburgh for 5 shillings farm letten unto Francis Tyler of York Co four lotts of ground in the sd City of Wmsburgh designed in the plot of the sd city by the figures 178, 179, 180 & 181 ... for the term of one year paying the yearly rent of one grain of Indian corn on 10 Oct if demanded ... . Wit: None. Ackn 20 May 1717 & admitted to record. Attest: Phi Lightfoot clerk. (Pg 163)

17 May 1717. Deed of Release. John Clayton & Wil Robertson feofees or trustees for the land appropriated for the building & erecting the City of Wmsburgh for £3 released unto Francis Tyler of York Co four lotts of ground in the sd City of Wmsburgh designed in the plot of the sd city by the figures 178, 179, 180 & 181 ... [same as above] ... if the sd Francis Tyler shall not within the space of 24 months build & finish upon each lott one good dwelling house then it shall & may be lawfull to & for the sd feofees or trustees into the granted premises & every part thereof to enter & the same to have again as of their former estate to have, hold & enjoy in like manner as they might otherwise have done if these presents had never been made ... . Wit: None. Ackn 20 May 1717 & admitted to record. Attest: Phi Lightfoot clerk. (Pg 164)

16 Nov 1716. Deed of Lease. John Clayton & Wil Robertson feofees & trustees for the land appropriated for the building & erecting the City of Wmsburgh for 5 shillings farm lett unto Tho Ravenscraft of York Co two lotts of ground in the sd City of Wmsburgh designed in the plot of the sd city by the figures 269 & 270 ... for the term of one year paying the yearly rent of one grain of Indian corn on 10 Oct if demanded ... . Wit: None. Ackn 20 May 1717 & admitted to record. Attest: Phi Lightfoot clerk. (Pg 165)

17 Nov 1716. Deed of Release. John Clayton & Wil Robertson feofees & trustees for the land appropriated for the building & erecting the City of Wmsburgh for 30 shillings released unto Tho Ravenscraft of York Co two lotts of ground in the sd City of Wmsburgh designed in the plot of the sd city by the figures 269 & 270 ... [same as above] ... if the sd Tho Ravenscraft shall not within the space of 24 months build & finish upon each lott one good dwelling house then it shall & may be lawfull to & for the sd feofees or trustees into the granted premises & every part thereof to enter & the same to have again as of their former estate to have, hold & enjoy in like manner as they might otherwise have done if these presents had never been made ... . Wit: None. Ackn 20 May 1717 & admitted to record. Attest: Phi Lightfoot clerk. (Pg 166)

1 May 1717. Deed of Lease. John Clayton & Wil Robertson feofees or trustees for the land appropriate for the building & erecting of the City of Wmsburgh for 5 shillings farm letten unto Francis Sharp of York Co two lotts of ground in the

sd City of Wmsburgh designed in the plot of the sd city by the figures 57 & 58 … for the term of one year paying the yearly rent of one grain of Indian corn on 10 Oct if demanded … . Wit: None. Ackn 20 May 1717 & admitted to record. Attest: Phi Lightfoot clerk. (Pg 167)

2 May 1717. Deed of Release. John Clayton & Wil Robertson feofees or trustees for the land appropriate for the building & erecting of the City of Wmsburgh for 30 shillings released unto Francis Sharp of York Co two lotts of ground in the sd City of Wmsburgh designed in the plot of the sd city by the figures 57 & 58 … [same as above] … if the sd Francis Sharp shall not within the space of 24 months build & finish upon each lott one good dwelling house then it shall & may be lawfull to & for the sd feofees or trustees into the granted premises & every part thereof to enter & the same to have again as of their former estate to have, hold & enjoy in like manner as they might otherwise have done if these presents had never been made … . Wit: None. Ackn 20 May 1717 & admitted to record. Attest: Phi Lightfoot clerk. (Pg 168)

20 Nov 1716. Quit Claim. To all persons to whom these presents shall come Saml Timson of New Kent Co gent & Tho Barbar the younger of co afsd gent & Mary his wife greetings, whereas Saml Timson gent late of York Co decd father of the sd Saml Timson & Mary w/o the sd Tho Barbar being in his lifetime seized in fee simple of a 200 a. tr of land in Bruton Parish being the remainder of the land late belonging to the sd Saml Timson decd on the Mill Swamp in Bruton Parish after 200 a. belonging to Jno Timson son of the sd Saml Timson decd were laid out bounded by Queens Cr Swamp, & being pt/o a tr of land purch by the sd Saml Timson decd of Saml Weldon gent decd & Sarah his wife which sd 200 a. of land bounded as afsd the sd Saml Timson decd did in & by his will dated 8 Jan 1694 devise & appoint to be sold by the executors of the sd will for the good & benefitt of the sd testators children, now these presents wit that the sd Saml Timson for the sum of £55 & the sd Tho Barbar & Mary his wife for £25, by these presents have each of them quit claimed unto the sd Wm Timson in his actuall possession now being the sd 200 a. of land bounded as afsd … . Wit: Jno Holloway, Wm Barbar, Wm Barbar Junr. Ackn 20 May 1717 by Saml Timson, Tho Barbar Junr & Mary his wife & the sd Mary (being first privately examined) relinquished her right of dower in the sd land & admitted to record. Attest: Phi Lightfoot clerk. (Pg 169)

13 Feb 1716. Deed of Lease. Wm Jones of Bruton Parish, York Co planter for 5 shillings leased to Richd Easter of same place planter a 40 a. tr of land in Bruton Parish at a place called Indian Field upon the br of a swamp issuing out of Queens Cr being pt/on the land purch by the sd Wm Jones of & from Ralph Graves of same parish bounded by the old Church, Jno Custis, Wm Jackson, Richd Easter, Old Church Spring Br, Wm Davis & Col Jenings … for the term

of one year ... . Wit: Michl Dewick, Hen Holdcraft, Basil Wagstaff. Ackn 17
Jun 1717 & admitted to record. Attest: Phi Lightfoot clerk. (Pg 170)

14 Feb 1716. Deed of Release. Wm Jones of Bruton Parish, York Co planter
for £17:10 released to Richd Easter of same place planter a 40 a. tr of land in
Bruton Parish ... [*same as above*] ... . Wit: Michl Dewick, Hen Holdcraft,
Basil Wagstaff. Ackn 17 Jun 1717 & admitted to record. Attest: Phi Lightfoot
clerk. (Pg 172)

14 Feb 1716. Bond. I Wm Jones of Bruton Parish, York Co am firmly bound
unto Richd Easter of same place planter for £35 ... the condition of this
obligation is such that whereas the afsd Wm Jones hath sold unto the sd Richd
Easter one 40 a. tr of land [*see above*] now if the sd Wm Jones shall & do well &
truly observe, perform, fullfill & keep all the articles, covenants, clauses, grants
& agreements mentioned in the sd deed of release then this obligation to be void
... . Wit: Michl Dewick, Hen Holdcraft, Basil Wagstaff. Ackn 17 Jun 1717 &
admitted to record. Attest: Phi Lightfoot clerk. (Pg 174)

13 Feb 1716. Deed of Lease. Wm Jones of Bruton Parish, York Co planter for
5 shillings leased unto Wm Davis of same place planter a 40 a. tr of land in
Bruton Parish at a place called Indian Field upon the brs of a swamp issuing out
of Queens Cr being pt/o the land purch by the sd Wm Jones of & from Ralph
Graves of same parish bounded by Graveners Spring Br, Old Church Spring Br
& Flax Hole Br ... for the term of one year ... . Wit: Mary Holdcraft, Ja
Stanup, Tho Holdcraft, Hen Holdcraft. Ackn 17 Jun 1717 & admitted to record.
Attest: Phi Lightfoot clerk. (Pg 175)

14 Feb 1716. Deed of Release. Wm Jones of Bruton Parish, York Co planter
for £17:10 released unto Wm Davis of same place planter a 40 a. tr of land in
Bruton Parish ... lately purch by the sd Wm Jones of & from Ralph Graves
being pt/o a greater tr formerly belonging to Ralph Graves father of the sd Ralph
Graves formerly of York Co decd ... [*same as above*] ... . Wit: Mary
Holdcraft, Ja Stanup, Hen Holdcraft, Tho Holdcraft. Ackn 17 Jun 1717 &
admitted to record. Attest: Phi Lightfoot clerk. (Pg 175)

14 Feb 1716. Bond. I Wm Jones of Bruton Parish, York Co am firmly bound
unto Wm Davis of same place planter for £35 ... the condition of this obligation
is such that whereas the afsd Wm Jones hath sold unto the afsd Wm Davis a 40
a. parcell of land [*see above*] now if the sd Wm Jones shall & do well & truly
observe, perform, fullfill & keep all the articles, covenants, clauses, grants &
agreements mentioned in the sd deed of release then this obligation to be void ...
. Wit: Mary Holdcraft, Ja Stanup, Tho Holdcraft, Hen Holdcraft. Ackn 17 Jun
1717 & admitted to record. Attest: Phi Lightfoot clerk. (Pg 178)

2 Jul 1716. Deed. Nathl Huggins of Gloucester Co weaver for £15 sold to Tho Nelson of York Town, York Co gent all his lott or ½ a. of land in York Town being pt/o the Port Land known by the number 57 as by the plot on the records of the sd co doth appear, the sd lott containing 10 poles in length & 8 poles in breadth bounded by the land of Wm Fuller, Jno Young, Nicho Phillips decd formerly belonging to Jno Penton & on the street opposite of land of Capt Lawr Smith ... . Wit: Michl Dewick, Matt Ballard, Jno Gibbons. Ackn 15 Jul 17617 & admitted to record. Attest: Phi Lightfoot clerk. (Pg 178)

2 Jul 1717. Bond. I Nathl Huggins of Gloucester Co weaver am firmly bound unto Tho Nelson of York Town, York Co for £30 ... the condition of this obligation is such that if the afsd Nathl Huggins shall well & truly observe, perform, fullfill, accomplish & keep all the covenants, grants, articles, clauses & agreements mentioned in one certain indenture of sale [see above] then this obligation to be void ... . Wit: Michl Dewick, Matt Ballard, Jno Gibbons. Ackn 15 Jul 1717 & admitted to record. Attest: Phi Lightfoot clerk. (Pg 180)

14 Jun 1717. Deed of Lease. Jno Washington of Gloucester Co gent for 5 shillings farm letten unto Philip Lightfoot of York Co gent all that 114 a. tr of land on the upper side of Martues Cr in York Hampton Parish adj Major Buckner, Jno Lewis esqr & Eliz his wife, Ballards Cr & Jno Smith, which sd tr of land came & descended to the sd Jno Washington as son & heir of Lawr Washington & Mildred his wife decd one of the daus & coheirs of Augustine Warner & Mildred his wife also decd as by one indenture of partition of lands of the sd Augustine Warner decd made jointly between Jno Lewis esqr & Eliz his wife surviving dau of the sd Augustine Warner & Mildred his wife decd of the one part & Jno Smith son & heir of Jno Smith & Mary his wife decd (another of the daus & coheirs of the sd Augustine Warner & Mildred his wife decd) of the second part & Jno Washington the party to these presents (son & heir of Lawr Washington & Mildred his wife decd) another of the daus & coheirs of the sd Augustine Warner & Mildred his wife decd) of the third part ...for one year paying the yearly rent of one ear of Indian corn on the last day of the sd year if demanded ... . Wit: Tho Reade, Tho Nelson, Michl Dewick, Drury Stith Junr. Ackn 15 Jul 1717 & admitted to record. Attest: Phi Lightfoot clerk. (Pg 180)

15 Jun 1717. Deed of Release. Jno Washington of Gloucester Co gent for £110 & £4 released unto Philip Lightfoot of York Co gent all that 114 a. tr of land ... [same as above] ... . Wit: Tho Reade, Tho Nelson, Michl Dewick, Drury Stith Junr. Ackn 15 Jul 1717 by Jno Washington & also at the same time appeared Tho Nelson gent who by vertue of a power of atty from Katherine Washington (w/o the sd Jno) relinquished her right of dower & admitted to record. Attest: Phi Lightfoot clerk. (Pg 181)

15 Jun 1717. Bond. I Jno Washington of Gloucester co gent am firmly bound unto Phi Lightfoot of York Co gent for £220 ... the condition of this obligation is such that if the afsd Jno Washington do & shall well & truly observe, perform, fullfill, accomplish & keep all the covenants, grants, articles, clauses, conditions & agreements mentioned in a pair of indentures of lease & release [see above] then this obligation to be void ... .Wit: Tho Reade, Tho Nelson, Michl Dewick, Drury Stith Junr. Ackn 15 Jul 1717 & admitted to record. Attest: Phi Lightfoot clerk. (Pg 183)

19 Apr 1717. Deed of Lease. John Clayton & Wil Robertson feofees or trustees for the land appointed for the building & erecting the City of Wmsburgh for 5 shillings farm letten unto Jno Tyler of York Co one lott of ground in the sd City of Wmsburgh denoted in the plan of the sd city by the figure 232 ... for the term of one year paying the rent of one ear of Indian corn at the feast of St. Michaell ye Archangel if demanded ... . Wit: None. Ackn 15 Jul 1717 & admitted to record. Attest: Phi Lightfoot clerk. (Pg 183)

20 Apr 1717. Deed of Release. John Clayton & Wil Robertson feofees or trustees for the land appointed for the building & erecting the City of Wmsburgh for 15 shillings released unto Jno Tyler of York Co one lott of ground in the sd City of Wmsburgh denoted in the plan of the sd city by the figure 232 ... [same as above] ... if the sd Jno Tyler shall not within the space of 24 months build & finish upon each lott one good dwelling house then it shall & may be lawfull to & for the sd feofees or trustees into the granted premises & every part thereof to enter & the same to have again as of their former estate to have, hold & enjoy in like manner as they might otherwise have done if these presents had never been made ... . Wit: None. Ackn 15 Jul 1717 & admitted to record. Attest: Phi Lightfoot clerk. (Pg 184)

31 May 1717. Deed of Lease. Wm Timson of York Co gent for 5 shillings farm lett unto James Shields of the City of Wmsburgh taylor three lotts of ground in the City of Wmsburgh designed in the plot of the sd city by the figures 46, 47 & 323 which sd three lotts were granted unto the sd Wm Timson by the feofees or trustees of the sd city by deeds of lease & release & also a 200 a. tr of land purch by the decd Saml Timson father of the sd Wm Timson from the also decd Saml Weldon of James City Co merchant & Sarah his wife by deed dated 19 Apr 1680 & transmitted by the will of the sd Saml Timson to the sd Wm Timson & Saml & Mary Timson his children equally amongst them to which 2/3 part of the sd Wm Timson has right from the sd Saml & Mary Timson & from Tho Barbar now husband to the sd Mary by deed dated 20 Nov 1716 ackn in York Co Court 20 May last, was lying within 4 miles of the City of Wmsburgh & is bounded by Queens Cr Swamp ... during the term of one year paying the rent of one grain of Indian corn upon the feast of St. Michael ye Arch Angell next coming if

demanded ... . Wit: Wm Lindsay, Jno Bates Junr, Abra Brodribb, Ralph White, Mary Dabbadie. Ackn 15 Jul 1717 & admitted to record. Attest: Phi Lightfoot clerk. (Pg 185)

1 Jun 1717. Deed of Release. Wm Timson of York Co gent for £300 released unto James Shields of the City of Wmsburgh taylor three lotts of ground in the City of Wmsburgh designed in the plot of the sd city by the figures 46, 47 & 323, also a 200 a. tr of land ... [*same as above*] ... also that Anna Marie the w/o the sd Wm Timson shall when required by the sd James Shield relinquish all her right of dower in the above granted premises unto the sd James Shields before York Co Court ... . Wit: Wm Lindsay, Jno Bates Junr, Abra Brodribb, Ralph White, Mary Dabbadie. Ackn 15 Jul 1717 by Wm Timson & admitted to record. Attest: Phi Lightfoot clerk. (Pg 186)

1 Jun 1717. Bond. I Wm Timson of York Co gent am firmly bound unto James Shield of the City of Wmsburgh taylor for £600 ... the condition of this obligation is such that if the afsd Wm Timson shall observe, perform, fullfill & keep all the covenants, grants, articles, clauses, conditions & agreements mentioned in deeds of lease & release [*see above*] then this obligation to be void ... . Wm Lindsay, Jno Bates Junr, Abra Broadribb, Ralph White, Mary Dabbadie. Ackn 15 Jul 1717 & admitted to record. Attest: Phi Lightfoot clerk. (Pg 188)

1 Jun 1717. Deed of Lease. Tho Jones, Henry Holdcraft & Jno Holloway all of VA attys of Wm Wharton of Great Brittain mariner son & heir & devisee of Richd Wharton late of VA formerly of the Co of Westmoreland in England esqr decd for 5 shillings farm letten unto Jno Marot of the City of Wmsburgh, VA ordinary keeper one lott of ½ a. of ground in the Duke of Gloucester Street in the City of Wmsburgh on the n side of the sd street opposite to the now dwelling house of the sd Marot adj to the lott of Susanna Allen & described in the plan or plot of the sd city by the number 56 & the mansion or dwelling house thereon now standing ... for the term of 6 months ... . Wit: Davis Bray, Jno Clayton. Ackn by the attys 15 Jul 1717 & admitted to record. Attest: Phi Lightfoot clerk. (Pg 189)

2 Jul 1717. Deed of Release. Tho Jones, Henry Holdcraft & Jno Holloway all of VA attys of Wm Wharton of Great Brittain mariner son & heir & devisee of Richd Wharton late of VA formerly of the Co of Westmoreland in England esqr decd for £40 released unto Jno Marot of the City of Wmsburgh, VA ordinary keeper one lott of ½ a. of ground in the City of Wmsburgh number 56 ... [*same as above*] ... . Wit: David Bray, Jno Clayton. Ackn 15 Jul 1717 by the attys & admitted to record. Attest: Phi Lightfoot clerk. (Pg 189)

15 Jun 1717. Deed of Lease. George Baskervyle of Charles Parish, York Co for 5 shillings farm letten unto Tho Roberts Junr of same place a 425 a. tr of land in Charles Parish together with the marsh adj whereon the sd Geo Baskervyle now liveth being pt/o a greater tr of land called Boar Quarter heretofore sold & conveyed to the sd George by Ralph Graves of Bruton Parish, York Co by deed dated 30 Nov 1714 bounded by the head of Boar Quarter Cr, Col Edmd Jenings, Wm Wise Junr & the old Poqusson River or Main Bay … for one year paying the yearly rent of one ear of Indian corn on the last day of the sd year if demanded … . Wit: Charles Thurman, Alles Thurman, Mary Norvell. Ackn 15 Jul 1717 & admitted to record. Attest: Phi Lightfoot clerk. (Pg 190)

16 Jun 1717. Deed of Release. George Baskervyle of Charles Parish, York Co for 300 lbs of sweet scented tobo released unto Tho Roberts Junr of same place a 425 a. tr of land in Charles Parish together with the marsh adj … [same as above] … . Wit: Charles Thurman, Alles Thurman, Mary Norvell. Ackn 15 Jul 1717 by Geo Baskervyle & also appeared Eliza the w/o the sd Geo who being first privately examined relinquished her right of dower & admitted to record. Attest: Phi Lightfoot clerk. (Pg 191)

16 Jun 1717. Bond. I Geo Baskervyle of Charles Parish, York Co planter am firmly bound unto Tho Roberts Junr of same place planter for £100 … the condition of this obligation is such that if the afsd Geo Baskervyle shall well & truly keep, perform, observe & fullfill all the clauses, articles, covenants, grants & agreements mentioned in one indenture of release [see above] then this obligation to be void … . Wit: Charles Thurman, Alles Thurman, Mary Norvell. Ackn 15 Jul 1717 & admitted to record. Attest: Phi Lightfoot clerk. (Pg 193)

5 Jun 1717. Deed. Jno Martin of York Hampton Parish, York Co mariner for 5 shillings farm letten unto Arthur Bickerdike of same place merchant all his lott or ½ a. of land in York Town containing 10 poles in length & 8 poles in breadth being pt/o the Port Land designed in the plot of the sd town by the number 39 … for the term of one year … . Wit: Richard Ambler, James Forsyth. Ackn 16 Sep 1717 by Cole Digges gent by vertue of a power of atty from Capt Jno Martin & admitted to record. Attest: Phi Lightfoot clerk. (Pg 193)

6 Jun 1717. Deed of Release. Jno Martin of York Hampton Parish, York Co mariner for £20 released unto Arthur Bickerdike of same place merchant all his lott or ½ a. of land in York Town number 39 … [same as above] … . Wit: Richard Ambler, James Forsyth. Ackn 16 Sep 1717 by Cole Digges gent by vertue of a power of atty from Capt Jno Martin & admitted to record. Attest: Phi Lightfoot clerk. (Pg 194)

6 Jun 1717. Bond. I Jno Martin of York Hampton Parish, York Co mariner am firmly bound unto Arthur Bickardike of same place merchant for £40 ... the condition of this obligation is such that if the afsd Jno Martin do & shall well & truly observe, perform, fullfill, accomplish & keep all the covenants, grants, articles, conditions, clauses & agreements mentioned in one pair of indentures of lease & release [see above] then this obligation to be void .... Wit: Richard Ambler, James Forsyth. Ackn 16 Sep 1717 by Cole Digges gent by vertue of a power of atty from Capt Jno Martin & is admitted to record. Attest: Phi Lightfoot clerk. (Pg 195)

13 Sep 1717. Deed of Lease. Jno Northern of Corratuck Precinct in NC for 5 shillings farm letten unto Benj Clifton of Charles Parish, York Co all his lott or ½ a. of land in York Town being pt/o the Port Land known by the number 32 as by the plot on the records of the sd co may appear, the sd lott containing 10 poles in length & 8 poles in breadth (formerly granted to Jno Northern father of the sd Jno Northern party to these presents) late of Charles Parish, York Co decd by deed under the hands & seals of Thos Ballard & Wm Buckner decd the feofees or trustees for the Port Land of York dated 24 Jun 1706, & by the death of the sd Jno Northern came & descended to the afsd Jno Northern as son & heir at law of the sd Jno Northern decd ... for the term of one year paying the yearly rent of one ear of Indian corn on the last day of the sd year if demanded .... Wit: Tho Roberts Junr, Jno Doswell Junr, Jno Hay. Ackn 16 Sep 1717 & admitted to record. Attest: Phi Lightfoot clerk. (Pg 196)

14 Sep 1717. Deed of Release. Jno Northern of Corratuck Precinct in NC (son & heir at law of Jno Northern late of Charles Parish, York Co decd) for £30 released to Benj Clifton of Charles Parish, York Co all his lott or ½ a. of land in York Town number 32 ... [same as above] .... Wit: Tho Roberts Junr, Jno Doswell Junr, Jno Hay. Ackn 16 Sep 1717 & admitted to record. Attest: Phi Lightfoot clerk. (Pg 197)

14 Sep 1717. Bond. I Jno Northern of Corratuck Precinct in NC am firmly bound unto Benj Clifton of Charles Parish, York Co for £60 ... the condition of this obligation is such that if the afsd Jno Northern do & shall well & truly observe, perform, fullfill, accomplish & keep all the covenants, grants, articles, clauses, conditions & agreements mentioned in one pair of indentures of lease & release [see above] then this obligation to be void .... Wit: Tho Roberts Junr, Jno Doswell Junr, Jno Hay. Ackn 16 Sep 1717 & admitted to record. Attest: Phi Lightfoot clerk. (Pg 198)

4 May 1717. Deed of Lease. Joseph Ring son & heir of Joseph Ring late of Hampton Parish, York Co gent decd for 5 shillings farm letten unto Joseph Walker of York Hampton Parish, co afsd merchant a 40 a. tr of land called

French Ordinary now in the tenor or occupation of Andrew Lester adj the land of Tho Buck, the land of sd Joseph Walker which he lately purch of Mary Bass, land of Tho Wade & the road that leads into Merchants Hundred ... for the term of one year ... . Wit: Phill Moody, Phi Lightfoot. Ackn 16 Sep 1717 & admitted to record. Attest: Phi Lightfoot clerk. (Pg 199)

5 May 1717. Deed of Release. Joseph Ring son & heir of Joseph Ring late of Hampton Parish, York Co gent decd for £25 released unto Joseph Walker of York Hampton Parish, co afsd merchant a 40 a. tr of land ... [same as above] ... . Wit: Phill Moody, Phi Lightfoot. Ackn 16 Sep 1717 & admitted to record. Attest: Phi Lightfoot clerk. (Pg 199)

5 May 1717. Bond. I Joseph Ring of York Hampton Parish, York Co am firmly bound unto Joseph Walker of same place merchant for £60 ... the condition of this obligation is such that if the afsd Joseph Ring shall well & truly observe, perform, fullfill, accomplish & keep al the covenants, conditions & agreements mentioned in one pair of indentures of lease & release [see above] then this obligation to be void ... . Wit: Phill Moody, Phi Lightfoot. Ackn 16 Sep 1717 & admitted to record. Attest: Phi Lightfoot clerk. (Pg 201)

16 Sep 1717. Deed. Lawr Smith & Tho Nelson gent trustees for the Port Land of York Town in York Co for 180 lbs of tobacco sold to Robt Ballard carpenter a lott or ½ a. of land in York Town being pt/o the Port Land known by the number 21 as by the plot of the sd town on the records of the sd co doth appear, the sd lott containing 10 poles in length & 8 poles in breadth ... provided that the sd Robt Ballard shall within 12 months begin to build & finish on the sd lott one good house to contain at least 20', wherein if he fail then this present grant to be void in law ... . Wit: None. Ackn 16 Sep 1717 & admitted to record. Attest: Phi Lightfoot clerk. (Pg 201)

28 Aug 1717. Deed of Lease. John Clayton & Wil Robertson feofees or trustees for the land appropriated for the building & erecting of the City of Wmsburgh for 5 shillings farm letten unto George Reddall of York Co one lott of ground in the sd City of Wmsburgh designed in the plott of the sd city by the figure 175 ... for the term of one year paying the yearly rent of one grain of Indian corn on 10 Oct if demanded ... . Wit: None. Ackn 18 Nov 1717 & admitted to record. Attest: Phi Lightfoot clerk. (Pg 202)

29 Aug 1717. Deed of Release. John Clayton & Wil Robertson feofees or trustees for the land appropriated for the building & erecting of the City of Wmsburgh for 15 shillings released unto George Reddall of York Co one lott of ground in the sd City of Wmsburgh designed in the plott of the sd city by the figure 175 ... [same as above] ... if the sd George Reddall shall not within the

space of 24 months build & finish upon each lott one good dwelling house then it shall & may be lawfull to & for the sd feofees or trustees into the granted premises & every part thereof to enter & the same to have again as of their former estate to have, hold & enjoy in like manner as they might otherwise have done if these presents had never been made … . Wit: None. Ackn 18 Nov 1717 & admitted to record. Attest: Phi Lightfoot clerk. (Pg 202)

4 Nov 1716. Deed of Lease. John Clayton & Wil Robertson feofees or trustees for the land appropriated for the building & erecting of the City of Wmsburgh for 5 shillings farm letten unto Wm Levingston of York Co gent three lotts of ground in the sd City of Wmsburgh designed in the plott of the sd city by the figures 163, 164 & 169 … for the term of one year paying the yearly rent of one grain of Indian corn on 10 Oct if demanded … . Wit: None. Ackn 19 Nov 1716 by Jno Clayton esqr & admitted to record. Attest: Michl Dewick clerk. Ackn 18 Nov 1717 by Wm Robertson gent & admitted to record. Attest: Phi Lightfoot clerk. (Pg 204)

5 Nov 1716. Deed of Release. John Clayton & Wil Robertson feofees or trustees for the land appropriated for the building & erecting of the City of Wmsburgh for £45 released unto Wm Levingston of York Co gent three lotts of ground in the sd City of Wmsburgh designed in the plott of the sd city by the figures 163, 164 & 169 … [*same as above*] … if the sd Wm Levingston shall not within the space of 24 months build & finish upon each lott one good dwelling house then it shall & may be lawfull to & for the sd feofees or trustees into the granted premises & every part thereof to enter & the same to have again as of their former estate to have, hold & enjoy in like manner as they might otherwise have done if these presents had never been made … . Wit: None. Ackn 19 Nov 1716 by Jno Clayton esqr & admitted to record. Attest: Michl Dewick clerk. Ackn 18 Nov 1717 by Wm Robertson gent & admitted to record. Attest: Phi Lightfoot clerk. (Pg 204)

13 Nov 1717. Deed of Lease. John Clayton & Wil Robertson feofees or trustees for the land appropriated for the building & erecting of the City of Wmsburgh for 5 shillings farm letten unto Jonathan Drewit of York Co four lotts of ground at Queen Mary Port & designed in the plott of the sd Port by the figures 5, 6, 30 & 31 … for the term of one year paying the rent of one grain of Indian corn on 10 Oct if demanded … . Wit: None. Ackn 18 Nov 1717 & admitted to record. Attest: Phi Lightfoot clerk. (Pg 206)

14 Nov 1717. Deed of Release. John Clayton & Wil Robertson feofees or trustees for the land appropriated for the building & erecting of the City of Wmsburgh for £3 released unto Jonathan Drewit of York Co four lotts of ground at Queen Mary Port & designed in the plott of the sd Port by the figures 5, 6, 30

& 31 ... [*same as above*] ... if the sd Jonathan Drewit shall not within the space of 24 months build & finish upon each lott one good dwelling house then it shall & may be lawfull to & for the sd feofees or trustees into the granted premises & every part thereof to enter & the same to have again as of their former estate to have, hold & enjoy in like manner as they might otherwise have done if these presents had never been made ... . Wit: None. Ackn 18 Nov 1717 & admitted to record. Attest: Phi Lightfoot clerk. (Pg 207)

24 Sep 1717. Deed. Francis Dursey eldest son & heir of Francis Dursey late of Bruton Parish, York Co decd for £35 sold to James Taylor of same place a plantation & 50 a. tr of land in Bruton Parish (being all that plantation & dividend of land which the afsd Francis Dursey the father dyed seized of & afterwards it fell & became due to this sd Francis Dursey as being eldest son & heir at law to his sd father) bounded by the land formerly of Saml Timson (now the land of James Shields), land of Geo Glascock, land of Richd Page & land of Jno Layton ... . Wit: Wm Taylor, Jno Taylor, Hen Holdcraft. Ackn 18 Nov 1717 & admitted to record. Attest: Phi Lightfoot clerk. (Pg 208)

24 Sep 1717. Bond. I Francis Dursey of Bruton Parish, York Co am firmly bound unto James Taylor of same place for £74 ... the condition of this obligation is such that whereas the afsd Francis Dursey hath sold & conveyed unto the sd James Taylor a plantation & 50 a. parcel of land by indenture of sale [*see above*], now if the sd Francis Dursey shall well & truly obey, observe, perform, fullfill & keep all the articles, covenants, grants, clauses & agreements mentioned in the sd indenture then this obligation to be void ... . Wit: Hen Holdcraft, Wm Taylor, Jno Taylor. Ackn 18 Nov 1717 & admitted to record. Attest: Phi Lightfoot clerk. (Pg 211)

15 Nov 1717. Deed of Lease. Saml Hyde of Bruton Parish, York Co son of Robt Hyde & Jane his wife dau of Capt Jno Underhill late of Hampton Parish, York Co for 5 shillings farm letten unto Joseph Walker of York Hampton Parish merchant all his 100 a. tr of land in York Hampton Parish in the tenor & occupation of Richd Cooke bounded by Filgates Cr, land of Tho Barbar, Baskervyles Swamp & land of sd Joseph Walker ... for the term of one year ... . Wit: Fran Tyler, H. Holdcraft, Godfrey Pole. Ackn 18 Nov 1717 & admitted to record. Attest: Phi Lightfoot clerk. (Pg 211)

16 Nov 1717. Deed of Release. Saml Hyde of Bruton Parish, York Co son of Robt Hyde & Jane his wife dau of Capt Jno Underhill late of Hampton Parish, York Co for £100 released unto Joseph Walker of York Hampton Parish merchant all his 100 a. tr of land in York Hampton Parish ... [*same as above*] ... . Wit: Fran Tyler, Godfrey Pole, H. Holdcraft. Ackn 18 Nov 1717 & admitted to record. Attest: Phi Lightfoot clerk. (Pg 212)

17 May 1717. Deed of Lease. M. Ingles & Wil Robertson feofees or trustees for the land appropriated for the building & erecting the City of Wmsburgh for 5 shillings farm letten unto Giles Moody of York Co four lotts of ground at Queen Mary's Port in the City of Wmsburgh designed in the plot of the sd Port by the figures 22, 23, 24 & 25 ... for the term of one year paying the yearly rent of one grain of Indian corn on 10 Oct if demanded ... . Wit: None. Ackn 18 Nov 1717 by Wm Robertson gent. Attest: Phi Lightfoot clerk. (Pg 214)

18 May 1717. Deed of Release. M. Ingles & Wil Robertson feofees or trustees for the land appropriated for the building & erecting the City of Wmsburgh for £3 released unto Giles Moody of York Co four lotts of ground at Queen Mary's Port in the City of Wmsburgh designed in the plot of the sd Port by the figures 22, 23, 24 & 25 ... if the sd Giles Moody shall not within the space of 24 months build & finish upon each lott one good dwelling house then it shall & may be lawfull to & for the sd feofees or trustees into the granted premises & every part thereof to enter & the same to have again as of their former estate to have, hold & enjoy in like manner as they might otherwise have done if these presents had never been made ... . Wit: None. Ackn 18 Nov 1717 by Wm Robertson gent. Attest: Phi Lightfoot clerk. (Pg 215)

5 May 1716. Deed of Lease. John Clayton & Wil Robertson feofees or trustees for the land appropriated for the building & erecting the City of Wmsburgh for 5 shillings farm letten unto Richd King of York Co nine lotts of ground in the sd City of Wmsburgh designed in the plot of the sd city by the figures 319, 320, 321, 322, 323, 324, 325, 326, 327 & 328 ... for the term of one year paying the yearly rent of one grain of Indian corn on 10 Oct if demanded ... . Wit: Phi Lightfoot, Fran Tyler, Graves Pack. Ackn 18 Nov 1717 & admitted to record. Attest: Phi Lightfoot clerk. (Pg 216)

6 May 1716. Deed of Release. John Clayton & Wil Robertson feofees or trustees for the land appropriated for the building & erecting the City of Wmsburgh for £6:15 released unto Richd King of York Co nine lotts of ground in the sd City of Wmsburgh designed in the plot of the sd city by the figures 319, 320, 321, 322, 323, 324, 325, 326, 327 & 328 ... [same as above] ... if the sd Richd King shall not within the space of 24 months build & finish upon each lott one good dwelling house then it shall & may be lawfull to & for the sd feofees or trustees into the granted premises & every part thereof to enter & the same to have again as of their former estate to have, hold & enjoy in like manner as they might otherwise have done if these presents had never been made ... . Wit: Phi Lightfoot, Fran Tyler, Grave Pack. Ackn 18 Nov 1717 & admitted to record. Attest: Phi Lightfoot clerk. (Pg 217)

6 Nov 1717. Deed. Jno May son & heir of Tho May & Margaret his wife (of Sussex Co adj to the Province of PA) late Margaret Spencer sister & heir at law of Eliz Spencer (late Eliz Powers decd) for £50 sold to Joseph Mountfort of York Hampton Parish, York Co a lott or ½ a. of land in York Town now in the possession of Philip Lightfoot gent & also of, in or to one Negro man slave named Guy, & likewise of, in or to all other lands or slaves within VA on this side of Cheseapeake Bay which were of the estate of the sd Eliz Powers decd … . Wit: Michl Dewick, Math Ballard, Edwd Young, Phi Lightfoot. Proved 16 Dec 1717 & admitted to record. Attest: Phi Lightfoot clerk. (Pg 218)

6 Nov 1717. I Jno May of Sussex Co adj to PA am firmly bound unto Joseph Mountfort of York Hampton Parish, York Co, VA for £240 … the condition of this obligation is such that whereas the afsd Jno May son & heir of Margaret May (late Margt Spencer heir at law of Eliza Spencer late Eliza Powers decd) hath sold & conveyed his right, title & claim of, in & to one lott of land in York Town & a Negro slave named Guy late the property of the sd Eliz Powers decd, now if the sd Jno May shall & do in all things well & truly observe, perform, fullfill, accomplish & keep all the covenants, grants, articles, conditions & agreements mentioned in one certain indenture [*see above*] then this obligation to be void … . Wit: Michl Dewick, Math Ballard, Edward Young, Phi Lightfoot. Proved 16 Dec 1717 & admitted to record. Attest: Phi Lightfoot clerk. (Pg 220)

20 Jan 1717. Deed. Lawrence Smith & Thomas Nelson gent trustees for the Portland of York Town in York Co for 180 lbs of tobacco sold to John Gibbons all that lott or ½ a. of land in York Town being pt/o the Port Land known by the number 67 as by the plott on the records of the sd co may appear the sd lott containing 10 poles in length & 8 poles in breadth … provided that the sd Jno Gibbons do & shall within 12 months build & finish on the sd lott one good house to contain at least 20' wherein if he fail then this present grant to be void in law … . Wit: None. Ackn 20 Jan 1717 & admitted to record. Attest: Phi Lightfoot clerk. (Pg 221)

20 Jan 1717. Deed. Lawrence Smith & Thos Nelson gent trustees for the Port Land of York Town in York Co for 180 lbs of tobacco sold to John Gibbons a lott or ½ a. of land in York Town being pt/o the Port Land known by the number 71 as by the plott on the records of the sd co may appear the sd lott containing 10 poles in length & 8 poles in breadth … provided that the sd John Gibbons do & shall within 12 months build & finish on the sd lott one good house to contain at least 20' wherein if he fail then this present grant to be void in law … . Wit: None. Ackn Jan 1717 & admitted to record. Attest: Phi Lightfoot clerk. (Pg 221)

51

20 Jan 1717. Deed. Lawrence Smith & Thos Nelson gent trustees for the Port Land of York Town in York Co for 180 lbs of tobacco sold to Saml Cooper one lott or ½ a. of land in York Town being pt/o the Port Land known by the number 9 as by the plott on the records of the sd co may appear, the sd lott containing 10 poles in length & 8 poles in breadth ... provided that the sd Saml Cooper do & shall within 12 months build & finish on the sd lott one good house to contain at least 20' wherein if he fail then this present grant to be void in law ... . Wit: None. Ackn 20 Jan 1717 & admitted to record. Attest: Phi Lightfoot clerk. (Pg 222)

16 Dec 1717. Deed. Lawrence Smith & Thos Nelson gent trustees for the Port Land of York Town in York Co for 180 lbs of tobacco sold to John Trotter a lott or ½ a. of land in York Town being pt/o the Port Land known by the number 15 as by the plott on the records of the sd co doth appear, the sd lott containing 10 poles in length & 8 poles in breadth ... provided that the sd John Trotter do & shall within 12 months build & finish on the sd lott one good house to contain at least 20' wherein if he fail then this present grant to be void in law ... . Wit: None. Ackn 20 Jan 1717 & admitted to record. Attest: Phi Lightfoot clerk. (Pg 223)

20 Jan 1717. Deed. Lawrence Smith & Thos Nelson gent trustees for the Port Land of York Town in York Co for 180 lbs of tobacco sold to Richard Cheshire merchant a lott or ½ a. of land in York Town being pt/o the Port Land known by the number 63 as by the plott in the records of the sd co may appear, the sd lott containing 10 poles in length & 8 poles in breadth ... provided that the sd Richard Cheshire do & shall within 12 months build & finish on the sd lott one good house to contain at least 20' wherein if he fail then this present grant to be void in law ... . Wit: None. Ackn 20 Jan 1717 & admitted to record. Attest: Phi Lightfoot clerk. (Pg 223)

20 Jan 1717. Deed. Lawrence Smith & Thos Nelson gent trustees for the Port Land of York Town in York Co for 180 lbs of tobacco sold to Richd Cheshire merchant a lott or ½ a. of land in York Town being pt/o the Port Land known by the number 59 as by the plott on the records of the sd co doth appear, the sd lott containing 10 poles in length & 8 poles in breadth ... provided that the sd Richard Cheshire do & shall within 12 months build & finish on the sd lott one good house to contain at least 20' wherein if he fail then this present grant to be void in law ... . Wit: None. Ackn 20 Jan 1717 & admitted to record. Attest: Phi Lightfoot clerk. (Pg 224)

20 Jan 1717. Deed. Lawrence Smith & Thos Nelson gent trustees for the Port Land of York Town in York Co of the one part & Joseph Walker of York Co gent of the other part, whereas Joseph Ring late of York Co one of the feofees

for the Portland was & died seized & possessed of one lott or ½ a. of land known in the plott of the sd town by the number 10 by vertue of an order of York Court dated 25 Nov 1692 specifying the sd lott to be granted & confirmed by the sd court to the sd Joseph Ring in consideration of his extraordinary care & trouble in the discharge of his office & place of feofee in trust as afsd (& for which sd lott there was never yet any deed granted by the feofees or trustees for the Port Land afsd the sd lott or ½ a. of land being by the sd Joseph Ring built upon according to the directions of the Act of Assembly, the sd lott containing 10 poles in length & 8 poles in breadth descending to Joseph Ring son & heir at law of the sd Joseph Ring decd & purch of the sd Joseph Ring by the sd Joseph Walker by deeds dated 15 & 16 Aug 1712, have granted & sold unto the sd Joseph Walker all the afsd lott or ½ a. of land in York Town ... . Wit: None. Ackn 20 Jan 1717 & admitted to record. Attest: Phi Lightfoot clerk. (Pg 225)

20 Jan 1717. Deed. Lawrence Smith & Thos Nelson gent trustees for the Port Land of York Town in York Co for 180 lbs of tobacco sold to Joseph Walker gent one lott or ½ a. of land in York Town being pt/o the Port Land known by the number 8 as by the plott on the records of the sd co doth appear, the sd lott containing 10 poles in length & 8 poles in breadth ... provided that the sd Joseph Walker do & shall within 12 months build & finish on the sd lott one good house to contain at least 20' wherein if he fail then this present grant to be void in law ... . Wit: None. Ackn 20 Jan 1717 & admitted to record. Attest: Phi Lightfoot clerk. (Pg 225)

13 Jul 1717. Deed of Lease. John Clayton & Wil Robertson feofees or trustees for the land appropriated for the building & erecting the City of Williamsburgh for 5 shillings farm letten unto David Cuningham of York Co two lotts of ground in the sd City of Williamsburgh designed in the plott of the sd city by the figures 337 & 338 ... for the term of one year paying the yearly rent of one ear of Indian corn at the Feast of St. Michael the Archangel if demanded ... . Wit: None. Ackn 20 Jan 1717 & admitted to record. Attest: Phi Lightfoot clerk. (Pg 226)

14 Jul 1717. Deed of Release. John Clayton & Wil Robertson feofees or trustees for the land appropriated for the building & erecting the City of Williamsburgh for 30 shillings released unto David Cuningham of York Co two lotts of ground in the sd City of Williamsburgh designed in the plott of the sd city by the figures 337 & 338 ... [same as above] ... if the sd David Cuningham shall not within the space of 24 months build & finish upon each lott one good dwelling house then it shall & may be lawfull to & for the sd feofees or trustees into the granted premises & every part thereof to enter & the same to have again as of their former estate to have, hold & enjoy in like manner as they might

otherwise have done if these presents had never been made ... . Wit: None. Ackn 20 Jan 1717 & admitted to record. Attest: Phi Lightfoot clerk. (Pg 227)

2 Sep 1717. Deed of Lease. John Clayton & Wil Robertson feofees or trustees for the land appropriated for the building & erecting the City of Williamsburgh for 5 shillings farm letten unto Saml Hyde of York Co one lott of ground in the City of Williamsburgh designed in the plott of the sd city by the figure 47 ... for the term of one year paying the yearly rent of one grain of Indian corn on 10 Oct if demanded ... . Wit: None. Ackn 16 Dec 1717. Attest: Phi Lightfoot clerk. (Pg 228)

3 Sep 1717. Deed of Release. John Clayton & Wil Robertson feofees or trustees for the land appropriated for the building & erecting the City of Williamsburgh for 15 shillings released unto Saml Hyde of York Co one lott of ground in the City of Williamsburgh designed in the plott of the sd city by the figure 47 ...[same as above] ... if the sd Samuel Hyde shall not within the space of 24 months build & finish upon each lott one good dwelling house then it shall & may be lawfull to & for the sd feofees or trustees into the granted premises & every part thereof to enter & the same to have again as of their former estate to have, hold & enjoy in like manner as they might otherwise have done if these presents had never been made ... . Wit: None. Ackn 16 Dec 1717. Attest: Phi Lightfoot clerk. (Pg 228)

10 Dec 1717. Deed of Lease. John Clayton & Wil Robertson feofees or trustees for the land appropriated for the building & erecting the City of Williamsburgh for 5 shillings farm letten unto Edward Ripping of York Co three lotts of ground in the sd City of Williamsburgh designed in the plott of the sd city by the figures 263, 264 & 265 ... for the term of one year paying the yearly rent of one grain of Indian corn on 10 Oct if demanded ... . Wit: None. Ackn 20 Jan 1717 & admitted to record. Attest: Phi Lightfoot clerk. (Pg 229)

11 Dec 1717. Deed of Release. John Clayton & Wil Robertson feofees or trustees for the land appropriated for the building & erecting the City of Williamsburgh for 45 shillings released unto Edward Ripping of York Co three lotts of ground in the sd City of Williamsburgh designed in the plott of the sd city by the figures 263, 264 & 265 ... [same as above] ... if the sd Edward Ripping shall not within the space of 24 months build & finish upon each lott one good dwelling house then it shall & may be lawfull to & for the sd feofees or trustees into the granted premises & every part thereof to enter & the same to have again as of their former estate to have, hold & enjoy in like manner as they might otherwise have done if these presents had never been made ... . Wit: None. Ackn 20 Jan 1717 & admitted to record. Attest: Phi Lightfoot clerk. (Pg 230)

13 Jan 1717. Deed of Lease. Williams Wise Junr of Charles Parish, York Co for 5 shillings farm lett unto Benja Clifton of same place a 50 a. tr of land in Oak Swamp in Charles Parish bounded by land of Henry Hayward & land John Eaton formerly sold by Robert Calvert to the sd Eaton, which tr of land was formerly conveyed by Robt Calvert to John Nicholson of Charles Parish & by the death of the sd John came & descended to Richd Nickson eldest son & heir of the sd John decd & afterwards was assigned & made over by the sd Richard to the sd William Wise Junr ... for the term of one year paying the yearly rent of one ear of Indian corn on the last day of the sd year if demanded ... . Wit: Giles Toniernoe, Jno Doswell Junr, Elias Love. Ackn 20 Jan 1717 & admitted to record. Attest: Phi Lightfoot clerk. (Pg 231)

14 Jan 1717/8. Deed of Release. Williams Wise Junr of Charles Parish, York Co for £10 released unto Benja Clifton of same place a 50 a. tr of land in Oak Swamp in Charles Parish ... [same as above] ... . Wit: Giles Tansernoy, Jno Doswell Junr, Elias Love. Ackn 20 Jan 1717 & admitted to record. Attest: Phi Lightfoot clerk. (Pg 232)

14 Jan 1717/8. Bond. I William Wise Junr of Charles Parish, York Co am firmly bound unto Benjamin Clifton of same place for £20 ... the condition of this obligation is such that if the afsd William Wise Junr do & shall well & truly observe, perform, accomplish, fulfill & keep all the covenants, grants, articles, clauses, conditions & agreements mentioned in one pair of indentures of lease & release [see above] then this obligation to be void ... . Wit: Giles Tavernor, Jno Doswell Junr, Elias Love. Ackn 20 Jan 1717 & admitted to record. Attest: Phi Lightfoot clerk. (Pg 233)

16 Dec 1717. Deed. Edward Ripping of the City of Williamsburgh for £10 sold to Henry Gill of same city three lotts or ½ acres of ground in the sd City of Williamsburgh denoted in the plan of the sd city by the figures 263, 264 & 265 ... . Wit: Tim Sullivant, Joseph Davenport, Elizabeth Davenport. Ackn 20 Jan 1717 & admitted to record. Attest: Phi Lightfoot clerk. (Pg 234)

16 Jan 1717. Deed of Lease. William Tabb of Charles Parish, York Co & Elizabeth his wife for 5 shillings farm lett unto Edward Tabb of Elizabeth City Co all that plantation & tr of land in Charles Parish late in the occupation of Daniel Taylor now decd & afterwards of Mary Taylor widow & relict of the sd Daniel Taylor now also decd, all which demised premises were & by the will of Edward Day decd formerly the husband of the afsd Mary Taylor given & bequeathed (after the decease of the sd Mary Taylor) to be divided between the sd William Tabb & Edward Tabb ... for the term of one year ... . Wit: Richard Slater, Gerard Roberts, Samuel Tomkins. Ackn 20 Jan 1717 & admitted to record. Attest: Phi Lightfoot clerk. (Pg 235)

17 Jan 1717. Deed of Release. William Tabb of Charles Parish, York Co &
Elizabeth his wife for £130 released unto Edward Tabb of Elizabeth City Co all
that plantation & tr of land in Charles Parish ... [same as above] ... . Wit:
Richard Slater, Gerard Roberts, Samuell Tompkins (Tomkins). Ackn 20 Jan
1717 by William Tabb & Elizabeth his wife & the sd Elizabeth relinquished her
right of dower & admitted to record. Attest: Phi Lightfoot clerk. (Pg 236)

16 Jan 1717. Bond. I William Tabb of Charles Parish, York Co am firmly
bound unto Edward Tabb of Elizabeth City Co, VA for £260 ... the condition of
this obligation is such that if the afsd William Tabb shall well & truly observe,
perform, fulfill & keep all the covenants, articles, contracts, clauses &
agreements mentioned in indentures of grant, release & confirmation [see above]
then this obligation to be void ... . Wit: Richard Slater, Gerard Roberts, Samuel
Tomkins. Ackn 20 Jan 1717 & admitted to record. Attest: Phi Lightfoot clerk.
(Pg 237)

15 Feb 1717. Deed. William Wade son & devisee of Thomas Wade late of
York Co decd for £105 sold to James Bates of Bruton Parish, York Co merchant
a 140 a. parcell of land in Bruton Parish near the place called Okn Neck being
pt/o the land late of the sd Thomas Wade decd & by his will dated in 1713 the sd
parcel of land was devised to the sd William Wade, bounded by the head of
Wades Spring Br, Perrymans Spring Br, land of John Bates, Oken Neck Mill
Road, sd Bates's line (formerly Perryman's), land of John Bates Junr & Joseph
Wade's land ... . Wit: Samll Wright, John Morison, William Pegram (Pegrim).
Ackn 17 Mar 1717 by William Wade & Ann the w/o the sd William
relinquished her right of dower & admitted to record. Attest: Phi Lightfoot
clerk. (Pg 238)

15 Nov 1717. Deed of Lease. Thomas Worldley of York Co for 5 shillings
farm lett unto Thomas Wooton of co afsd all my plantation & 10 a. tr of land on
the head of a br of Chismans Cr between the lands of Thomas Edmunds, John
Read, Edward Corley & the afsd Thomas Wooten ... for the term of one year ...
. Wit: Thomas Chisman, John Chapman. Ackn 17 Mar 1717 & admitted to
record. Attest: Phi Lightfoot clerk. (Pg 240)

15 Nov 1717. Deed of Release. Thomas Worldley of York Co for £12 released
unto Thomas Wooton of co afsd all my plantation & 10 a. tr of land ... [same as
above] ... . Wit: Thomas Chisman, John Chapman. Ackn 17 Mar 1717 &
admitted to record. Attest: Phi Lightfoot clerk. (Pg 241)

15 Nov 1717. Bond. I Thomas Worldley of York Co am firmly bound unto
Thomas Wooton of co afsd for £24 ... the condition of this obligation is such
that if the afsd Thomas Worldley shall well & truly obey, observe, perform,

fulfill & keep all the covenants, articles, contracts, clauses & agreements mentioned in indentures of grant, release & confirmation [*see above*] then this obligation to be void … . Wit: Thomas Chisman, John Chapman. Ackn 17 Mar 1717 & admitted to record. Attest: Phi Lightfoot clerk. (Pg 242)

18 Apr 1718. Deed. William Sheldon of York Co having custody by execution as sub sher of one Negro girl called Betty for £21 have sold unto the sd Richd Cheshire the afsd Negro girle as a slave to serve him & his heirs … . Wit: Saml Seldon, John Lowry. Ackn 16 Jun 1718 & admitted to record. Attest: Phi Lightfoot clerk. (Pg 243)

13 Jun 1718. Deed of Lease. John Clayton & Hugh Norvell feofees or trustees for the land appropriated for the building & erecting the City of Williamsburgh for 5 shillings farm lett unto Ambrose Cobbs of York Co two lotts of ground in the sd City of Williamsburgh designed in the plan of the sd city by the figures 43 & 44 … for the term of one year paying the yearly rent of one grain of Indian corn on 10 Oct if demanded … . Wit: None. Ackn 16 Jun 1718 & admitted to record. Attest: Phi Lightfoot clerk. (Pg 243)

14 Jun 1718. Deed of Release. John Clayton & Hugh Norvell feofees or trustees for the land appropriated for the building & erecting the City of Williamsburgh for £1:10 released unto Ambrose Cobbs of York Co two lotts of ground in the sd City of Williamsburgh designed in the plan of the sd city by the figures 43 & 44 … [*same as above*] … if the sd Ambrose Cobbs shall not within the space of 24 months build & finish upon each lott one good dwelling house then it shall & may be lawfull to & for the sd feofees or trustees into the granted premises & every part thereof to enter & the same to have again as of their former estate to have, hold & enjoy in like manner as they might otherwise have done if these presents had never been made … . Wit: None. Ackn 16 Jun 1718 & admitted to record. Attest: Phi Lightfoot clerk. (Pg 244)

13 Jun 1718. Deed of Lease. David Cuningham of York Co for 5 shillings leased unto Timothy Sullivant of co afsd one lott of ground in the City of Williamsburgh designed in the plot of the sd city by the figure 338 … for the term of one year paying the yearly rent of one grain of Indian corn on 10 Oct if demanded … . Wit: R. Hickman, Joseph Hanker. Ackn 16 Jun 1718 & admitted to record. Attest: Phi Lightfoot clerk. (Pg 245)

14 Jun 1718. Deed of Release. David Cuningham of York Co for 50 shillings released unto Timothy Sullivant of co afsd one lott of ground in the City of Williamsburgh designed in the plot of the sd city by the figure 338 … [*same as above*] … . Wit: R. Hickman, Joseph Hanker. Ackn 16 Jun 1718 & admitted to record. Attest: Phi Lightfoot clerk. (Pg 245)

7 Jul 1717. Deed of Lease. John Clayton & Wil Robertson feofees or trustees for the land appropriated for the building & erecting the City of Williamsburgh for 5 shillings farm lett unto John Brush of James City Co two lotts of ground in the sd City of Williamsburgh designed in the plott of the sd city by the figures 165 & 166 ... for the term of one year paying the yearly rent of one grain of Indian corn on 10 Oct if demanded .... Wit: None. Ackn 21 Jul 1718 & admitted to record. Attest: Phi Lightfoot clerk. (Pg 246)

8 Jul 1717. Deed of Release. John Clayton & Wil Robertson feofees or trustees for the land appropriated for the building & erecting the City of Williamsburgh for 30 shillings released unto John Brush of James City Co two lotts of ground in the sd City of Williamsburgh designed in the plott of the sd city by the figures 165 & 166 ... [same as above] ... if the sd John Brush shall not within the space of 24 months build & finish upon each lott one good dwelling house then it shall & may be lawfull to & for the sd feofees or trustees into the granted premises & every part thereof to enter & the same to have again as of their former estate to have, hold & enjoy in like manner as they might otherwise have done if these presents had never been made .... Wit: None. Ackn 21 Jul 1718 & admitted to record. Attest: Phi Lightfoot clerk. (Pg 247)

15 Jul 1718. Deed of Lease. John Bates Junr of Bruton Parish, York Co merchant for 5 shillings leased unto James Bates of same place a 65 a. tr of land being the land formerly belonging to George Tindal late of York Co decd & by the sd George Tindall devised to the sd John Bates June in fee simple as by the sd will duly proved in York Co Court dated 2 Sep 1701, bounded by the sd George Tindall, John Bates Senr, Joseph Bansafield, the Great Swamp, Skimmino Mill Damm, Beverdam Swamp & James Bates' Spring Br, it to be held & taken for 64 a. according to a late survey made by Simon Jeffreys ...for the term of one year paying the yearly rent of one ear of Indian corn at the feast of St. Michael the Archangel if demanded .... Wit: Wil Lindsay, Edward Ripping, Wm Gordon. Ackn 15 Sep 1718 & admitted to record. Attest: Phi Lightfoot clerk. (Pg 248)

16 Jul 1718. Deed of Release. John Bates Junr of Bruton Parish, York Co merchant for £50 released unto James Bates of same place a 65 a. tr of land ... [same as above] .... Wit: Wil Lindsay, Wm Gordon, Edward Ripping. Ackn 15 Sep 1718 & admitted to record. Attest: Phi Lightfoot clerk. (Pg 249)

15 Sep 1718. Deed. John Lewis & Sarah his wife sister & sole heiress of George Glascock late of York Co decd for £30 sold to John Taylor of co afsd planter a 50 a. tr of land in Bruton Parish near the place call Mill Swamp bounded by the land of James Taylor, land of James Shields his Spring Br, Matthew Pierce, the main runn of the Great Swamp, land of Major Custis &

John Layton's line, it being the land formerly of George Glascock decd who was father of the sd Sarah & after his death the same land did descend & fall to the sd George Glascock son & heir of the sd George who is lately decd & the same land now fallen & become due to the sd Sarah as being the only surviving sister & heir to the sd George Glascock & now sold by the sd James Lewis & Sarah his wife to the sd John Taylor in fee ... . Wit: Wil Lindsay, Ralph Graves, Wm Tibbs. Ackn 15 Sep 1718 by the sd James Lewis & Sarah his wife & the sd Sarah being also privately examined relinquished her right of dower & is admitted to record. Attest: Phi Lightfoot clerk. (Pg 250)

14 Nov 1718. Deed of Lease. John Wills of Mulberry Island Parish, York Co (*sic*) & Elizabeth his wife for 5 shillings farm letten unto Thomas Nelson of York Hampton Parish, York Co gent ½ of an acre of land whereon a water mill called Mountforts Mill now standing in York Hampton Parish together with the ½ of the sd mill & all manner of going & running geers belonging & used to & with the sd mill & likewise all manner of other goods, chattels, utensils, implements & tools whatsoever of the sd John Wills remaining or being of, in or upon the sd parcel of land ... for the term of one year ... . Wit: Wil Lindsay, Geo Allen, Benja Clifton. Ackn 17 Nov 1718 & admitted to record. Attest: Phi Lightfoot clerk. (Pg 252)

15 Nov 1718. Deed of Release. John Wills of Mulberry Island Parish, York Co (*sic*) & Elizabeth his wife for £50 released unto Thomas Nelson of York Hampton Parish, York Co gent ½ of an acre of land whereon a water mill called Mountforts Mill now standing ... [*same as above*] ... . Wit: Wil Lindsay, Geo Allen, Benja Clifton. Ackn by John Wills 17 Nov 1718 & admitted to record. (Pg 253)

15 Nov 1718. Bond. I John Wills of Mulberry Island Parish, Warwick Co gent am firmly bound unto Thomas Nelson of York Hampton Parish, York Co gent for £100 ... the condition of this obligation is such that if the afsd John Wills shall well & truly obey, observe, perform, fulfill & keep all the covenants, articles, contracts & agreements mentioned in indentures of grant, release & confirmation [*see above*] then this obligation to be void ... . Wit: Wil Lindsay, Geo Allen, Benja Clifton. Ackn 17 Nov 1718 & admitted to record. Attest: Phi Lightfoot clerk. (Pg 254)

17 Nov 1718. Deed. Lawrence Smith & Thomas Nelson gent trustees for the Port Land of York Town in York Co for 180 lbs of tobacco sold to Philip Lightfoot gent a lott or ½ a. of land in York Town being pt/o the Port Land known by the number 7 as by the plot on the records of the sd co doth appear, the sd lott containing 10 poles in length & 8 Poles in breadth ... provided that the sd Philip Lightfoot do & shall within 12 months begin to build & finish on

the sd lott one good house to contain at least 20' wherein if he fail then this present grant to be void in law ... . Wit: None. Ackn 17 Nov 1718 & admitted to record. Attest: Phi Lightfoot clerk. (Pg 255)

14 Nov 1718. Deed of Lease. John Eaton & Elizabeth his wife of York Hampton Parish, York Co for 5 shillings farm letten to Benjamin Clifton of Charles Parish, York Co all their 50 a. tr of land in Charles Parish as appears by a pattent thereof granted by Sir William Berkeley then Governor of VA dated 10 Nov 1673 bounded by Finch his Dam & Edmund Hudson, (then granted to Robert Draper) & 50 a. of land in Charles Parish as appears by a deed of sale granted by Edward Hudson to the sd Robert Draper dated 16 Nov 1672 bounded by land formerly called Owen Davis's, John Drury, John Mackanree & Thomas Hynds ... for the term of one year paying the yearly rent of one ear of Indian corn on 10 Dec if demanded ... . Wit: Wil Lindsay, Thos Ray, Charles Calthorp, John Welch. Ackn 17 Nov 1718 by John Eaton & Elizabeth his wife & the sd Elizabeth being also privately examined relinquished her right of dower & admitted to record. Attest: Phi Lightfoot clerk. (Pg 255)

15 Nov 1718. Deed of Release. John Eaton & Elizabeth his wife of York Hampton Parish, York Co for £76 released to Benjamin Clifton of Charles Parish, York Co two trs of land ... [same as above] ... . Wit: Wil Lindsay, Thos Ray, Charles Calthorp, John Welch. Ackn 17 Nov 1718 by John Eaton & Elizabeth his wife & the sd Elizabeth being also privately examined relinquished her right of dower & admitted to record. Attest: Phi Lightfoot clerk. (Pg 257)

15 Nov 1718. Bond. We John Eaton & Elizabeth my wife of York Hampton Parish, York Co are firmly bound unto Benjamin Clifton of Charles Parish, co afsd for £152 ... the condition of this obligation is such that if the afsd John Eaton & Elizabeth his wife do & shall well & truly observe, perform, fulfill, accomplish & keep all the covenants, grants, articles, clauses, conditions & agreements mentioned in one pair of indentures of lease & release [see above] then this obligation to be void ... . Wit: Wil Lindsay, Thos Ray, Chas Calthorp, John Welch. Ackn 17 Nov 1718 by John Eaton & Eliza his wife & admitted to record. Attest: Phi Lightfoot clerk. (Pg 258)

14 Nov 1718. Deed of Lease. William Wise Junr of Charles Parish, York Co for 5 shillings farm letten unto Charles Powers of Elizabeth City Co a 200 a. tr of land in Charles Parish together with the marsh thereto adj being pt/o a great tr of land called Boar Quarter heretofore sold to George Baskervyle by Ralph Graves of Bruton Parish, York Co by deed dated 30 Nov 1714 & so conveyed to the sd William Wise Junr bounded by Charles Thurman, Col Edmund Jenings & land of Will Blackston now in the tenure & occupation of John Lyell ... during the term of one year paying the yearly rent of one ear of Indian corn on the last

day of the sd year if demanded ... . Wit: Starkey More, Anthony Lambe, Christian Mackeny. Ackn 17 Nov 1718 by William Wise & also appeared Eliza his wife & relinquished her right of dower & admitted to record. Attest: Phi Lightfoot clerk. (Pg 259)

15 Nov 1718. Deed of Release. William Wise Junr of Charles Parish, York Co for £50 released unto Charles Powers of Elizabeth City Co a 200 a. tr of land in Charles Parish together with the marsh thereto adj ... [same as above] ... . Wit: Starkey Moore, Anthony Lambe, Christian Mackeney. Ackn 17 Nov 1718 by William Wise & also appeared Elizabeth the w/o the sd William Wise & relinquished her right of dower & admitted to record. Attest: Phi Lightfoot clerk. (Pg 260)

15 Nov 1718. Bond. I William Wise Junr of Charles Parish, York Co am firmly bound unto Charles Powers of Elizabeth City Co for £100 ... the condition of this obligation is such that if the afsd William Wise Junr shall well & truly observe, perform, fulfill, accomplish & keep all the covenants, grants, articles, clauses, conditions & agreements mentioned in one pair of indentures of lease & release [see above] then this obligation to be void ... . Wit: Starkey Moore, Anthony Lambe, Christian Mackeney. Ackn 17 Nov 1718 & admitted to record. Attest: Phi Lightfoot clerk. (Pg 262)

9 Aug 1718. Deed of Lease. Bartlett Morland & Elizabeth his wife of Surry Co for 5 shillings farm letten unto William Cross of York Hampton Parish, York Co planter all their ½ pt/o 310 a. of land held & enjoyed by the sd Bartlett Morland & Elizabeth his wife in York Hampton Parish called Essex Lodge, which sd ½ pt/o 310 a. is pt/o a greater tr of land given & devised by the will of Thomas Hill decd to his son John Hill & in case of his death (without issue) to be divided amongst his daus (the sd Elizabeth being one) as by the sd will dated 8 Aug 1710 remaining in the records of York Co Court ... for the term of one year paying the yearly rent of one ear of Indian corn on the last day of the sd year if demanded ... . Wit: Wil Lindsay, William Mainyard, Joseph Mountfort. Ackn 17 Nov 1718 by Bartlett Morland & Elizabeth his wife the sd Elizabeth being also privately examined relinquished her right of dower & admitted to record. Attest: Phi Lightfoot clerk. (Pg 262)

10 Aug 1718. Deed of Release. Bartlett Morland & Elizabeth his wife of Surry Co for £78 released unto William Cross of York Hampton Parish, York Co planter all their ½ pt/o 310 a. of land ... [same as above] ... . Wit: Wil Lindsay, William Mainyard, Joseph Mountfort. Ackn 17 Nov 1718 by Bartlett Morland & Elizabeth his wife & the sd Elizabeth being also privately examined relinquished her right of dower & admitted to record. Attest: Phi Lightfoot clerk. (Pg 263)

10 Aug 1718. Bond. I Bartlett Morland of Surry Co am firmly bound unto William Cross of York Co planter for £156 ... the condition of this obligation is such that if the afsd Bartlett Morland shall well & truly observe, perform, fulfill, accomplish & keep all the covenants, grants, articles, clauses, conditions & agreements mentioned in one pair of indentures of lease & release [*see above*] then this obligation to be void ... . Wit: Wil Lindsay, William Mainyard, Joseph Mountfort. Ackn 17 Nov 1718 & admitted to record. Attest: Phi Lightfoot clerk. (Pg 265)

12 Dec 1718. Deed of Lease. John Clayton & Hugh Norvell feofees or trustees for the land appropriated for the building & erecting the City of Williamsburgh for 5 shillings farm letten unto John Davis of York Co two lotts of ground in Queen Mary's Port in the sd City of Williamsburgh designed in the platt of the sd city by the figures 1 & 2 ... for the term of one year paying the yearly rent of one grain of Indian corn on 10 Oct if demanded ... . Wit: None. Ackn 15 Dec 1718 & admitted to record. Attest: Phi Lightfoot clerk. (Pg 265)

13 Dec 1718. Deed of Release. John Clayton & Hugh Norvell feofees or trustees for the land appropriated for the building & erecting the City of Williamsburgh for 30 shillings released unto John Davis of York Co two lotts of ground in Queen Mary's Port in the sd City of Williamsburgh designed in the platt of the sd city by the figures 1 & 2 ... [*same as above*] ... if the sd John Davis shall not within the space of 24 months build & finish upon each lott one good dwelling house then it shall & may be lawfull to & for the sd feofees or trustees into the granted premises & every part thereof to enter & the same to have again as of their former estate to have, hold & enjoy in like manner as they might otherwise have done if these presents had never been made ... . Wit: None. Ackn 15 Dec 1718 & admitted to record. Attest: Phi Lightfoot clerk. (Pg 266)

10 Nov 1718. Deed. William Robertson of the City of Williamsburgh for £50 sold to John Brown of same city gent all that parcel of ground in the City of Williamsburgh (being pt/o the sd Robertson's lott whereon he now lives) adj Lott 27 which joyns on Duke of Glocester Street & the Capitol Square, the Barbars Shop & Sullivant's poles to his corner port on the Main Street ... . Wit: William Hamilton, Wil Buckner, James Frazer. Ackn 19 Jan 1718 & admitted to record. Attest: Phi Lightfoot clerk. (Pg 267)

16 Jan 1718. Deed of Lease. John Clayton & Hugh Norvell feofees or trustees for the land appropriated for the building & erecting the City of Williamsburgh for 5 shillings farm letten unto Saml Cobbs of York Co one lott of ground in the sd City of Williamsburgh designed in the plot of the sd city by the figure 235 ... for the term of one year paying the yearly rent of one grain of Indian corn on 10

62

Oct if demanded ... . Wit: None. Ackn 16 Feb 1718 & admitted to record. Attest: Phi Lightfoot clerk. (Pg 268)

17 Jan 1718. Deed of Release. John Clayton & Hugh Norvell feofees or trustees for the land appropriated for the building & erecting the City of Williamsburgh for 15 shillings released unto Saml Cobbs of York Co one lott of ground in the sd City of Williamsburgh designed in the plot of the sd city by the figure 235 ... [*same as above*] ... if the sd Saml Cobbs shall not within the space of 24 months build & finish upon each lott one good dwelling house then it shall & may be lawfull to & for the sd feofees or trustees into the granted premises & every part thereof to enter & the same to have again as of their former estate to have, hold & enjoy in like manner as they might otherwise have done if these presents had never been made ... . Wit: None. Ackn 16 Feb 1718 & admitted to record. Attest: Phi Lightfoot clerk. (Pg 268)

14 Feb 1718. Deed. David Cuningham of York Co for £10 sold to John Blair of the City of Williamsburgh one lott or ½ a. of ground in the City of Williamsburgh denoted in the plan of the sd city by the figure 337 ... . Wit: Patrick Ferguson, Ambrose Cobbs, Robert Cobbs Junr. Ackn 16 Feb 1718 & admitted to record. Attest: Phi Lightfoot clerk. (Pg 270)

13 Feb 1718. Deed of Lease. Martha Sebrell of York Hampton Parish, York Co widow & Samuel Sebrell of same place planter for 5 shillings farm let unto Joseph Walker of same place esqr all that messuage & 50 a. tr of land & premises in the parish afsd bounded by Underhill's Line & Mr. Barbar's line ... for the term of one year paying the rent of one ear of Indian corn if demanded ... . Wit: Godfrey Pole, Richard Parr, Thomas Colace. Ackn 16 Feb 1718 by Samuel Sebrel & Martha Sebrell not appearing was proved to be her act & deed & also appeared Mary the w/o the sd Samuel & relinquished her right of dower & admitted to record. Attest: Phi Lightfoot clerk. (Pg 271)

14 Feb 1718. Deed of Release. Martha Sebrell of York Hampton Parish, York Co widow & Samuel Sebrell of same place planter for £30 released unto Joseph Walker of same place esqr all that messuage & 50 a. tr of land & premises ... [same as above] ... . Wit: Godfrey Pole, Richard Parr, Thomas Coleue. Ackn 16 Feb 1718 by Samuel Sebrel & Martha Sebrell not appearing was proved to be her act & deed & also appeared Mary the w/o the sd Samuel & relinquished her right of dower & admitted to record. Attest: Phi Lightfoot clerk. (Pg 271)

14 Feb 1718. Bond. We Martha & Samuel Sebrell of York Hampton Parish, York Co are firmly bound unto Joseph Walker esqr of same place for £70 ... the condition of this obligation is such that if the afsd Martha & Samuel Sebrell shall well & truly observe, perform, fulfill, accomplish & keep all the covenants,

grants, articles, clauses & conditions mentioned in one pair of indentures of lease & release [*see above*] then this obligation to be void .... Wit: Godfrey Pole, Richard Paar, Thomas Coleue. Ackn 16 Feb 1718 by Samuel Sebrell & Martha Sebrell not appearing was proved to be her act & deed & admitted to record. Attest: Phi Lightfoot clerk. (Pg 273)

13 Feb 1718. Deed of Lease. Edward Powers of Yorkhampton Parish, York Co inn keeper for 5 shillings farm letten unto Philip Lightfoot of same place merchant all his lott or ½ a. of land in the Town of York on the Main Street known in the plot of the sd town by the figure 37 which lott was made over & conveyed by deed to Micajah Perry & Richard Perry of London merchants by Joseph Mountfort son & heir at law of Thomas Mountfort decd & by vertue of a power of atty made by the sd Micajah & Richard Perry to William Buckner of York Town in VA gent & Nathaniel Burwell of Glocester Co gent joyntly & severally dated 6 Nov 1710 sold & conveyed by the sd William Buckner unto the afsd Edward Powers by deeds of lease & release dated 14 & 15 Jul 1712 ... for the term of one year .... Wit: Wil Lindsay, Wm Gordon, Edward Ripping. Ackn 16 Feb 1718 by Edward Powers & also appeared Eliza w/o the sd Edward & relinquished her right of dower & admitted to record. Attest: Phi Lightfoot clerk. (Pg 273)

14 Feb 1718. Deed of Release. Edward Powers of Yorkhampton Parish, York Co inn keeper for £110 released unto Philip Lightfoot of same place merchant all his lott or ½ a. of land in the Town of York on the Main Street known in the plot of the sd town by the figure 37 together with all the buildings ... [*same as above*] .... Wit: Wil Lindsay, Wm Gordon, Edward Ripping. Ackn 16 Feb 1718 by Edward Powers & also appeared Eliza w/o the sd Edward & relinquished her right of dower & admitted to record. Attest: Phi Lightfoot clerk. (Pg 274)

16 Feb 1718/19. Bond. I Edward Powers of Yorkhampton Parish, York Co am firmly bound unto Philip Lightfoot of same place for £220 ... the condition of this obligation is such that if the afsd Edward Powers shall well & truly observe, perform, accomplish, fulfill & keep all the covenants, grants, articles, clauses, conditions & agreements mentioned in a pair of indentures of lease & release [*see above*] then this obligation to be void .... Wit: Wil Lindsay, Edward Ripping, Wm Gordon. Ackn 16 Feb 1718 & admitted to record. Attest: Phi Lightfoot clerk. (Pg 275)

9 Mar 1719. Deed. Samuel Hyde of York Co for £10 sold to Joseph Freeman of same co one lott or ½ a. of ground in the City of Williamsburgh designed in the plott of the sd city by the figure 47 adj on the Great Street between the storehouse of Archibald Blair & the house of Henry Gill ... excepting out of the

sd premises one piece of the sd lott of ground on the n end thereof of the breadth of the sd lott & 30' in length ... . Wit: Tho Jones, Jno Harris, Hen Bowcock. Ackn 16 Mar 1718 (*sic*) & admitted to record. Attest: Phi Lightfoot clerk. (Pg 276)

7 Mar 1718. Deed of Lease. Joseph Walker of Yorkhampton Parish, York Co gent for 5 shillings farm letten unto William Huet of Mulberry Island Parish, Warwick Co a 300 a. tr of land in Yorkhampton Parish bounded by Baskerviles Swamp, the Gleab Br, Filgates Cr, William Barbar & Baskerviles Spring Br ... for the term of one year ... . Wit: Wm Barbar, Will Barbar Junr, Robt Petters. Ackn 18 May 1719 & admitted to record. Attest: Phi Lightfoot clerk. (Pg 277)

8 Mar 1718. Deed of Release. Joseph Walker of Yorkhampton Parish, York Co gent for £340 released unto William Huet of Mulberry Island Parish, Warwick Co a 300 a. tr of land in Yorkhampton Parish ... [*same as above*] ... . Wit: Wm Barbar, Will Barbar Junr, Robt Petters. Ackn 18 May 1719 & admitted to record. Attest: Phi Lightfoot clerk. (Pg 278)

8 Mar 1718. Bond. I Joseph Walker of Yorkhampton Parish, York Co gent am firmly bound unto William Huet of Mulberry Island Parish, Warwick Co for £1,000 ... the condition of this obligation is such that if the afsd Joseph Walker shall well & truly observe, perform, fulfill, accomplish & keep all the grants, covenants, articles, clauses, conditions & agreements mentioned in one pair of indentures [*see above*] then this obligation to be void ... . Wit: Wm Barbar, Will Barbar Junr, Robt Petters. Ackn 18 May 1719 & admitted to record. Attest: Phi Lightfoot clerk. (Pg 279)

7 May 1719. Deed. Philip Lightfoot of York Co for 50 shillings sold to William Anthony of same co a piece of ground described in the platt thereof by the number 7 containing 40' square at the w corner of the sd lott ... provided that the sd William Anthony shall build a house on the sd piece of ground according to law ... . Wit: Wil Lindsay. Ackn 18 May 1719 & admitted to record. Attest: Phi Lightfoot clerk. (Pg 280)

16 May 1719. Deed of Lease. John Chapman of Yorkhampton Parish, York Co planter for 5 shillings leased to William Wise of Charles Parish, co afsd planter a 70 a. tr of land in Charles Parish pt/o a pattent of land belonging to James Calthorp bounded according to a survey made by Lt Col Miles Cary surveyor dated 10 Feb 1700 adj the sd Calthorp's line & Booth Nutting, which tr of land came to the sd James Calthorp as heir at law after the expiration of an intail thereof by the will of his decd father James Calthorp the partys in the sd will being all decd without issue as by the sd will dated 10 Oct 1688 on the records of York Co Court proved 26 May 1690 being sold by the sd James Calthorp to

the afsd John Chapman ... for the term of one year paying the rent of one grain of Indian corn upon the feast of St. Michael the Arch Angel next ensuing if demanded ... . Wit: Wm Trotter, John Trotter, John Roberts. Ackn 18 May 1719 by John Chapman & also appeared Elizabeth w/o the sd John & relinquished her right of dower & admitted to record. Attest: Phi Lightfoot clerk. (Pg 281)

18 May 1719. Deed of Release. John Chapman of Yorkhampton Parish, York Co planter for £50 released to William Wise of Charles Parish, co afsd planter a 70 a. tr of land in Charles Parish ... [*same as above*] ... . Wit: Wm Trotter, John Trotter, John Roberts. Ackn 18 May 1719 by John Chapman & also appeared Elizabeth w/o the sd John & relinquished her right of dower & admitted to record. Attest: Phi Lightfoot clerk. (Pg 282)

18 May 1719. Deed. I John Chapman of Yorkhampton Parish, York Co planter am firmly bound unto William Wise of Charles Parish, co afsd planter for £100 ... the condition of this obligation is such that if the afsd John Chapman do well & truly observe, perform, fulfill & keep all the covenants, grants, articles & agreements mentioned in a pair of indentures [*see above*] then this obligation to be void ... . Wit: Wm Trotter, John Trotter, John Roberts. Ackn 18 May 1719 & admitted to record. Attest: Phi Lightfoot clerk. (Pg 284)

8 Dec 1718. Deed of Gift. David Stoner of York Co planter for natural love & affection which he beareth unto his loving wife Jane Stoner & for her better maintainance & support in time to come & in consideration of the promise of his sd wife to take on her as far as she may be capable the management of his worldly affairs & to provide for his subsistence during his natural life & for other good & valuable considerations hath give unto Philip Ludwell of James City Co esqr all his lands & all other real estate whatsoever in this Colony, Great Britain or elsewhere ... also all the goods, chattels, moveables & other personal estate of what nature soever ... to the use & behoof of his wife during her naturall life & after her decease to the use & behoof of his son Daniel Stoner forever ... . Wit: Richd Kendall, Tho Hansford, Wm Gordon. Proved 15 Jun 1719 & admitted to record. Attest: Phi Lightfoot clerk. (Pg 285)

8 Dec 1718. Deed. Philip Ludwell of James City Co, VA esqr send greeting, whereas David Stoner of York Co planter by his deed of sale [*see above*] did give unto me all his lands & other his real & personal estate, now know ye that I the sd Philip Ludwell esqr do hereby ackn & confess that all the sd estate & premises is by the recited deed conveyed unto yet nevertheless it is so taken & the sd premises are so to me conveyed only upon trust & confidence in me reposed by Jane Stoner w/o the sd David Stoner & for her use, behoof & benefit as in & by the sd recited deed is more fully expressed & for no other use, intent

or purpose whatsoever … . Wit: Wm Gordon, Tho Hansford, Richd Kendall. This deed from Philip Ludwell to Jane Stoner was proved 14 Jun 1719 & admitted to record. Attest: Phi Lightfoot clerk. (Pg 286)

12 Jun 1719. Quit Claim. Between John Clayton & Wil Robertson feofees or trustees for the land appropriated for the building & erecting the City of Williamsburgh of the one part & Philip Ludwell of James City Co esqr of the other part, whereas Chickeley Corbin Thacker & Mongo Ingles gent two of the trustees for the sd City of Williamsburgh by their deeds of lease & release dated 27 & 28 Apr 1707 did grant & release unto John Redwood of York Co four lotts or ½ acres of ground in the sd City of Williamsburgh denoted in the plan of the sd city by the figures 61, 62, 272 & 273, which four lotts afterwards were conveyed by the sd John Redwood to the afsd Philip Ludwell esqr, but it doth not appear that the sd lease & release granted to the sd John Redwood have been ackn & recorded nor can now be by reason of the death of Mongo Ingles one of the sd trustees by means whereof some doubt in law suits may arise & whereas the sd Philip Ludwell esqr is willing to quit his claim & pretensions to two of the sd four lotts, viz, those denoted by the figures 272 & 273 & to accept of a release & confirmation of the remaining two lotts mentioned in the sd deed of lease & release granted to the afsd John Redwood, now this indenture wit that the sd feofees or trustees for the considerations above mentioned & for 30 shillings have quit claimed to the sd Philip Ludwell all those two lotts or ½ acres of land in the sd City of Williamsburgh & now in the actuall possession of the sd Philip Ludwell denoted in the plan of the sd city by the figures 61 & 62 … . Wit: None. Ackn 15 Jun 1719 & admitted to record. Attest: Phi Lightfoot clerk. (Pg 286)

15 Jun 1719. Deed of Mortgage. Joseph Freeman of the City of Williamsburgh, York Co joyner for £131 sold to Thomas Jones of same place merchant a lott or ½ a. of ground in Williamsburgh afsd described in the plott of the sd city by the figure 47 & adj on the Great Street between the storehouse now in the tenure of Archibald Blair gent & the house now in the tenure of Henry Gill shoemaker …excepting out of the afsd lott one piece thereof of the breadth of the sd lott & of the length of 30' & lying on the n end of the sd lott … provided that if the sd Joseph Freeman shall well & truly pay to the sd Thomas Jones at the Capitol in the sd City of Williamsburgh the full sum of £138:17 at or upon 15 Jun 1720 then this present indenture shall cease … . Wit: John Clayton, Frans Tyler, Wil Lindsay. Ackn 15 Jun 1719 by Joseph Freeman & also appeared Dorcas w/o the sd Joseph & being first privately examined relinquished her right of dower recorded. Attest: Phi Lightfoot clerk. (Pg 288)

14 Jun 1719. Deed of Lease. Joseph Freeman of the City of Williamsburgh, York Co joyner for 5 shillings leased to Thomas Jones of same place merchant a

lott or ½ a. of ground in Williamsburgh described in the plott of the sd city by the figure 47 ... [*same as above*] ... for the term of one day paying the rent of one grain of Indian corn at the feast of the Nativity if demanded ... . Wit: John Clayton, Frans Tyler, Wil Lindsay. Ackn 15 Jun 1719 by Joseph Freeman & also appeared Dorcas w/o the sd Joseph & being first privately examined relinquished her right of dower recorded. Attest: Phi Lightfoot clerk. (Pg 290)

11 Jun 1719. Deed. Samuel Cooper of the Town & Co of York with the consent & freewill of my wife Ann, for love & friendship have given unto John Mattock of same place pt/o that lott of Port Land in York Town known by the number 9 as was ackn to me by the trustees of the afsd Port Land which part is bounded by the Port Land that points toward York River & to run from thence 61' 8" on the line that binds on the street towards my now dwelling house, which contains 8,140 sq ft ... . Wit: John Young, Francis Ellingsworth. Ackn 15 Jun 1719 by Samuel Cooper & also appeared Ann the w/o the sd Samuel & relinquished her right of dower & admitted to record. Attest: Phi Lightfoot clerk. (Pg 291)

11 Jun 1719. Bond. I Samuel Cooper of York Town & Ann my wife do stand joyntly & separately firmly bound unto John Mattocke of same town for £300 ... the condition of this obligation is such that if the afsd John Mattocke shall forever peaceably & quietly have, hold, use, occupy, possess & enjoy all that messuage of Port Land in York Town to be given, granted & confirmed by the sd Samuel Cooper & Ann his wife in & by a deed of gift [*see above*] then this obligation to be void ... . Wit: John Young, Francis Ellingsworth. Ackn 15 Jun 1719 by Samuel Cooper & Ann his wife & admitted to record. Attest: Phi Lightfoot clerk. (Pg 292)

1 Jun 1719. Deed of Lease. John Clayton & Wil Robertson feofees or trustees for the land appropriated for the building & erecting the City of Williamsburgh for 5 shillings farm letten unto George Gilbert of York Co four lotts of ground in Queen Mary Port designed in the plott of the sd port by the figures 26, 27, 28 & 29 ... during the term of one year paying the yearly rent of one grain of Indian corn on 10 Oct if demanded ... . Wit: None. Ackn 20 Jul 1719 & admitted to record. Attest: Phi Lightfoot clerk. (Pg 293)

2 Jun 1719. Deed of Release. John Clayton & Wil Robertson feofees or trustees for the land appropriated for the building & erecting the City of Williamsburgh for £3 released unto George Gilbert of York Co four lotts of ground in Queen Mary Port designed in the plott of the sd port by the figures 26, 27, 28 & 29 ... [*same as above*] ... if the sd George Gilbert shall not within the space of 24 months build & finish upon each lott one good dwelling house then it shall & may be lawfull to & for the sd feofees or trustees into the granted premises &

68

every part thereof to enter & the same to have again as of their former estate to have, hold & enjoy in like manner as they might otherwise have done if these presents had never been made ... . Wit: None. Ackn 20 Jul 1719 & admitted to record. Attest: Phi Lightfoot clerk. (Pg 293)

17 Jul 1719. Deed of Lease. John Clayton & Wil Robertson feofees or trustees for the land appropriated for the building & erecting the City of Williamsburgh for 5 shillings farm letten unto John Holloway of York Co gent two lotts of ground in the sd City of Wmsburgh designed in the platt of the sd city by the figures 33 & 338 ... during the term of one year paying the yearly rent of one grain of Indian corn on 10 Oct if demanded ... . Wit: None. Ackn 20 Jul 1719 & admitted to record. Attest: Phi Lightfoot clerk. (Pg 295)

18 Jul 1719. Deed of Release. John Clayton & Wil Robertson feofees or trustees for the land appropriated for the building & erecting the City of Williamsburgh for 15 shillings released unto John Holloway of York Co gent two lotts of ground in the sd City of Wmsburgh designed in the platt of the sd city by the figures 33 & 338 ... if the sd John Holloway shall not within the space of 24 months build & finish upon each lott one good dwelling house then it shall & may be lawfull to & for the sd feofees or trustees into the granted premises & every part thereof to enter & the same to have again as of their former estate to have, hold & enjoy in like manner as they might otherwise have done if these presents had never been made ... . Wit: None. Ackn 20 Jul 1719 & admitted to record. Attest: Phi Lightfoot clerk. (Pg 295)

17 Jul 1719. Deed of Lease. Samuel Cobbs & Edith his wife of York Co for 5 shillings leased unto Samuel Boush Junr of Norfolk Co two lotts of land in the City of Williamsburgh adj the Main Street, Pallace Street & the Market Place, the same being taken up by the sd Cobbs & ackn by the feofees for the sd city as per deed dated 5 Feb 1716 ... for the term of one year paying the yearly rent of one peper corn at the feast of St. John the Baptist if demanded ... . Wit: Frans Tyler, Saml Weldon, Ralph Gough. Ackn 20 Jul 1719 & admitted to record. Attest: Phi Lightfoot clerk. (Pg 297)

18 Jul 1719. Deed of Release. Samuel Cobbs & Edith his wife of York Co for £40 released unto Samuel Boush Junr of Norfolk Co two lotts of land in the City of Williamsburgh ... [same as above] ... . Wit: Frans Tyler, Saml Weldon, Ralph Gough. Ackn 20 Jul 1719 & admitted to record. Attest: Phi Lightfoot clerk. (Pg 297)

2 Apr 1719. Deed of Lease. John Clayton & Wil Robertson feofees or trustees for the land appropriated for the building & erecting the City of Williamsburgh for 5 shillings farm letten unto Bridget Menetrie of York Co two lotts of ground

in the sd City of Williamsburgh designed in the plott of the sd city by the figures 272 & 273 ... during the term of one year paying the yearly rent of one grain of Indian corn on 10 Oct if demanded ... . Wit: None. Ackn 20 Jul 1719 & admitted to record. Attest: Phi Lightfoot clerk. (Pg 298)

3 Apr 1719. Deed of Release. John Clayton & Wil Robertson feofees or trustees for the land appropriated for the building & erecting the City of Williamsburgh for 30 shillings released unto Bridget Menetrie of York Co two lotts of ground in the sd City of Williamsburgh designed in the plott of the sd city by the figures 272 & 273 ... if the sd Bridget Menetrie shall not within the space of 24 months build & finish upon each lott one good dwelling house then it shall & may be lawfull to & for the sd feofees or trustees into the granted premises & every part thereof to enter & the same to have again as of their former estate to have, hold & enjoy in like manner as they might otherwise have done if these presents had never been made ... . Wit: None. Ackn 20 Jul 1719 & admitted to record. Attest: Phi Lightfoot clerk. (Pg 299)

14 Jul 1719. Deed. Lawrence Smith & Thomas Nelson gent trustees for the Port Land of York Town in York Co for 180 lbs of tobacco sold to William Lindsay of York Co a lott or ½ a. of land in York Town being pt/o the Port Land known by the number 8 as by the plott on the records of the sd co doth appear, the sd lott containing 10 poles In length & 8 poles in breadth (which sd lott was lately in the possession of Joseph Walker of York Co gent but he not complying with the law in building thereon elapsed the same) ... provided that the sd William Lindsay shall within 12 months build & finish on the sd lott one good house to contain at least 20' wherein if he fail then this present grant to be void in law ... . Wit: None. Ackn 20 Jul 1719 & admitted to record. Attest: Phi Lightfoot clerk. (Pg 301)

15 Jul 1719. Deed. William Lindsey of York Town, York Co for £10 sold to Joseph Walker of sd co gent one lott or ½ a. of land in York Town being pt/o the Port Land known by the number 8 ... [same as above] ... formerly in the possession of the sd Joseph Walker ... . Wit: Wm Gordon, F. Hayward. Ackn 20 Jul 1719 & admitted to record. Attest: Phi Lightfoot clerk. (Pg 302)

13 Aug 1719. Deed of Lease. Benjamin Clifton of York Co planter for 5 shillings farm letten to Thomas Nelson & Joseph Walker of York Town merchants all his lott or ½ a. of land in York Town being pt/o the Portland known by the number 25 containing 10 poles in length & 8 in breadth as by the records of the sd co doth appear, which hereby demised premises were by deed dated 8 Jan 1706 by Thomas Ballard & William Buckner gent then trustees for the Port land of York Town granted unto Daniel Taylor gent & by the sd Daniel Taylor & Mary his wife by deed dated 25 Jun 1707 were granted unto James

Sclater clerk & by the sd James Sclater & Mary his wife by deeds dated 14 & 15
Sep 1716 were granted unto Benjamin Clifton party to these presents ... for the
term of one year paying at the end of the sd term the rent of one ear of Indian
corn if demanded ... . Wit: Nath Hoggard, Robt Ballard, Jno Ballard. Ackn 17
Aug 1719 by Benja Clifton & also appeared Sarah w/o the sd Clifton &
relinquished her right of dower & admitted to record. Attest: Phi Lightfoot
clerk. (Pg 303)

14 Aug 1719. Deed of Release. Benjamin Clifton of York Co planter for £100
released to Thomas Nelson & Joseph Walker of York Town merchants all his
lott or ½ a. of land in York Town being pt/o the Portland known by the number
25 ... [same as above] ... . Wit: Nath Hoggard, Robt Ballard, Jno Ballard.
Ackn 17 Aug 1719 by Benja Clifton & also appeared Sarah w/o the sd Clifton &
relinquished her right of dower & admitted to record. Attest: Phi Lightfoot
clerk. (Pg 304)

14 Aug 1719. Bond. I Benjamin Clifton of York Co planter am firmly bound
unto Thomas Nelson & Joseph Walker of York Town merchants for £200 ... the
condition of this obligation is such that if the afsd Benjamin Clifton shall well &
truly obey, observe, perform, fullfill & keep all the covenants, articles, contracts
& agreements mentioned in indentures of lease & release [see above] then this
obligation to be void ... . Wit: Nath Hoggard, Robt Ballard, Jno Ballard. Ackn
17 Aug 1719 by Benja Clifton & Sarah his wife & admitted to record. Attest:
Phi Lightfoot clerk. (Pg 305)

21 Sep 1719. Deed. Bridgett Menetree of James City Co widow for £30 sold to
Lewis Delony of York Co carpenter two lotts or ½ acres of ground in the City of
Wmsburgh being the next two lotts adj eastward on the lott of John Pasture &
are numbered 272 & 273 ... . Wit: Sarah Adkison, Mathew Cumings, Joseph
Davenport. Ackn 21 Sep 1719 & admitted to record. Attest: Phi Lightfoot
clerk. (Pg 306)

19 Sep 1719. Deed of Lease. William Andrews of Nancemond Co clerk for 5
shillings farm letten unto Richard Baker of York Town, York Co all his pt/o the
lot or ½ a. of land in York Town & distinquish'd by the number 44 containing 8
poles 3' in length & 8 poles in breadth adj to the lot of George Burton decd
(which lot of the sd Geo Burton is now in the possession of Christopher Haines
& joynes in the Main Street from Major Wm Buckner), which sd land being pt/o
the Portland was by the will of John Andrews decd (dated 1 Mar 1717/8)
devised unto the sd William Andrews (the remaining pt/o the sd lot or 30' across
the upper end adj to the lot of Humphry Moody being given & devised unto
William Kern by the sd Jno Andrews ... for the term of one year ... . Wit: Wm

Rogers, Wm Richardson. Ackn 21 Sep 1719 & admitted to record. Attest: Phi Lightfoot clerk. (Pg 307)

21 Sep 1719. Deed of Release. William Andrews of Nancemond Co clerk for £21 released unto Richard Baker of York Town, York Co all his pt/o the lot or ½ a. of land in York Town & distinquish'd by the number 44 ... [*same as above*] .... Wit: Wm Rogers, Wm Richardson. Ackn 21 Sep 1719 & admitted to record. Attest: Phi Lightfoot clerk. (Pg 307)

1 Sep 1719. Bond. I William Andrews of Nancemond Co clerk am firmly bound unto Richd Baker (Bayker) of York Town, York Co taylor for £42 ... the condition of this obligation is such that if the afsd William Andrews do & shall well & truly observe, perform, fullfill & keep all the conditions, covenants, grants, articles, causes & agreements mentioned in one pare of indentures of lease & release [*see above*] then this obligation to be void .... Wit: Wm Rodgers, Wm Richardson. Ackn 21 Sep 1719 & admitted to record. Attest: Phi Lightfoot clerk. (Pg 308)

19 Sep 1719. Deed of Lease. Wm Andrews of Nancemond Co clerk for 5 shillings farm letten unto John Gibbons (Gibbins) of York Town, York Co planter two lotts or ½ acres of land in York Town distinquish'd by the numbers 64 & 65 the lot No. 64 containing 10 poles in length & 8 in breadth opposite to the lott & now dwelling house of Wm Gordon, the other lott or ½ a. adj the afsd lott, which sd two lotts (being pt/o the Portland designed in the plott of the sd town) whereby the will of John Andrews decd (dated 1 Mar 1717/8) given & devis'd to the sd Wm Andrews ... for the term of one year .... Wit: Wm Sheldon, Wm Rodgers. Ackn 21 Sep 1719 & admitted to record. Attest: Phi Lightfoot clerk. (Pg 309)

21 Sep 1719. Deed of Release. Wm Andrews of Nancemond Co clerk for £72 released unto John Gibbons of York Town, York Co planter two lotts or ½ acres of land in York Town distinquish'd by the numbers 64 & 65 ... [*same as above*] .... Wit: Wm Sheldon, Wm Rodgers. Ackn 21 Sep 1719 & admitted to record. Attest: Phi Lightfoot clerk. (Pg 309)

21 Sep 1719. Bond. Wm Andrews of Nacemond Co clerk am firmly bound to John Gibbons of York Town, York Co for £144 ... the condition of this obligation is such that if the afsd Wm Andrews shall well & truly observe, perform, fulfill, accomplish & keep all the conditions, covenants, grants, articles, clauses & agreements mentioned in one pair of indentures of lease & release [*see above*] then this obligation to be void ....Wit: Wm Sheldon, Wm Rogers. Ackn 21 Sep 1719 & admitted to record. Attest: Phi Lightfoot clerk. (Pg 311)

72

14 Nov 1719. Deed. William Heron of York Hampton Parish, York Co planter for 20 shillings sold to Richard Baker of York Town, parish & co afsd all his pt/o a lott containing 30' of ground in York Town adj to Humphrey Moody's lott & being pt/o a lott lately purch by the sd Richard Baker of William Andrews known by the number 44 which was bequeathed unto the sd William Heron by John Andrews decd … . Wit: Wm Lindsay, Wm Craig, Seamer Powell. Ackn 16 Nov 1719 & admitted to record. Attest: Phi Lightfoot clerk. (Pg 311)

13 Nov 1719. Deed of Lease. Daniell Mackintosh of York Hampton Parish, York Co for 5 shillings farm lett unto Benjamin Clifton of Charles Parish, co afsd all his 100 a. tr of land in Charles Parish known by the name of Knivetons Plantation bounded by the cr that comes out of Old Poguoson adj Richard Slater's orphan's land, Thomas Tomer's tobo house & Anthony Robinson … during the term of one year paying the yearly rent of one ear of Indian corn on the last day of the year if demanded … . Wit: Edmund Sweny, John Robinson, John Hay. Ackn 16 Nov 1719 & admitted to record. Attest: Phi Lightfoot clerk. (Pg 312)

14 Nov 1719. Deed of Release. Daniell Mackintosh of York Hampton Parish, York Co for £72:12 released unto Benjamin Clifton of Charles Parish, co afsd all his 100 a. tr of land in Charles Parish known by the name of Knivetons Plantation … [same as above] … . Wit: Edmund Sweny, John Robinson, John Hay. Ackn 16 Nov 1719 & admitted to record. (Pg 313)

14 Nov 1719. Bond. I Daniell Mackintosh of York Hampton Parish, York Co am firmly bound unto Benja Clifton of Charles Parish, co afsd for £160 … the condition of this obligation is such that if the afsd Daniell Mackintosh do & shall well & truly observe, perform, fulfill, accomplish & keep all the covenants, grants, articles, clauses, conditions & agreements mentioned in one pair of indentures of lease & release [see above] then this obligation to be void … . Wit: Edmund Sweny, John Robinson, John Hay. Ackn 16 Nov 1719 & admitted to record. Attest: Phi Lightfoot clerk. (Pg 315)

27 Nov 1719. Deed of Gift. John Lorrain for good will & affection have given to my son in law Richard Cliff of York Co blacksmith (after my decease) two Negro girles the one named Judy the other Hannah together with what increase they may have … . Wit: Nicholas Hulston, Uriah Hudson, Denes Ranols, George Strahan. Proved 21 Dec 1719 & admitted to record. Attest: Phi Lightfoot clerk. (Pg 315)

13 Nov 1719. Deed of Lease. John Clayton & Wil Robertson feofees or trustees for the land appropriated for the building & erecting the City of Williamsburgh for 5 shillings farm letten unto John Tyler gent of James City Co

two lotts in the City of Williamsburgh designed in the platt of the sd city by the figures 176 & 177 ... during the term of one year paying the yearly rent of one grain of Indian corn on 10 Oct if demanded ... . Wit: None. Ackn 18 Jan 1719 & admitted to record. Attest: Phi Lightfoot clerk. (Pg 316)

1 Nov 1719 (*sic*). Deed of Release. John Clayton & Wil Robertson feofees or trustees for the land appropriated for the building & erecting the City of Williamsburgh for 30 shillings released unto John Tyler gent of James City Co two lotts ... [*same as above*] ... if the sd John Tyler shall not within the space of 24 months build & finish upon each lott one good dwelling house then it shall & may be lawfull to & for the sd feofees or trustees into the granted premises & every part thereof to enter & the same to have again as of their former estate to have, hold & enjoy in like manner as they might otherwise have done if these presents had never been made ... . Wit: None. Ackn 18 Jan 1719 & admitted to record. Attest: Phi Lightfoot clerk. (Pg 317)

6 Jan 1719. Deed of Lease. John Clayton & Wil Robertson feofees or trustees for the land appropriated for the building & erecting the City of Williamsburgh for 5 shillings farm letten unto Michael Archer of the City of Williamsburgh gent one lott of ground in the sd city of Williamsburgh designed in the platt of the sd city by the figure 48 ... for the term of one year paying the yearly rent of one grain of Indian corn on 10 Oct if demanded ... . Wit: M. Robertson. Ackn 18 Jan 1719 & admitted to record. Attest: Phi Lightfoot clerk. (Pg 318)

7 Jan 1719. Deed of Release. John Clayton & Wil Robertson feofees or trustees for the land appropriated for the building & erecting the City of Williamsburgh for 15 shillings released unto Michael Archer of the City of Williamsburgh gent one lott of ground in the sd city of Williamsburgh designed in the platt of the sd city by the figure 48 ... [*same as above*] ... if the sd Michael Archer shall not within the space of 24 months build & finish upon each lott one good dwelling house then it shall & may be lawfull to & for the sd feofees or trustees into the granted premises & every part thereof to enter & the same to have again as of their former estate to have, hold & enjoy in like manner as they might otherwise have done if these presents had never been made ... . Wit: M. Robertson. Ackn 18 Jan 1719 & admitted to record. Attest: Phi Lightfoot clerk. (Pg 319)

6 Jan 1719. Deed of Lease. John Clayton & Wil Robertson feofees or trustees for the land appropriated for the building & erecting the City of Williamsburgh for 5 shillings farm letten unto John Blair of Williamsburgh merchant four lotts in the sd city designed in the platt of the sd city by the figures 34, 41, 42 & 339 ... for the term of one year paying the yearly rent of one grain of Indian corn on 10 Oct if demanded ... . Wit: None. Ackn 18 Jan 1719 & admitted to record. Attest: Phi Lightfoot clerk. (Pg 320)

2 Jan 1719. Deed of Release. John Clayton & Wil Robertson feofees or trustees for the land appropriated for the building & erecting the City of Williamsburgh for £3 released unto John Blair of Williamsburgh merchant four lotts in the sd city designed in the platt of the sd city by the figures 34, 41, 42 & 339 ... [*same as above*] ... if the sd John Blair shall not within the space of 24 months build & finish upon each lott one good dwelling house then it shall & may be lawfull to & for the sd feofees or trustees into the granted premises & every part thereof to enter & the same to have again as of their former estate to have, hold & enjoy in like manner as they might otherwise have done if these presents had never been made ... . Wit: None. Ackn 18 Jan 1719 & admitted to record. Attest: Phi Lightfoot clerk. (Pg 320)

12 Jan 1719. Deed of Lease. John Clayton & Wil Robertson feofees or trustees for the land appropriated for the building & erecting the City of Williamsburgh for 5 shillings farm letten unto Thomas Jones of the City of Williamsburgh gent twelve lotts of ground in the sd City of Williamsburgh designed in the platt of the sd city by the figures, 313, 314, 315, 316, 317, 318, 41, 42, 34, 339, 360 & 361 ... for the term of one year paying the yearly rent of one grain of Indian corn on 10 Oct if demanded ... . Wit: None. Ackn 18 Jan 1719 & admitted to record. Attest: Phi Lightfoot clerk. (Pg 322)

13 Jan 1719. Deed of Release. John Clayton & Wil Robertson feofees or trustees for the land appropriated for the building & erecting the City of Williamsburgh for unto Thomas Jones of the City of Williamsburgh gent twelve lotts of ground in the sd City of Williamsburgh designed in the platt of the sd city by the figures, 313, 314, 315, 316, 317, 318, 41, 42, 34, 339, 360 & 361 ... [*same as above*] ... if the sd Thomas Jones shall not within the space of 24 months build & finish upon each lott one good dwelling house then it shall & may be lawfull to & for the sd feofees or trustees into the granted premises & every part thereof to enter & the same to have again as of their former estate to have, hold & enjoy in like manner as they might otherwise have done if these presents had never been made ... . Wit: None. Ackn 18 Jan 1719 & admitted to record. Attest: Phi Lightfoot clerk. (Pg 322)

15 Jan 1719. Deed of Lease. John Clayton & Wil Robertson feofees or trustees for the land appropriated for the building & erecting the City of Williamsburgh for 5 shillings farm letten unto Daniel Pegram of York Co one lott of ground in the sd city designed in the platt of the sd city by the figure 183 ... for the term of one year paying the yearly rent of one grain of Indian corn on 10 Oct if demanded ... . Wit: None. Ackn 18 Jan 1719 & admitted to record. Attest: Phi Lightfoot clerk. (Pg 323)

16 Jan 1719. Deed of Release. John Clayton & Wil Robertson feofees or trustees for the land appropriated for the building & erecting the City of Williamsburgh for 15 shillings released unto Daniel Pegram of York Co ... [*same as above*] ... if the sd Daniel Pegram shall not within the space of 24 months build & finish upon each lott one good dwelling house then it shall & may be lawfull to & for the sd feofees or trustees into the granted premises & every part thereof to enter & the same to have again as of their former estate to have, hold & enjoy in like manner as they might otherwise have done if these presents had never been made ... . Wit: None. Ackn 18 Jan 1719 & admitted to record. Attest: Phi Lightfoot clerk. (Pg 324)

21 Sep 1719. Deed of Gift. I Nicholas Martin of Charles Parish, York Co for love, good will & affection that I have towards my loving son in law John Bond of Mulberry Island Parish, Warwick Co have given unto the sd John Bond all my goods, wares, jewels, moneys, chattels, lands & all other things that shall prove to belong unto me either in the afsd parish or elsewhere on consideration that the sd John Bond & his heirs shall oblige themselves by bond & security to provide for & maintain the sd Nicholas Martin with sufficient & decent maintainance with diet, washing, lodging & all other things necessary for the needfull use of the sd Nicholas Martin ... . Wit: Thomas Chisman, John Davis. Ackn 18 Jan 1719 & admitted to record. Attest: Phi Lightfoot clerk. (Pg 325)

21 Sep 1719. Bond. We John Bond, Joseph Stacy & John Leughelling (Lewelling) of York Co are firmly indebted unto Nicholas Martin of sd co in the penal sum of £50 in consideration of a deed of gift [*see above*] ... the condition of this obligation is such that if the afsd John Bond his heirs, &c do perform the conditions mentioned in the abovesd deed of gift then this obligation to be made void ... . Wit: Tho Chisman, John Davis. Ackn 18 Jan 1719 by John Bond & Joseph Stacy & admitted to record. Attest: Phi Lightfoot clerk. (Pg 326)

16 Jan 1719. Deed. Between Mary Jones widow of Orlando Jones late of York Co gent decd of the one part & John James Flournoy of the City of Williamsburgh watchmaker of the other part, wit that whereas the sd Orlando Jones at the time of his decease was possessed in fee of two lotts of ground in the sd City of Williamsburgh denoted in the plan of the sd city by the figures 16 & 17, as by deeds of lease & release from the feofees of the sd city dated 18 & 19 Oct 1716, & whereas the sd Orlando Jones did by his will constitute Baldwin Mathews of York Co gent together with the sd Mary Jones executor of his sd will with full power to make sale of the afsd lotts & premises, & whereas the sd Baldwin Mathews for certain reasons hath relinquished his part in the executorship whereby the execution of the sd testament & the power of the selling the afsd lotts & premises is devolved upon the sd Mary Jones, she the sd Mary Jones for £100 hath sold unto the sd John James Flournoy all the afsd two

lotts with the houses ... . Wit: Jno Harris, Lewis Contesse, Francis Flournoy. Ackn 21 Mar 1719/20 & admitted to record. Attest: Phi Lightfoot clerk. (Pg 326)

16 Sep 1719. Deed of Gift. We James Parsons & Dorothy his wife of Charles Parish, York Co for natural love & effections have given unto our son James Parsons Junr all that plantacon & parsell of land which descended to us from our father Armiger Wade containing 41 a. 23 chain as by a platt of Major Wm Buckner's ... . Wit: John Robinson, Samll Hawkins, John Parsons. Ackn 21 Mar 1719/20 by James Parsons & Dorothy his wife & the sd Dorothy being also privately examined relinquished her right of dower & admitted to record. Attest: Phi Lightfoot clerk. (Pg 327)

3 Nov 1718. Deed of Lease. Gilbert Sheldon of Queens Square in Middlesex Co esqr only son & heir of Daniel Sheldon late of London esqr for 5 shillings farm letten unto Joseph Walker of York Co, VA esqr a 618 a. tr of land, 475 a. part whereof are mentioned in & excepted out of a pattent for 1,927 a. of land granted unto George Ludlow esqr dated 26 Jul 1646 were sold unto Robert Kinsey which sd lands & the residue of the hereby demised premises are also comprised & mentioned in one deed poll dated 12 Jun 1685 whereby the sd lands are sold by Wm Cole of Warwick Co, VA unto the sd Daniel Sheldon which sd Daniel Sheldon by his will dated 16 Feb 1696 bequeathed the same to the sd Gilbert Sheldon his only son party to these presents ... for the term of one year ... . Wit: Christo Smyth, William Halladay, John Walker. Ackn 21 Mar 1719/20 by Cole Digges esqr by vertue of a power of atty from Gilbert Sheldon esqr & admitted to record. Attest: Phi Lightfoot clerk. (Pg 328)

4 Nov 1718. Deed of Release. Gilbert Sheldon of Queens Square in Middlesex Co esqr only son & heir of Daniel Sheldon late of London esqr for £107:10 released unto Joseph Walker of York Co, VA esqr a 618 a. tr of land ... [*same as above*] ... . Wit: Christo Smyth, William Halladay, John Walker. Ackn 21 Mar 1719/20 by Cole Digges esqr by vertue of a power of atty from Gilbert Sheldon esqr & admitted to record. Attest: Phi Lightfoot clerk. (Pg 329)

4 Nov 1718. Bond. I Gilbert Sheldon of Queens Square in Middlesex Co esqr am firmly bound unto Joseph Walker of York Co, VA esqr for £700 ... the condition of this obligation is such that if the afsd Gilbert Sheldon shall well & truly observe, obey, perform, fulfill & keep all the articles, clauses, covenants, grants, conditions & agreements mentioned in indentures of lease & release [*see above*] then this obligation to be void ... . Wit: Christo Smyth, William Halladay, John Walker. Ackn 21 Mar 1719/20 by Cole Digges esqr by vertue of a power of atty from Gilbert Sheldon esqr & admitted to record. Attest: Phi Lightfoot clerk. (Pg 331)

2 Feb 1719. Deed of Lease. John Clayton & Wil Robertson feofees or trustees for the land appropriated for the building & erecting the City of Wmsburgh for 5 shillings farm letten unto Jno Davis of Bruton Parish, York Co a lott of ground in the sd City of Wmsburgh designed in the platt of the sd city by the figure 175 ... for one year paying the yearly rent of one grain of Indian corn on 10 Oct if demanded ... . Wit: None. Ackn 16 May 1720 & admitted to record. Attest: Phi Lightfoot clerk. (Pg 331)

3 Feb 1719. Deed of Release. John Clayton & Wil Robertson feofees or trustees for the land appropriated for the building & erecting the City of Wmsburgh for 15 shillings released unto Jno Davis of Bruton Parish, York Co a lott of ground in the sd City of Wmsburgh designed in the platt of the sd city by the figure 175 ... [same as above] ... if the sd Jno Davis shall not within the space of 24 months build & finish upon each lott one good dwelling house then it shall & may be lawfull to & for the sd feofees or trustees into the granted premises & every part thereof to enter & the same to have again as of their former estate to have, hold & enjoy in like manner as they might otherwise have done if these presents had never been made ... . Wit: None. Ackn 16 May 1720 & admitted to record. Attest: Phi Lightfoot clerk. (Pg 332)

14 Jun 1720. Deed of Lease. Francis Tyler of York Co gent for 5 shillings farm lett unto James Roscow of Warwick Co esqr a lott of ground in the City of Williamsburgh denoted in the plan of the sd city by the figure 262 ... for the term of one year paying the rent of one grain of Indian corn on the first of Christmas if demanded ... . Wit: None. Ackn 20 Jun 1720 & admitted to record. Attest: Phi Lightfoot clerk. (Pg 332)

15 Jun 1720. Deed of Release. Francis Tyler of York Co gent for £80 released unto James Roscow of Warwick Co esqr a lott of ground in the City of Williamsburgh denoted in the plan of the sd city by the figure 262 ... [same as above] ... . Wit: None. Ackn 20 Jun 1720 & admitted to record. Attest: Phi Lightfoot clerk. (Pg 333)

16 Jun 1720. Deed of Lease. John Welch & Elizabeth his wife of Charles Parish, York Co for 5 shillings farm lett unto Edmund Sweny of same place all their 125 a. tr of land in Charles Parish, which sd tr of land is pt/o a 600 a. tr of land taken up & patented by John Clark as by the pattent dated 10 Aug 1669 & by the death of the sd John Clark the sd land fell to his son Nicholas Clark & at the death of the sd Nicholas the sd land descended by inheritance to his two daus as coheirs of the sd land (of which the sd Elizabeth Welch w/o the sd John Welch is one) which sd 125 a. of land is bounded by Dedmans Runn & land of Elizabeth Doswell widow & relict of John Doswell decd ... during the term of one year paying the yearly rent of one ear of Indian corn on the last day of the sd

year if demanded ... . Wit: Robt Shield Junr, Bennit Tompkins. Ackn 20 Jun 1720 by John Welch & Eliza his wife & the sd Eliza being privately examined relinquished her dower & admitted to record. Attest: Phi Lightfoot clerk. (Pg 334)

17 Jun 1720. Deed of Release. John Welch & Elizabeth his wife of Charles Parish, York Co for £90 released unto Edmund Sweny of same place all their 125 a. tr of land in Charles Parish ... [*same as above*] ... . Wit: None. Ackn 20 Jun 1720 by John Welch & Eliza his wife & the sd Eliza being privately examined relinquished her dower & admitted to record. Attest: Phi Lightfoot clerk. (Pg 335)

17 Jun 1720. Bond. I John Welch of York Co am firmly bound unto Edmund Sweny of same place for £180 ... the condition of this obligation is such that if the afsd John Welch shall well & truly observe, perform, fulfill, accomplish & keep all the covenants, grants, articles, clauses, conditions & agreements mentioned in one pair of indentures of lease & release [*see above*] then this obligation to be void ... . Wit: Robt Shield Junr, Bennit Tompkins. Ackn 20 Jun 1720 & admitted to record. Attest: Phi Lightfoot clerk. (Pg 336)

14 Jul 1720. Deed of Lease. Thomas Ray of Charles Parish, York Co & Chrismas Ray of Abbington Parish, Glocester Co for 5 shillings farm lett unto William Wise of Charles Parish, co afsd a 91 a. tr of land in Charles Parish together with the marsh thereto adj bounded according to a survey made 9 Sep 1685 for Chrismas Ray father to the sd Thomas & Chrismas Ray by Lawr Smith surveyor adj land of Thomas Nutting & land of Peter Starky ... for the term of one year paying the yearly rent of one ear of Indian corn on the last day of the sd year if demanded ... . Wit: Benja Clifton, James Parsons, Sam Hyde. Ackn 18 Jul 1720 by Thomas Ray & Sarah w/o the sd Thos relinquished her right of dower & admitted to record. Attest: Phi Lightfoot clerk. (Pg 336)

16 Jul 1720. Deed of Release. Thomas Ray of Charles Parish, York Co & Chrismas Ray of Abbington Parish, Glocester Co for £85 released unto William Wise of Charles Parish, co afsd a 91 a. tr of land in Charles Parish ... [*same as above*] ... . Wit: Benja Clifton, James Parsons, Sam Hyde. Ackn 18 Jul 1720 by Thomas Ray & Sarah w/o the sd Thos relinquished her right of dower & admitted to record. Attest: Phi Lightfoot clerk. (Pg 337)

16 Jul 1720. Bond. We Thomas Ray of Charles Parish, York Co & Chrismas Ray of Abbington Parish, Glocester Co are firmly bound unto William Wise of Charles Parish, York Co for £170 ... the condition of this obligation is such that if the afsd Thomas Ray & Chrisman Ray shall well & truly observe, perform, fulfill, accomplish & keep all the covenants, grants, articles, clauses, conditions

& agreements mentioned in one pair of indentures of lease & release [*see above*] then this obligation to be void ... . Wit: Benja Clifton, James Parsons, Sam Hyde. Ackn 18 Jul 1720 & admitted to record. Attest: Phi Lightfoot clerk. (Pg 339)

18 Jul 1720. Deed of Gift. Elizabeth Moss of Charles Parish, York Co widow for love & affection have given to my loving sons James & Benja Moss £20 each but in case any of my sd sons should die before they come of age then the sd £20 to return to the survivor of my sd two sons & if it should please god both my sd sons should depart this life before they come of age then the sd £40 to revert to me the sd Eliza Moss & be again of my proper estate ... . Wit: None. Ackn 15 Aug 1720 & admitted to record. Attest: Phi Lightfoot clerk. (Pg 339)

19 Dec 1720. Deed of Gift. I Mary Davis of Charles Parish, York Co widow relict of John Davis of same place decd who by his will gave to me & my heirs a tr of land in the same parish called the White Ridge. I do out of tender love & affection to my brother Saml Spurr & his two sons Jno & Saml my two niphews give to them the afsd tr of land to be equally divided between them after my decease or to the surviver & his heirs forever & this I do freely ... . Wit: Jas Sclater, Wm Tabb, Jas Sclater Junr. Ackn 19 Dec 1720 & admitted to record. Attest: Phi Lightfoot clerk. (Pg 340)

11 Jan 1720. Deed of Lease. Christopher Haynes & Ann his wife of Mulberry Island Parish, Warwick Co for 5 shillings farm lett unto Richard Ambler of Yorkhampton Parish, York Co merchant all their lott or ½ a. of land in the Town of York abutting on the Main Street, Philip Lightfoot's land, land of Richard Baker & opposite to Thomas Nelson's & described in the plot of the sd town by the figure 43 which sd lott of land was purch by George Burton from Thomas Ballard & Wm Buckner feofees or trustees for the Port Land in York Town by deed dated 10 Jun 1706, & came & descended to the sd Ann as dau & heiress at law of the sd George Burton decd ... during the term of one year ... . Wit: Wil Lindsay, Richd Baker. Ackn by Christo Haynes & Ann his wife 16 Jan 1720 & admitted to record. Attest: Phi Lightfoot clerk. (Pg 340)

12 Jan 1720. Deed of Release. Christopher Haynes & Ann his wife of Mulberry Island Parish, Warwick Co for £30 released unto Richard Ambler of Yorkhampton Parish, York Co merchant all their lott or ½ a. of land in the Town of York ... [*same as above*] ... . Wit: Wil Lindsay, Richd Baker. Ackn 16 Jan 1720 by Christopher Haynes & Ann his wife & the sd Ann being privately examined relinquished her right of dower & admitted to record. Attest: Phi Lightfoot clerk. (Pg 341)

12 Jan 1720. Bond. I Christopher Haynes of Mulberry Island Parish, Warwick Co am firmly bound unto Richard Ambler of the Town & Co of York for £60 ... the condition of this obligation is such that if the afsd Christo Haynes shall well & truly observe, perform, fulfill, accomplish & keep all the covenants, grants, articles, clauses, conditions & agreements mentioned in one pair of indentures of lease & release [*see above*] then this obligation to be void ... . Wit: Wil Lindsay, Richard Baker. Ackn 16 Jan 1720 & admitted to record. Attest: Phi Lightfoot clerk. (Pg 343)

17 Feb 1720. Deed of Lease. John Davis of York Co carpenter for 5 shillings farm lett unto Christopher DeGraffenried of the City of Williamsburgh a lott or ½ a. of ground in the City of Williamsburgh & denoted in the plan of the sd City by the figure 175 ... for the term of one year paying the rent of one grain of Indian corn at the feast of Christmas if demanded ... . Wit: Wil Lindsay, James Keith. Ackn 20 Feb 1720 & admitted to record. Attest: Phi Lightfoot clerk. (Pg 343)

18 Feb 1720. Deed of Release. John Davis of York Co carpenter for £5 released unto Christopher DeGraffenried of the City of Williamsburgh a lott or ½ a. of ground in the City of Williamsburgh & denoted in the plan of the sd City by the figure 175 ... [*same as above*] ... . Wit: Wil Lindsay, James Keith. Ackn 20 Feb 1720 & admitted to record. Attest: Phi Lightfoot clerk. (Pg 344)

13 Dec 1720. Deed of Lease. Francis Tyler of York Co gent for 5 shillings farm letten unto Gawin Corbin of Middlesex Co esqr four lotts of ground in the City of Williamsburgh denoted in the plan of the sd city by the figures 178, 179, 180 & 181 ... for the term of one year paying the rent of one pepper corn upon the fest of Christmas if demanded ... . Wit: Benja Weldon, Henry Powers, Benja Edwards. Ackn 20 Feb 1720 & admitted to record. Attest: Phi Lightfoot clerk. (Pg 345)

14 Dec 1720. Deed of Release. Francis Tyler of York Co gent for £124 released to Gawin Corbin of Middlesex Co esqr four lotts of ground in the City of Williamsburgh denoted in the plan of the sd city by the figures 178, 179, 180 & 181 ... [*same as above*] ... . Wit: Benja Weldon, Henry Powers, Benja Edwards. Ackn 20 Feb 1720 & admitted to record. Attest: Phi Lightfoot clerk. (Pg 345)

20 Feb 1720. Deed of Lease. Stephen Fuller of New Kent Co planter for 5 shillings farm letten unto John Gibbons of York Town, York Co planter all that lott or ½ a. of land in York Town distinguished by the number 54 containing 10 poles in length & 8 poles in breadth bounded upon Mr. Cheshire's lotts adj to the street that leads to the now dwelling house of Thomas Nelson ... which sd lott

(being pt/o the Port Land) was given & bequeathed unto the sd Stephen Fuller by the will of his father Edwd Fuller ... for the term of one year .... Wit: None. Ackn 20 Feb 1720 & admitted to record. Attest: Phi Lightfoot clerk. (Pg 346)

20 Feb 1720. Deed of Release. Stephen Fuller of New Kent Co planter for £15 released unto John Gibbons of York Town, York Co planter all that lott or ½ a. of land in York Town distinguished by the number 54 ... [*same as above*] .... Wit: None. Ackn 20 Feb 1720 by Stephen Fuller & also appeared Eliza w/o the sd Stephen & being privately examined relinquished her right of dower & admitted to record. Attest: Phi Lightfoot clerk. (Pg 347)

20 Feb 1720. Bond. I Stephen Fuller of New Kent Co planter am firmly bound unto John Gibbons of York Town, York Co for £30 ... the condition of this obligation is such that if the afsd Stephen Fuller shall well & truly observe, perform, fulfill, accomplish & keep all the conditions, covenants, grants, articles, clauses & agreements mentioned in one pair of indentures of lease & release [*see above*] then this obligation to be void .... Wit: None. Ackn 20 Feb 1720 & admitted to record. Attest: Phi Lightfoot clerk. (Pg 348)

16 Dec 1720. Deed of Lease. William Robertson & Samuel Cobbs of York Co gent surviving executors of the will of David Cuningham late of sd co barber decd for 5 shillings leased to George Newton of Norfolk Co gent all that lott of land in the City of Williamsburgh near the Capitol in York Co designed in the plot of the sd city by the figure 280 ... for the term of one year paying the rent of one grain of Indian corn on the feast of St. John the Baptist if demanded .... Wit: None. Ackn 20 Feb 1720 & admitted to record. Attest: Phi Lightfoot clerk. (Pg 348)

17 Dec 1720. Deed of Release. William Robertson & Samuel Cobbs of York Co gent surviving executors of the will of David Cuningham late of sd co barber decd for £75 released to George Newton of Norfolk Co gent all that lott of land in the City of Williamsburgh near the Capitol in York Co designed in the plot of the sd city by the figure 280 ... [*same as above*] .... Wit: None. Ackn 20 Feb 1720 & admitted to record. Attest: Phi Lightfoot clerk. (Pg 349)

16 Dec 1720. Deed of Lease. Wm Robertson & Saml Cobbs of York Co gent surviving executors of the will of David Cuningham late of sd co barber decd for 5 shillings leased to Nathaniel Newton of Norfolk Co gent all that lott of land in the City of Williamsburgh near the Capitol in York Co designed in the plot of the sd city by the figure 279 ... for the term of one year paying the rent of one grain of Indian corn on the feast of St. John the Baptist if demanded .... Wit:

None. Ackn 20 Feb 1720 & admitted to record. Attest: Phi Lightfoot clerk. (Pg 350)

17 Dec 1720. Deed of Release. Wm Robertson & Saml Cobbs of York Co gent surviving executors of the will of David Cuningham late of sd co barber decd for £75 released to Nathaniel Newton of Norfolk Co gent all that lott of land in the City of Williamsburgh near the Capitol in York Co designed in the plot of the sd city by the figure 279 ... [*same as above*] ... . Wit: None. Ackn 20 Feb 1720 & admitted to record. Attest: Phi Lightfoot clerk. (Pg 350)

9 Jan 1720. Deed of Lease. John Clayton & Wil Robertson feofees or trustees for the land appropriated for the building & erecting the City of Williamsburgh for 5 shillings farm letten unto Saml Cobbs of York Co one lott of ground in the sd City of Williamsburgh designed in the plot of the sd city by the figure 52 ... for the term of one year paying the yearly rent of one grain of Indian corn on 10 Oct if demanded ... . Wit: None. Ackn 20 Feb 1720 & admitted to record. Attest: Phi Lightfoot clerk. (Pg 351)

10 Jan 1720. Deed of Release. John Clayton & Wil Robertson feofees or trustees for the land appropriated for the building & erecting the City of Williamsburgh for 15 shillings released unto Saml Cobbs of York Co one lott of ground in the sd City of Williamsburgh designed in the plot of the sd city by the figure 52 ... [*same as above*] ... if the sd Saml Cobbs shall not within the space of 24 months build & finish upon each lott one good dwelling house then it shall & may be lawfull to & for the sd feofees or trustees into the granted premises & every part thereof to enter & the same to have again as of their former estate to have, hold & enjoy in like manner as they might otherwise have done if these presents had never been made ... . Wit: None. Ackn 20 Feb 1720 & admitted to record. Attest: Phi Lightfoot clerk. (Pg 352)

11 Jul 1720. Deed of Lease. John Clayton & Wil Robertson feofees or trustees for the land appropriated for the building & erecting the City of Williamsburgh for 5 shillings farm letten unto John Holloway of York Co gent two lotts of ground in the sd City of Wmsburgh designed in the platt of the sd city by the figures 331 & 332 ...during the term of one year paying the yearly rent of one grain of Indian corn on 10 Oct if demanded ... . Wit: None. Ackn 20 Feb 1720 & admitted to record. Attest: Phi Lightfoot clerk. (Pg 353)

12 Jul 1720. Deed of Release. John Clayton & Wil Robertson feofees or trustees for the land appropriated for the building & erecting the City of Williamsburgh for 30 shillings released unto John Holloway of York Co gent two lotts of ground in the sd City of Wmsburgh designed in the platt of the sd city by the figures 331 & 332 ... [*same as above*] ... if the sd John Holloway

shall not within the space of 24 months build & finish upon each lott one good dwelling house then it shall & may be lawfull to & for the sd feofees or trustees into the granted premises & every part thereof to enter & the same to have again as of their former estate to have, hold & enjoy in like manner as they might otherwise have done if these presents had never been made ... . Wit: None. Ackn 20 Feb 1720 & admitted to record. Attest: Phi Lightfoot clerk. (Pg 353)

18 Jul 1720. Deed of Lease. John Clayton & Wil Robertson feofees or trustees for the land appropriated for the building & erecting the City of Williamsburgh for 5 shillings farm letten unto Lewis Holland of Wmsburgh merchant nine lotts of ground in Queen Marys Port designed in the platt of the sd Port by the figures 36, 37, 38, 39, 13, 14, 64, 65 & 68 ... for the term of one year paying the yearly rent of one grain of Indian corn on 10 Oct if demanded ... . Wit: None. Ackn 20 Feb 1720 & admitted to record. Attest: Phi Lightfoot clerk. (Pg 355)

19 Jul 1720. Deed of Release. John Clayton & Wil Robertson feofees or trustees for the land appropriated for the building & erecting the City of Williamsburgh for £6:15 released unto Lewis Holland of Wmsburgh merchant nine lotts of ground in Queen Marys Port designed in the platt of the sd Port by the figures 36, 37, 38, 39, 13, 14, 64, 65 & 68 ... [same as above] ... if the sd Lewis Holland shall not within the space of 24 months build & finish upon each lott one good dwelling house then it shall & may be lawfull to & for the sd feofees or trustees into the granted premises & every part thereof to enter & the same to have again as of their former estate to have, hold & enjoy in like manner as they might otherwise have done if these presents had never been made ... . Wit: None. Ackn 20 Feb 1720 & admitted to record. Attest: Phi Lightfoot clerk. (Pg 355)

13 Aug 1720. Deed of Lease. George Gilbert of York Co planter for 5 shillings farm letten unto Graves Packe of co afsd gent four lotts of ground in Queen Mary's Port in Wmsburgh designed in the plot of the sd Port by the figures 26, 27, 28 & 29 ... for the term of one year paying the yearly rent of one grain of Indian corn on 10 Oct if demanded ... . Wit: R?. Armistead, Wm Perkins, Daniel Short. Ackn 20 Mar 1720 & admitted to record. Attest: Phi Lightfoot clerk. (Pg 356)

14 Aug 1720. Deed of Release. George Gilbert of York Co planter for £39 released unto Graves Packe of co afsd gent four lotts of ground in Queen Mary's Port in Wmsburgh designed in the plot of the sd Port by the figures 26, 27, 28 & 29 ... [same as above] ... which four lotts were heretofore granted to the sd George Gilbert by deeds of lease & release dated 1 & 2 Jun 1719 by John Clayton esqr & Wm Robertson gent feofees or trustees appropriated for the building & erecting the City of Williamsburgh ... . Wit: Po (or R?) Armistead,

84

Wm Perkins, Daniel Short. Ackn 20 Mar 1720 & admitted to record. Attest: Phi Lightfoot clerk. (Pg 357)

13 Jan 1721. Deed of Lease. Charles Rowan & Lidia his wife of York Hampton Parish, York Co for 5 shillings leased unto Beuford Pleasant of Charles Parish co afsd a messuage & 15 a. tr of land in Charles Parish being pt/o a piece of land formerly belonging to Joseph Potter of Charles Parish & by the sd Joseph Potter's will devised the same unto his dau Lidia Potter now Lidia Rowan ... during the term of one year ... . Wit: Richd Bellamee, Sarah Bellamee, Jno Wythe. Ackn 20 Mar 1720 by Charles Rowan & Lidia his wife & admitted to record. Attest: Phi Lightfoot clerk. (Pg 358)

14 Jan 1721. Deed of Release. Charles Rowan & Lidia his wife of York Hampton Parish, York Co for £15 released unto Beuford Pleasant of Charles Parish co afsd a messuage & 15 a. tr of land in Charles Parish ... [same as above] ... . Wit: Richd Bellamee, Sarah Bellamee, Jno Wythe. Ackn 20 Mar 1720 by Charles Rowan & Lidia his wife & the sd Lydia being privately examined relinquished her right of dower & admitted to record. Attest: Phi Lightfoot clerk. (Pg 359)

15 Jan 1720/21. Bond. We Charles Rowan & Lidia his wife are firmly indebted unto Beauford Pleasants in the penal sum of £30 ... the condition of this obligation is such that if the afsd Charles Rowen & Lidia his wife do keep & perform all clauses, articles, conditions & agreements made in one deed of lease [see above] then this obligation to be void ... . Wit: Richd Bellamee, Sarah Bellamee. Ackn 20 Mar 1720 by Charles Rowan & Lidia his wife & admitted to record. Attest: Phi Lightfoot clerk. (Pg 360)

20 Mar 1720. Deed of Gift. John Dowsing of Mulberry Island Parish, Warwick Co, VA bricklayer for good will & paternal affection have given unto my son Robert Dowsing of same place bricklayer ½ of my lott of ground in York being pt/o the Port Land known in the plot of the sd town by the figure 33, that ½ of the sd lott which lyes towards the cr at the back of the town being the outside half, which sd lott I formerly purch of Thomas Ballard & William Buckner gent trustees for the Port Land of the sd town by deed dated 24 Aug 1707 ... . Wit: Wil Lindsay, Wm Gordon. Ackn 20 Mar 1720 & admitted to record. Attest: Phi Lightfoot clerk. (Pg 360)

20 Mar 1720/21. Deed of Gift. William Wise of Charles Parish, York Co have given unto my beloved son Robert Wise & his heirs all that tr of land I bought of Charles Calthorp decd, to witt, I give him as afsd all that land on the s side of the rode that runs by the Widow Grey's & from thence to Elizabeth Nutting's, with that tr of land I bought of Thomas Ray together with the tr of land John

Chapman bought of James Calthorp decd adj thereto (& in case my sd son Robert Wise should die without issue I freely give the afsd land unto my loving son Charles Wise & to his heirs) ... . Wit: Thos Kerby, Jno Sclater, Edmund Sweny. Ackn 20 mar 1720 & admitted to record. Attest: Phi Lightfoot clerk. (Pg 361)

7 May 1721. Deed of Lease. Thomas Sandifer of Charles Parish, York Co & his wife Elizabeth Sandifer for 5 shillings farm lett unto Eliza Heyward widow of same place all his 70 a. tr of land in Oaken Swamp in Charles Parish which was given to my father Jno Sandifer & from my father to me by inheritance ... for the term of one year paying the yearly rent of one ear of Indian corn on 10 Oct if demanded ... . Wit: Robt Beluin, Wm Heyward, Wm Trotter. Ackn 15 May 1721 by Thos Sandifer & Eliza his wife & admitted to record. Attest: Phi Lightfoot clerk. (Pg 362)

8 May 1721. Deed of Release. Thomas Sandifer of Charles Parish, York Co & his wife Elizabeth Sandifer for £25 released unto Eliza Heyward widow of same place all his 70 a. tr of land in Oaking Swamp in Charles Parish ... [same as above] ... (except my mother's right of dower in the afsd premises) ... . Wit: Robt Beluin, Wm Heyward, Wm Trotter. Ackn 15 May 1721 by Thos Sandifer & Eliza his wife & the sd Eliza relinquished her right of dower & admitted to record. Attest: Phi Lightfoot clerk. (Pg 262)

8 May 1721. Bond. I Thomas Sandifer of Yorkhampton Parish, York Co am firmly bound unto Eliza Heyward of Charles Parish, York Co for £50 ... the condition of this obligation is such that if the afsd Thomas Sandifer shall well & truly observe, perform, fulfill, accomplish & keep all the covenants, grants, articles, clauses, conditions & agreements mentioned in one pair of indentures of lease & release [see above] then this obligation to be void ... . Wit: Robert Beluin, Wm Hayward, Wm Trotter. Ackn 15 May 1721 & admitted to record. Attest: Phi Lightfoot clerk. (Pg 264)

21 Apr 1721. Deed of Lease. Elinor Thebaut widow devisee of John Thebaut late of Yorkhampton Parish, carpenter decd for 5 shillings farm letten unto Samuel Hyde of same place planter a 50 a. tr of land in the parish afsd being the same plantation which the sd John Thebaut purch of John Anderson by deed dated 11 Dec 1710 bounded by the lines late of Robert Hyde & lines late of Major Lewis Burwell ... for the term of one year paying the rent of one grain of Indian corn at the expiration of the afsd term if demanded ... . Wit: Frans Tyler, Wm Gordon, Henry Power, Joseph Davenport. Ackn 15 May 1721 & admitted to record. Attest: Phi Lightfoot clerk. (Pg 364)

22 Apr 1721. Deed of Release. Elinor Thebaut widow devisee of John Thebaut late of Yorkhampton Parish, carpenter decd for £25 released unto Samuel Hyde of same place planter a 50 a. tr of land in the parish afsd ... [*same as above*] ... . Wit: Frans Tyler, Wm Gordon, Henry Power, Joseph Davenport. Ackn 15 May 1721 & admitted to record. Attest: Phi Lightfoot clerk. (Pg 365)

16 May 1721. Deed of Lease. Robt Cobbs of Bruton Parish, York Co planter for 5 shillings farm lett unto Mathew Pierce of same place planter a 45 a. tr of land being pt/o a tr of land whereon the sd Robt now dwells in the afsd parish & is separated therefrom by the following bounds n side of the Widdow Gibson's Spring Br, the dividing line between Major Jno Holloway & the sd Pierce, near Major Custis's Mill Swamp, the Main Runn, sd Pierce's Spring Br & the sd Cobbs ... during the term of one year paying the rent of one grain of Indian corn at the feast of Christmas next if demanded ... . Wit: Jno Rice, Jno Pegram, Jos Devenport. Ackn 19 Jun 1721 & admitted to record. Attest: Phi Lightfoot clerk. (Pg 365)

17 May 1721. Deed of Release. Robt Cobbs of Bruton Parish, York Co planter for £45 released unto Mathew Pierce of same place planter a 45 a. tr of land ... [*same as above*] ... . Wit: Jno Rice, Jno Pegram, Jos Devenport. Ackn 19 Jun 1721 & admitted to record. Attest: Phi Lightfoot clerk. (Pg 366)

17 Jul 1721. Deed. John Dowsing of Mullberry Island Parish, Warwick Co bricklayer for £14 sold to Robert Dowsing of same place a lott of ground in York Town being pt/o the Port Land known in the platt of the sd town by the figure 33, to witt, that ½ of the sd lott which lyes to the ne which sd lott the sd John Dowsing formerly purch of Thomas Ballard & William Buckner gent trustees for the Port Land of the sd town by deed dated 24 Aug 1707, & the sd John Dowsing having by deed of gift dated 20 Mar 1720/1 given unto the sd Robt Dowsing the other half of the sd lott ... . Wit: Wm Lindsay, Wm Gordon. Ackn 17 Jul 1721 & admitted to record. Attest: Phi Lightfoot clerk. (Pg 367)

10 Jul 1721. Deed of Lease. Miles Wills & Emanuel Wills of Mulberry Island Parish, Warwick Co gent for 5 shillings farm letten unto William Stark of Yorkhampton Parish, York Co merchant all their lott or ½ a. of land in York Town containing 10 poles in length & 8 in breadth being pt/o the Port Land designed in the plot of the sd town by the number [?] ... for the term of one year ... . Wit: Jno Wills, Seamer Powell. Ackn 17 Jul 1721 & admitted to record. Attest: Phi Lightfoot clerk. (Pg 368)

11 Jul 1721. Deed of Release. Miles Wills & Emanuel Wills of Mulberry Island Parish, Warwick Co gent for £30 released unto William Stark of Yorkhampton Parish, York Co merchant all their lott or ½ a. of land in York

Town ... [*same as above*] ... . Wit: Jno Wills, Seamer Powell. Ackn 17 Jul
1721 & admitted to record. Attest: Phi Lightfoot clerk. (Pg 369)

11 Jul 1721. Bond. We Miles Wills & Emanuel Wills of Mulberry Island
Parish, Warwick Co are firmly bound unto William Stark of Yorkhampton
Parish, York Co for £60 ... the condition of this obligation is such that if the afsd
Miles Wills & Emanuel Wills shall well & truly observe, perform, fulfill,
accomplish & keep all the covenants, grants, articles, clauses, conditions &
agreements mentioned in one pair of indentures of lease & release [*see above*]
then this obligation to be void ... . Wit: John Wills, Seamore Powell. Ackn 17
Jul 1721 & admitted to record. Attest: Phi Lightfoot clerk. (Pg 370)

20 Nov 1722. Deed of Gift. Mary Jackson of Bruton Parish, York Co widdow
for good will that I bear & divers other good considerations have given unto
Robt Crawley son of Nathaniel Crawley late of sd parish decd all that plantation
& 500 a. tr of land in the place called the Indian Field in the afsd parish which
was granted together with 300 a. more to Joseph White by patent dated 20 Apr
1694 & by the will of the sd Joseph dated 25 Feb 1705/6 devised in fee to me the
then w/o the sd Joseph ... during his natural life & no longer & further for the
considerations afsd I do give unto the sd Robert Crawley nine Negro slaves, viz,
Samson, Ben, Simon, Sambo, Jack, Kate, Sarah, Lucy & Betty, together with
such increase as they shall hereafter produce forever. Also know ye that I the sd
Mary Jackson as well in consideration of the natural love & affection which I
have & bear unto my loving dau Elizabeth Jackson as for other good
considerations have given unto the sd Elizabeth Jackson two Negro slaves by
name Harry & Jenny together with the increase which they shall hereafter
produce, to her forever. And further know ye that I the sd Mary Jackson for &
in consideration of the natural love & affection which I have & bear unto my
loving sons Phipps Jackson & Ambrose Jackson do give unto the sd Phipps
Jackson & Ambrose Jackson & their heirs forever all my right & title which I
shall may or ought to have of & in all the plantation & tr of land & premises
herein above granted to Robert Crawley immediately after the decease of the sd
Robert in the manner following, to the sd Ambrose Jackson to have the mannour
house with all other the houses thereto belonging & ½ of the sd tr of land, & the
sd Phipps Jackson to have the other ½ pt/o the sd land to be laid out & divided
(in case of their disagreement) by two freeholders of the co indifferently chosen
by the sd Phipps & Ambrose to divide & assign the sd dividends, nevertheless
reserving & always saving to myself full power to dispose or sell the right I may
have in reversion to the sd lands after the decease of the sd Robert Crawley & to
such other person as I shall hereafter think fit ... . Wit: None. Ackn 20 Nov
1721 & admitted to record. Attest: Phi Lightfoot clerk. (Pg 371)

16 xber 1721. Deed of Release. Jno Stockner of York Hampton Parish, York Co for £25 released to Joseph Walker of same place merchant all his 50 a. tr of land in the sd parish bounded by the road, land of Arthur Dickeson, land late of Capt Phil Moody, the Black Swamp, land of William Barbar & land of the sd Joseph Walker which he lately purch of Martha & Samuel Sebrell & which two parcels of land together are the land mentioned in a patent dated at James City 12 Jun 1663 & thereby given & granted unto Wm Grimes ... . Wit: Giles Moody, H. Hopkins, Godfrey Pole. Ackn 18 xber 1721 & admitted to record. Attest: Phi Lightfoot clerk. (Pg 372)

15 xber 1721. Deed of Lease. John Stockner of York Hampton Parish, York Co for 25 shillings farm letten unto Joseph Walker of same place merchant all that 50 a. tr of land ... [same as above] ... . Wit: Giles Moody, H. Hopkins, Godfrey Pole. Ackn 18 xber 1721 & admitted to record. Attest: Phi Lightfoot clerk. (Pg 373)

16 xber 1721. Bond. I John Stockner of York Hampton Parish, York Co am firmly bound unto Joseph Walker of same place in the penal sum of £50 ... the condition of this obligation is such that if the afsd Jno Stockner shall well & truly observe, perform & keep all the clauses, covenants, articles & provisos menconed in deeds of lease & release [see above] then this obligation to be void ... . Wit: Giles Moody, H. Hopkins, Godfrey Pole. Ackn 18 xber 1721 & admitted to record. Attest: Phi Lightfoot clerk. (Pg 373)

12 Jan 1721. Deed of Lease. Jno Moss & Eliza his wife & Eliza his mother of York Hampton Parish, York Co for 5 shillings leased unto John Trotter of York Town, co afsd one lott of land known by the number 65 containing ½ a. of land in the Town & Parish of York ... for the term of one year ... . Wit: Jno Mattocke, Robt Kerby Junr, Jno Addustun Rogers, Peter Manson. Ackn 15 Jan 1721/2 by John Moss, Eliza Moss his wife & Eliza Moss his mother & admitted to record. Attest: Phi Lightfoot clerk. (Pg 374)

12 Jan 1721. Deed of Release. Jno Moss & Eliza his wife & Eliza his mother of York Hampton Parish, York Co for a competent sum of mony released unto John Trotter of York Town, co afsd one lott of land known by the number 65 containing ½ a. of land in the Town & Parish of York ... [same as above] ... . Wit: Jno Mattocke, Robt Kerby Junr, Jno Addustun Rogers, Peter Manson. Ackn 15 Jan 1721 by Jno Moss & Eliz Moss his wife & Eliza Moss his mother & the sd Eliza his wife being privately examined released her right of dower & admitted to record. Attest: Phi Lightfoot clerk. (Pg 374)

12 Jan 1721. Bond. We John Moss & Eliza his wife & Eliz his mother of York Hampton Parish, York Co do severally stand & are firmly bound unto John

Trotter of York Town in parish & co afsd for £64 ... the condition of this obligation is such that if the afsd John Moss, Eliza his wife & Eliza his mother doth forever after acquit all their right & title, interest, profit, claim & demand of a lott of land in York Town known by the number 65 being by them sold as appears by a pair of indentures of lease & release [see above] then this obligation to be void ... . Wit: Jno Mattocke, Robert Kerby Junr, Jno Addustun Rogers, Peter Manson. Ackn 15 Jan 1721 by the partys & admitted to record. Attest: Phi Lightfoot clerk. (Pg 376)

9 Jan 1721/2. Deed. Wm Biggs & Mary his wife of York Hampton Parish, York Co for £18 sold to Wm Gordon of same place one Negro boy slave named Frank aged 7 years ... . Wit: Danl Fisher, Lawr Smith, Wm Harwood, Lucinda Smith, Thos Frayser. Ackn 15 Jan 1721/2 & admitted to record. Attest: Phi Lightfoot clerk. (Pg 376)

16 Sep 1721. Deed of Release. John Clayton & Wm Robertson feofees or trustees for the land appropriated for the building & erecting the City of Williamsburgh for £3 released unto Jonathan Drewit of York Co four lotts of ground at Queen Marys Port designed in the plan of the sd Port by the figures 2, 4, 9 & 8 ... if the sd Jonathan Drewit shall not within the space of 24 months build & finish upon each lott one good dwelling house then it shall & may be lawfull to & for the sd feofees or trustees into the granted premises & every part thereof to enter & the same to have again as of their former estate to have, hold & enjoy in like manner as they might otherwise have done if these presents had never been made ... . Wit: None. Ackn 19 Feb 1721 & admitted to record. Attest: Phi Lightfoot clerk. (Pg 377)

15 Sep 1721. Deed of Lease. John Clayton & Wm Robertson feofees or trustees for the land appropriated for the building & erecting the City of Williamsburgh for 5 shillings leased unto Jonathan Drewit of York Co four lotts of ground at Queen Marys Port designed in the plan of the sd Port by the figures 2, 4, 9 & 8 ... [same as above] ... . Ackn 19 Feb 1721 & admitted to record. Attest: Phi Lightfoot clerk. (Pg 378)

7 Feb 1721. Deed of Release. Joseph Freeman of the City of Wmsburgh, York Co joyner for £135 released unto Thomas Jones of the same city merchant all that lott or ½ a. of ground in Williamsburgh described in the plot of the sd city by the figure 47 & adj on the Great Street between the storehouse now in the tenure of Archibald Blair gent & the house now in the tenure of Michael Archer, excepting out of the sd lott one piece of ground on the n end thereof the breadth of the sd lott & 30' in length which sd lott with the exception afsd was by Samuel Hyde conveyed to the sd Joseph Freeman by deed dated 9 Mar 1718 ... . Wit: Michl Archer, John Tyler, Charles Prince. Ackn 19 Feb 1721 by Joseph

Freeman & Dorcas the w/o the sd Joseph being privately examined relinquished her right of dower & admitted to record. Attest: Phi Lightfoot clerk. (Pg 378)

16 Feb 1721. Deed of Lease. Joseph Freeman of the City of Wmsburgh, York Co joyner for 5 shillings leased unto Thomas Jones of the same city merchant all that lott or ½ a. of ground in Williamsburgh described in the plot of the sd city by the figure 47 ... [same as above] ... for one year paying the rent of one ear of Indian corn on the last day of the sd term if demanded ... . Wit: Michl Archer, Jno Tyler, Cha Prince. Ackn 19 Feb 1721 by Joseph Freeman & admitted to record. Attest: Phi Lightfoot clerk. (Pg 380)

17 Feb 1721. Deed. John Lewelling & Mary my wife of Charles Parish, York Co for a valuable consideration already recd have sold unto John Johnson of same place a parcel or ½ of land in the sd parish adj the swamp below Chismans Mill, line of John Bond formerly called Nicho Martin's line, Emuses Run & the line of John Wills formerly known to be the line of Thomas Harwood, the sd parcel of land being pt/o a dividend of land belonging to Robt Everit ... . Wit: John Moss, James Burton, Cha Cox. Ackn 19 Feb 1721 by John Lewelling & Mary his wife & admitted to record. Attest: Phi Lightfoot clerk. (Pg 380)

17 Feb 1721. Bond. We John Lewelling & Mary his wife of Charles Parish, York Co are firmly bound & indebted unto Jno Johnson of same place in the penal sum of £100 ... the condition of this obligation is such that if the afsd John Lewelling & Mary his wife do perform all articles, clauses & conditions concerning a bargain of sale of land [see above] then this obligation to be void ... . Wit: John Moss, James Burton, Chas Cox. Ackn 19 Feb 1721 & admitted to record. Attest: Phi Lightfoot clerk. (Pg 381)

19 Feb 1721. Deed of Gift. Sarah Burnham of Charles Parish, York Co for love, good will & affection have given unto my loving children Thos Pescod, Robt Pescod, Rachel Pescod & George Pescod two Negro women named Bess & Sarah, I give the sd Negro Bess wholly & solely unto my son Thomas after my death & the other Negro named Sarah & her increase unto my afsd children Thomas, Robert, Rachel & George to them & their heirs forever after my death ... . Wit: Robt Shield Junr, John Johnson. Ackn 19 Feb 1721 & admitted to record. Attest: Phi Lightfoot clerk. (Pg 381)

19 Mar 1721/2. Deed of Release. John Wills of Mulberry Island Parish, Warwick Co for £70 released unto Eliza Hayward of Charles Parish, York Co a tr of land in Charles Parish formerly belonging to Michael Bartlet of Charles Parish decd which sd land was given to the sd Bartlet by the will of Robert Everit decd 19 Jan 1681 containing 200 a. of land according to a survey made 25 8ber 1683 for Michael Bartlet afsd by Lawr Smith surveyor adj Col Miles Cary

& Mr. Harwood's line ... . Wit: Thos Chisman, Wm Harwood, Jno Robinson. Ackn 19 Mar 1721 by John Wills & Eliza his wife & the sd Eliza being privately examined relinquished her right of dower & admitted to record. Attest: Phi Lightfoot clerk. (Pg 381)

17 Mar 1721. Deed of Lease. John Wills of Mulberry Island Parish, Warwick Co for 5 shillings leased unto Eliza Hayward of Charles Parish, York Co a 200 a. tr of land in Charles Parish ... [same as above] ... . Wit: Thos Chisman, Willm Harwood, Jno Robinson. Ackn 19 Mar 1721 by Jno Wills & Eliza his wife & admitted to record. Attest: Phi Lightfoot clerk. (Pg 383)

19 Mar 1721/2. Bond. I John Wills & Eliza my wife of Mulberry Island Parish, Warwick Co are firmly holden unto Eliza Hayward of Charles Parish, York Co for £140 ... the condition of this obligation is such that if the afsd Jno Wills & Eliza his wife do & shall well & truly observe, perform, fulfill, accomplish & keep all the covenants, grants, articles, claims & agreements mentioned in one pair of indentures of lease & release [see above] then this obligation to be void ... . Wit: Thos Chisman, Wm Harwood, Jno Robinson. Ackn 19 Mar 1721 by Jno Wills & Eliza his wife & admitted to record. Attest: Phi Lightfoot clerk. (Pg 384)

4 Aug 1722. Deed of Release. Thomas Jones of the City of Wmsburgh merchant for £130 released unto Christopher DeGraffenried of same place gent all that lott or ½ a. of ground in Wmsburgh described in the plat of the sd city by the figure 47 adj to the Great Street between the storehouse now in the tenure of Archibald Blair gent & the house now in the tenure of Michael Archer, excepting out of the sd lott one piece of ground on the n end thereof the breadth of the sd lot & 30' in length, which sd lot or ½ a. of ground (with the excepting afsd) was by Saml Hyde conveyed to Joseph Freeman & by the sd Freeman conveyed to the sd Thos Jones by deeds of lease & release dated 16 & 17 Feb 1721 ... . Wit: H. Hacker, Peter Scott, Chas Prince. Ackn 20 Aug 1722 & admitted to record. Attest: Phi Lightfoot clerk. (Pg 384)

3 Aug 1722. Deed of Lease. Thomas Jones of the City of Wmsburgh merchant for 5 shillings leased unto Christopher DeGraffenried of same place gent all that lott or ½ a. of ground in Wmsburgh described in the plat of the sd city by the figure 47 ... [same as above] ... for the term of one year paying the rent of one ear of Indian corn on the last day of the sd term if demanded ... . Wit: H. Hacker, Peter Scott, Chas Prince. Ackn 20 Aug 1722 & admitted to record. Attest: Phi Lightfoot clerk. (Pg 386)

15 Dec 1722. Deed of Lease. John Mattocke (Maddocks) (Mattocks) & Ann his wife of York Hampton Parish, York Co for 5 shillings leased to John Gomer of

same place one lott of Port Land containing ½ a. known by the number 9 ...
during the term of one year ... . Wit: John Trotter, Thos Wootten. Ackn 17
Dec 1722 by John Mattock & Ann his wife & admitted to record. (Pg 386)

14 Dec 1722. Deed of Release. John Mattocke (Maddocks) (Mattocks) & Ann
his wife of York Hampton Parish, York Co for £47:10 released to John Gomer
of same place one lott of Port Land containing ½ a. known by the number 9 ...
[same as above] ... . Wit: John Trotter, Thos Wooton. Ackn 17 Dec 1722 by
John Mattocke & Ann his wife & admitted to record. Attest: Phi Lightfoot
clerk. (Pg 387)

12 Dec 1722. Deed of Lease. William Forgason (Ferguson) & Hope his wife of
Charles Parish, York Co for 5 shillings farm letten unto Benjamin Clifton of
same place all that 50 a. tr of land in Charles Parish known by the name of Owen
Davises plantation bounded by Fincher Dam, Thomas Hynd's land & land of
Clifton afsd, which sd 50 a. of land was given to the sd William Forgason by
Owen Davis his grandfather who was the sole heir ... during the term of one
year paying the rent of one ear of Indian corn on the last day of the sd year if
demanded ... . Wit: Jno Hay, Thos Hinde, Ann Grouse Ackn 17 xber 1722 by
Wm Ferguson & Hope his wife & admitted to record. Attest: Phi Lightfoot
clerk. (Pg 388)

13 Dec 1722. Deed of Release. William Forgason (Ferguson) & Hope his wife
of Charles Parish, York Co for £50 released unto Benjamin Clifton of same
place all that 50 a. tr of land in Charles Parish ... [same as above] ... . Wit: Jno
Hay, Thomas Hinde, Ann Grouse. Ackn 17 Dec 1722 by Wm Ferguson & Hope
his wife the sd Hope being privately examined released her right of dower &
admitted to record. Attest: Phi Lightfoot clerk. (Pg 389)

13 Dec 1722. Bond. I Wm Ferguson (Forgason) & Hope my wife of Charles
Parish, York Co are firmly bound unto Benja Clifton of same place for £100 ...
the condition of this obligation is such that if the afsd Wm Ferguson & Hope his
wife do & shall well & truly observe, perform, fulfill, accomplish & keep all the
covenants, grants, articles, clauses, conditions & agreements mentioned in one
pair of indentures of lease & release [see above] then this obligation to be void
... . Wit: Jno Hay, Thos Hinde, Ann Grouse. Ackn 17 xber 1722 & admitted to
record. Attest: Phi Lightfoot clerk. (Pg 390)

15 7ber 1722. Deed of Release. John Clayton & Wm Robertson feofees or
trustees for the land appropriated for the building & erecting the City of
Williamsburgh for 45 shillings released unto Henry Cary of James City Co gent
three lotts of ground in the sd City of Williamsburgh numbered in the plan of the
sd city by the figures 316, 317 & 318 bounded by Henry Street & Prince George

Street ... if the sd Henry Cary shall not within the space of 24 months build & finish upon each lott one good dwelling house then it shall & may be lawfull to & for the sd feofees or trustees into the granted premises & every part thereof to enter & the same to have again as of their former estate to have, hold & enjoy in like manner ... . Wit: None. Ackn 18 Feb 1722 & admitted to record. Attest: Phi Lightfoot clerk. (Pg 391)

14 Sep 1722. Deed of Lease. John Clayton & Wm Robertson feofees or trustees for the land appropriated for the building & erecting the City of Williamsburgh for 5 shillings leased unto Henry Cary of James City Co gent three lotts of ground in the sd City of Williamsburgh numbered in the plan of the sd city by the figures 316, 317 & 318 ... [same as above] ... for the term of one year paying the yearly rent of one grain of Indian corn on 10 Oct if demanded ... . Wit: None. Ackn 18 Feb 1722 & admitted to record. Attest: Phi Lightfoot clerk. (Pg 392)

6 Feb 1722. Deed of Release. John Clayton & Wm Robertson feofees or trustees for the land appropriated for the building & erecting the City of Williamsburgh for £3:15 released unto Christopher Jackson of James City Co gent five lots of ground in the sd City of Williamsburgh designed in the plot of the sd city by the figures 43, 42, 313, 314 & 315 ... if the sd Christopher Jackson shall not within the space of 24 months build & finish upon each lott one good dwelling house then it shall & may be lawfull to & for the sd feofees or trustees into the granted premises & every part thereof to enter & the same to have again as of their former estate to have, hold & enjoy in like manner ... . Wit: Geo Allen, Joseph Davenport, R. Hickman. Ackn 18 Feb 1723 & admitted to record. Attest: Phi Lightfoot clerk. (Pg 392)

5 Feb 1722. Deed of Lease. John Clayton & Wm Robertson feofees or trustees for the land appropriated for the building & erecting the City of Williamsburgh for 5 shillings leased unto Christopher Jackson of James City Co gent five lots of ground in the sd City of Williamsburgh designed in the plot of the sd city by the figures 43, 12, 313, 314 & 315 ... [same as above] ... for the term of one year paying the yearly rent of one grain of Indian corn on 10 Oct if demanded ... . Wit: Geo Allen, Joseph Davenport, R. Hickman. Ackn 18 Feb 1723 & admitted to record. Attest: Phi Lightfoot clerk. (Pg 393)

18 Mar 1722. Deed. Between Thomas Nelson of York, York Co gent of the one part & Joseph Walker of same co esqr of the other part, whereas Benjamin Clifton by a deed dated 14 Aug 1719 did convey unto the sd Thomas Nelson & Joseph Walker all that lot or ½ a. of land in York Town being pt/o the Port Land then known by the number 25, by virtue of which sd recited conveyance the sd Thomas Nelson & Joseph Walker are now jointly seized as well of one

messuage called The Swan now in the tenure & occupacon of Robert Wills
which hath been build by the sd Thomas Nelson & Joseph Walker upon the sd
lott of ground since the same was conveyed to them by the sd Benjamin Clifton,
now this indenture wit that the sd Thomas Nelson & Joseph Walker for severing
the joint tenanty between them do by these presents agree to & with each other
in manner & form following, that is to say that he the sd Joseph Walker shall
have hold & enjoy ½ pt/o the sd messuage lot or ½ a. of ground, & the sd
Thomas Nelson shall have hold & enjoy the other ½ of the same messuage & ½
a. of ground & premises, & the sd Thomas Nelson doth release & confirm to the
sd Joseph Walker the sd ½ pt/o the sd messuage & premises, & the sd Joseph
Walker doth release & confirm to the sd Thomas Nelson the other ½ pt/o the sd
messuage & premises … . Wit: None. Ackn 18 Mar 1722 by Thomas Nelson
& Joseph Walker gent to each other & admitted to record. Attest: Phi Lightfoot
clerk. (Pg 394)

16 May 1723. Deed of Lease. David Morce of James City Co for 5 shillings
farm letten unto Philip Lightfoot of Yorkhampton Parish, York Co gent all that
100 a. tr of land in Yorkhampton Parish lately in the tenure & occupation of Jno
Rhodes & Robert Roberts adj the road leading over the Beaver Dams, land of
Capt William Barbar, land late of James Causby decd, Ulys or Kings Cr & land
of Robert Roberts, which land was sold & conveyed by John Dennit to Jane
Morce mother of the sd David by deed dated 14 Dec 1689 & by the sd Jane
Morce assigned & made over to her son John Morce which sd land afterwards
came & descended to the sd David Morce as brother & heir at law to the sd John
Morce … for the term of one year paying the yearly rent of one ear of Indian
corn on the last day of the sd year if demanded … . Wit: Daniel Fisher, Thos
Frayser, Wm Gordon, H. Wythe, John Buckner. Ackn 17 Jun 1723 & admitted
to record. (Pg 395)

17 May 1723. Deed of Release. David Morce of James City Co for £45
released unto Philip Lightfoot of Yorkhampton Parish, York Co gent all that 100
a. tr of land in Yorkhampton Parish … [same as above] … . Wit: Daniel
Fisher, Thos Frayser, Wm Gordon, H. Wythe, John Buckner. Ackn 17 Jun 1723
by David Morce & also appeared Thomas Nelson gent who by vertue of a power
of atty from Mary w/o the sd David Morce relinquished here right of dower &
admitted to record. (Pg 396)

17 May 1723. Bond. I David Morce of James City Co am firmly bound unto
Philip Lightfoot of York Co gent for £90 … the condition of this obligation is
such that if the afsd David Morce do & shall well & truly observe, perform,
fulfill, accomplish & keep all the covenants, grants, articles, clauses, conditions
& agreements mentioned in one pair of indentures of lease & release [see above]
then this obligation to be void … . Wit: Thos Frayser, Daniel Fisher, Wm

Gordon, H. Wythe, John Buckner. Ackn 17 Jun 1723 & admitted to record. (Pg 398)

12 Jul 1723. Deed of Lease. Samuel Cobbs of the City of Wmsburgh merchant for 5 shillings farm let unto Christopher Degraffenried of same city dancing master one lot of ground in the sd City of Williamsburgh designed in the plan of the sd city by the figure 235 with all houses thereon ... for the term of one year paying the rent of one grain of Indian corn at the feast of Christmas next ensuing if demanded .... Wit: None. Ackn 15 Jul 1723 & admitted to record. Attest: Phi Lightfoot clerk. (Pg 398)

13 Jul 1723. Deed of Release. Samuel Cobbs of the City of Wmsburgh merchant for £22:10 released unto Christopher Degraffenried of same city dancing master one lot of ground in the sd City of Williamsburgh designed in the plan of the sd city by the figure 235 with all houses thereon ... [same as above] .... Wit: None. Ackn 15 Jul 1723 & admitted to record. Attest: Phi Lightfoot clerk. (Pg 399)

25 Jan 1722. Deed of Lease. John Clayton & Wil Robertson feofees or trustees for the land appropriated for the building & erecting the City of Williamsburgh for 5 shillings farm letten unto Thomas Jones of James City Co gent five lots of ground lying at Queen Mary's Port in the sd city designed in the plot of the sd Port by the figures 58, 59, 60, 61 & 62 ... for the term of one year paying the yearly rent of one grain of Indian corn on 10 Oct if demanded .... Wit: None. Ackn 15 Jul 1723 & admitted to record. Attest: Phi Lightfoot clerk. (Pg 400)

26 Jan 1722. Deed of Release. John Clayton & Wil Robertson feofees or trustees for the land appropriated for the building & erecting the City of Williamsburgh for £3:15 released unto Thomas Jones of James City Co gent five lots of ground lying at Queen Mary's Port in the sd city designed in the plot of the sd Port by the figures 58, 59, 60, 61 & 62 ... [same as above] ... if the sd Thomas Jones shall not within the space of 24 months build & finish upon each lott one good dwelling house then it shall & may be lawfull to & for the sd feofees or trustees into the granted premises & every part thereof to enter & the same to have again as of their former estate to have, hold & enjoy in like manner .... Wit: None. Ackn 15 Jul 1723 & admitted to record. Attest: Phi Lightfoot clerk. (Pg 400)

12 Jul 1723. Deed of Lease. John Welch & Elizabeth his wife of York Co for 5 shillings farm letten unto Thomas Nelson of York Town & Co gent all that 300 a. tr of land in Charles Parish now in the tenure & occupacon of the sd John Welch & Elizabeth his wife (except one parcel thereof containing 100 a. within certain bounds laid off & conveyed to Edmund Sweny by deed dated 17 Jun

1720) abutting upon new Poquoson River & land of Edmund Sweny, which sd tr of land or ½ pt/o a tr of land containing 600 a. granted to John Clark by patent dated 10 Aug 1669 from whom the same lands descended to Nicho Clark son & heir at law to the sd John Clark & afterwards by the death of the sd Nicho Clark without will came & descended to Mary late the w/o Edward Worley & the afsd Eliza w/o the sd John Welch as being the only daus & coheirs at law to the sd Nicho Clark ... for the term of one year paying the yearly rent of one ear of Indian corn on the last day of the sd year if demanded ... . Wit: Lawr Smith, John Ballard, Edward Baptist. Ackn 15 Jul 1723 by John Welch & Elizabeth his wife & admitted to record. Attest: Phi Lightfoot clerk. (Pg 401)

13 Jul 1723. Deed of Release. John Welch & Elizabeth his wife of York Co for £150 released unto Thomas Nelson of York Town & Co gent all that 300 a. tr of land in Charles Parish ... [*same as above*] ... . Wit: Law Smith, John Ballard, Edward Baptist. Ackn 15 Jul 1723 by John Welch & Elizabeth his wife & the sd Eliza being privately examined relinquished her right of dower & admitted to record. Attest: Phi Lightfoot clerk. (Pg 402)

15 Jul 1723. Bond. I John Welch of York Co am firmly bound unto Thomas Nelson of same co gent for £300 ... the condition of this obligation is such that if the afsd John Welch & Elizabeth his wife shall well & truly observe, perform, fulfill, accomplish & keep all the covenants, grants, articles, clauses, conditions & agreements mentioned in one pair of indentures of lease & release [*see above*] then this obligation to be void ... . Wit: Law Smith, John Ballard, Edward Baptist. Ackn 15 Jul 1723 by John Welch & admitted to record. Attest: Phi Lightfoot clerk. (Pg 404)

1 Jul 1723. Deed. Col Alexander Spotswood late Leiut Governour of VA for £36 sold to John Randolph of the City of Wmsburgh gent all that messuage & ½ a. of land in the City of Wmsburgh contiguous to the gardens of Archibald Blair ... . Wit: John Clayton, Graves Pack, David Bray, Lewis Burwell, John Brown. Ackn 15 Jul 1723 & admitted to record. Attest: Phi Lightfoot clerk. (Pg 404)

8 Mar 1722. Deed of Lease. John Clayton & Wil Robertson feofees or trustees for the land appropriated for the building & erecting the City of Williamsburgh for 5 shillings farm letten unto George Allen of James City Co gent three lots of ground in the City of Wmsburgh designed in the plot of the sd city by the figures 231, 186 & 187 ... for the term of one year paying the yearly rent of one grain of Indian corn on 10 Oct if demanded ... . Wit: None. Ackn 19 Aug 1723 & admitted to record. Attest: Phi Lightfoot clerk. (Pg 405)

9 Mar 1722. Deed of Release. John Clayton & Wil Robertson feofees or trustees for the land appropriated for the building & erecting the City of

Williamsburgh for £2:5 released unto George Allen of James City Co gent three lots of ground in the City of Wmsburgh designed in the plot of the sd city by the figures 231, 186 & 187 ... [*same as above*] ... if the sd George Allen shall not within the space of 24 months build & finish upon each lott one good dwelling house then it shall & may be lawfull to & for the sd feofees or trustees into the granted premises & every part thereof to enter & the same to have again as of their former estate to have, hold & enjoy in like manner ... . Wit: None. Ackn 19 Aug 1723 & admitted to record. Attest: Phi Lightfoot clerk. (Pg 406)

14 Mar 1722. Deed of Lease. John Clayton & Wil Robertson feofees or trustees for the land appropriated for the building & erecting the City of Williamsburgh for 5 shillings farm letten unto John Davis of York Co two lots of ground in Queen Marys Port designed in the plot of the sd Port by the figures 11 & 12 ... during the term of one year paying the yearly rent of one grain of Indian corn on 10 Oct if demanded ... . Wit: None. Ackn 19 Aug 1723 & admitted to record. (Pg 407)

15 Mar 1722. Deed of Release. John Clayton & Wil Robertson feofees or trustees for the land appropriated for the building & erecting the City of Williamsburgh for 30 shillings released unto John Davis of York Co two lots of ground in Queen Marys Port designed in the plot of the sd Port by the figures 11 & 12 ... [*same as above*] ... if the sd John Davis shall not within the space of 24 months build & finish upon each lott one good dwelling house then it shall & may be lawfull to & for the sd feofees or trustees into the granted premises & every part thereof to enter & the same to have again as of their former estate to have, hold & enjoy in like manner ... . Wit: None. Ackn 19 Aug 1723 & admitted to record. Attest: Phi Lightfoot clerk. (Pg 408)

1 Apr 1723. Deed of Lease. John Clayton & Wil Robertson feofees or trustees for the land appropriated for the building & erecting the City of Williamsburgh for 5 shillings farm letten unto Jonathan Drewit of York Co two lots of ground in Queen Marys Port designed in the plot of the sd Port by the figures 32 & 33 ... during the term of one year paying the yearly rent of one grain of Indian corn on 10 Oct if demanded ... . Wit: None. Ackn 19 Aug 1723 & admitted to record. Attest: Phi Lightfoot clerk. (Pg 409)

2 Apr 1723. Deed of Release. John Clayton & Wil Robertson feofees or trustees for the land appropriated for the building & erecting the City of Williamsburgh for 30 shillings released unto Jonathan Drewit of York Co two lots of ground in Queen Marys Port designed in the plot of the sd Port by the figures 32 & 33 ... [*same as above*] ... if the sd Jonathan Drewit shall not within the space of 24 months build & finish upon each lott one good dwelling house then it shall & may be lawfull to & for the sd feofees or trustees into the granted

premises & every part thereof to enter & the same to have again as of their former estate to have, hold & enjoy in like manner ... . Wit: None. Ackn 19 Aug 1723 & admitted to record. Attest: Phi Lightfoot clerk. (Pg 410)

12 Dec 1723. Deed. William Robertson of York Co gent for £200 sold to John Grymes of Middlesex Co esqr all that dwelling house with the out houses thereunto belonging wherein the sd William Robertson lately dwelt in the City of Wmsburgh & being pt/o two lots of ground denoted in the place of the sd city by the figures 26 & 27 & bounded by Francis Street, the Capitol Square & pt/o the sd lots formerly sold to Doctor John Brown, the other pt/o the sd lots sold to John Marot decd, & the lot late of the sd John Marot & now in the tenure & occupacon of Anne Sullivan ... . Wit: Wil Toplis, Jno Randolph, Graves Pack. Ackn 16 Dec 1723 & admitted to record. Attest: Phi Lightfoot clerk. (Pg 411)

12 Dec 1723. Deed. William Robertson of York Co for £80 sold to John Holloway of the City of Wmsburgh in same co esqr four lots of ground in the City of Wmsburgh denoted in the plan of the sd city by the figures 286, 237, 207 & 208 being the lots whereon the sd William Robertson's windmill stands together with the sd windmill & houses ... . Wit: Wil Toplis, John Randolph, Graves Pack. Ackn 16 Dec 1723 & admitted to record. Attest: Phi Lightfoot clerk. (Pg 412)

15 Nov 1723. Deed of Lease. Thomas Ravenscroft of James City Co gent & Elizabeth his wife for 5 shillings farm letten unto Cole Diggs of York Co esqr two lots or two ½ acres of land in the City of Wmsburgh in or upon the s side of Duke of Gloucester Street designed in the plot thereof by the numbers 17 & 18 ... for the term of one year ... . Wit: Hen Power, Richard Ambler. Ackn 16 Dec 1723 by Thomas Ravenscroft & Elizabeth his wife & the sd Elizabeth being privately examined relinquished her right of dower & admitted to record. Attest: Phi Lightfoot clerk. (Pg 412)

16 Nov 1723. Deed of Release. Thomas Ravenscroft of James City Co gent & Elizabeth his wife for £200 released unto Cole Diggs of York Co esqr two lots or two ½ acres of land in the City of Wmsburgh in or upon the s side of Duke of Gloucester Street designed in the plot thereof by the numbers 17 & 18 ... [*same as above*] ... . Wit: Hen Power, Richard Ambler. Ackn 16 Dec 1723 by Thomas Ravenscroft & Elizabeth his wife & the sd Elizabeth being privately examined relinquished her right of dower & admitted to record. Attest: Phi Lightfoot clerk. (Pg 413)

16 Nov 1723. Bond. I Thomas Ravenscroft of James City Co am firmly bound unto Cole Diggs of York Co esqr for £400 ... the condition of this obligation is such that if the afsd Thomas Ravenscroft shall well & truly observe, perform,

fulfill, accomplish & keep all the covenants, grants, articles, clauses, conditions & agreements mentioned in one pair of indentures of lease & release [*see above*] then this obligation to be void ... . Wit: Henry Power, Richard Ambler. Ackn 16 Dec 1723 & admitted to record. Attest: Phi Lightfoot clerk. (Pg 414)

27 Feb 1723. Deed of Lease. Henry Cary of the City of Wmsburgh gent for 5 shillings farm letten unto David Menetrie of same city bricklayer a lot of ground in the sd City of Wmsburgh designed in the plot of the sd city by the figure 317 ... for the term of one year paying the rent of one grain of Indian corn on the feast of Christmas next if demanded ... . Wit: Henry Walker, Benja Morris, Elinor Tinsey. Ackn 16 Mar 1723 & admitted to record. Attest: Phi Lightfoot clerk. (Pg 414)

28 Feb 1723. Deed of Release. Henry Cary of the City of Wmsburgh gent for £10 released unto David Menetrie of same city bricklayer a lot of ground in the sd City of Wmsburgh designed in the plot of the sd city by the figure 317 ... [*same as above*] ... . Wit: Henry Walker, Benja Morris, Elinor Tinsey. Ackn 16 Mar 1723 & admitted to record. Attest: Phi Lightfoot clerk. (Pg 415)

10 Mar 1723. Deed of Lease. Henry Cary of the City of Williamsburgh gent for 5 shillings farm letten unto Benjamin Harrison of Charles City Co gent one lot of ground in the City of Wmsburgh & designed in the plot of the sd city by the figure 318 ... during the term of one year paying the rent of one pepper corn at the feast of Christmas next ensuing if demanded ... . Wit: None. Ackn 16 Mar 1723 & admitted to record. Attest: Phi Lightfoot clerk. (Pg 416)

11 Mar 1723. Deed of Release. Henry Cary of the City of Williamsburgh gent for £10 released unto Benjamin Harrison of Charles City Co gent one lot of ground in the City of Wmsburgh & designed in the plot of the sd city by the figure 318 ... [*same as above*] ... . Wit: None. Ackn 16 Mar 1723 & admitted to record. Attest: Phi Lightfoot clerk.(Pg 416)

30 Jan 1723. Deed of Lease. John Clayton & Wil Robertson feofees or trustees for the land appropriated for the building & erecting the City of Williamsburgh for 5 shillings farm letten unto John Holloway of York Co esqr one lot of ground in the City of Wmsburgh designed in the plot of the sd city by the figure 53 ... for the term of one year paying the yearly rent of one grain of Indian corn on 10 Oct if demanded ... . Wit: None. Ackn 18 May 1724 & admitted to record. Attest: Phi Lightfoot clerk. (Pg 417)

31 Jan 1723. Deed of Release. John Clayton & Wil Robertson feofees or trustees for the land appropriated for the building & erecting the City of Williamsburgh for 15 shillings released unto John Holloway of York Co esqr

one lot of ground in the City of Wmsburgh designed in the plot of the sd city by the figure 53 ... [*same as above*] ... if the sd John Holloway shall not within the space of 24 months build & finish upon each lott one good dwelling house then it shall & may be lawfull to & for the sd feofees or trustees into the granted premises & every part thereof to enter & the same to have again as of their former estate to have, hold & enjoy in like manner ... . Wit: None. Ackn 18 May 1724 & admitted to record. Attest: Phi Lightfoot clerk. (Pg 418)

28 Mar 1724. Deed of Lease. Alexander Gary of Wilminton Parish, James City Co for 5 shillings farm let unto Thomas Lark of Bruton Parish, York Co a 25 a. tr of land in Bruton Parish being a plantacon whereon Thomas Hickham one lived & was purch of John Bates Senr by the sd Alexander Gary, bounded by the w most br of Scimino Mill Swamp & Robert Ivory ... for the term of one year paying one ear of Indian corn if demanded ... . Wit: Jno Humphrys, David Walker, Anthony Metcalf. Ackn 18 May 1724 by Alexander Gary & also appeared Mary the w/o the sd Gary & relinquished her right of dower & admitted to record. Attest: Phi Lightfoot clerk. (Pg 419)

30 Mar 1724. Deed of Release. Alexander Gary of Wilminton Parish, James City Co for £10 released unto Thomas Lark of Bruton Parish, York Co a 25 a. tr of land in Bruton Parish ... [*same as above*] ... . Wit: Jno Humphrys, David Walker, Anthony Metcalf. Ackn 18 May 1724 by Alexander Gary & also appeared Mary the w/o the sd Gary & relinquished her right of dower & admitted to record. Attest: Phi Lightfoot clerk. (Pg 419)

30 Mar 1724. Bond. I Alexander Gary of Wilminton Parish, James City Co am firmly bound unto Thomas Lark of Bruton Parish, York Co for £50 ... the condition of this obligation is such that if the afsd Alexr Gary shall well & truly perform, execute, observe, fulfill & keep all the covenants, grants, agreements, articles, promises & provisions mentioned in certain lease & release [*see above*] then this obligacon to be void ... . Wit: Jno Humphrys, David Walker, Anthony Metcalf. Ackn 18 May 1724 & admitted to record. Attest: Phi Lightfoot clerk. (Pg 420)

15 May 1724. Deed of Lease. John Holloway of the City Wmsburgh gent for 5 shillings leased unto Henry Bowcock of the sd city one lott or ½ a. of ground in the sd City of Wmsburgh designed in the plat of the sd city by the figure 53 ... during the term of one year paying the rent of one ear of Indian corn at the feast of Saint Michael the Arch Angel if demanded ... . Wit: None. Ackn 18 May 1724 & admitted to record. Attest: Phi Lightfoot clerk. (Pg 421)

16 May 1724. Deed of Release. John Holloway of the City Wmsburgh gent for £70 released unto Henry Bowcock of the sd city one lott or ½ a. of ground in the

sd City of Wmsburgh designed in the plat of the sd city by the figure 53 ...
[*same as above*] ... . Wit: None. Ackn 18 May 1724 & admitted to record.
Attest: Phi Lightfoot clerk. (Pg 421)

26 Jun 1724. Deed of Lease. John Daniel of Bruton Parish, York Co for 5
shillings farm letten unto William Stone of same place a 100 a. tr of land in the
afsd parish it being the land that John Daniel the grandfather of the sd John
Daniel bought of William Gantlett as per his deed dated 8 Dec 1665, bounded by
the run of Reedy Swamp, the Lower Landing, Pinkethman Eaton & the sd
Daniel ... for the term of one year paying the yearly (rent) on 10 Nov one ear of
Indian corn if demanded ... . Wit: J. Humphrys, Ralph Graves, Edmund Cobbs,
Wm Taylor. Ackn 20 Jul 1724 & admitted to record. Attest: Phi Lightfoot
clerk. (Pg 422)

30 Jun 1724. Deed of Release. John Daniel of Bruton Parish, York Co for £70
released unto William Stone of same place a 100 a. tr of land in the afsd parish
... [*same as above*] ... . Wit: J. Humphrys, Ralph Graves, Edmund Cobbs, Wm
Taylor. Ackn 20 July 1724 & admitted to record. Attest: Phi Lightfoot clerk.
(Pg 422)

20 Jul 1724. Deed. John Holloway of the City of Wmsburgh esqr for £30 sold
to John Randolph of same city esqr all that messuage & lot or ½ a. of land in the
City of Wmsburgh adj to the lot whereon the sd John Randolph now lives which
the sd John Holloway lately purch of William Robertson of the City of
Wmsburgh gent ... . Wit: Phi Lightfoot. Ackn 20 Jul 1724 & admitted to
record. Attest: Phi Lightfoot clerk. (Pg 423)

20 Jul 1724. Deed. John Randolph of the City of Wmsburgh esqr for £30 sold
to Archibald Blair of same city gent all that messuage & lot or ½ a. of land in the
City of Wmsburgh adj to the garden of the sd Archibald which the sd John lately
purch of the Honble Alexander Spotswood esqr ... . Wit: Dudley Diggs, Phi
Lightfoot. Ackn 20 Jul 1724 & admitted to record. Attest: Phi Lightfoot clerk.
(Pg 424)

6 Jul 1724. Deed of Lease. John Brooke late of York Town marriner for 5
shillings leased to Thomas Nelson gent one lot or ½ a. of land in the Town of
York designed in the plat of the sd town by the figure [*blank*] ... for the term of
one year paying the rent of one ear of Indian corn at the feast of St. Michael the
Archangel if demanded ... . Wit: Wil Toplis, James Simmons, John Ballard,
John Thruston. Ackn 20 Jul 1724 by John Gibbons by virtue of a power of atty
from Jno Brooke & admitted to record. Attest: Phi Lightfoot clerk. (Pg 425)

7 Jul 1724. Deed of Release. John Brooke late of York Town marriner for £100 released to Thomas Nelson gent one lot or ½ a. of land in the Town of York designed in the plat of the sd town by the figure [*blank*] ... . Wit: Wil Toplis, James Simmons, John Ballard, John Thruston. Ackn 20 Jul 1724 by John Gibbons by virtue of a power of atty from Jno Brooke & admitted to record. Attest: Phi Lightfoot clerk. (Pg 425)

7 Jul 1724. Bond. I John Brooke of York Town, York Co marriner am firmly bound unto Thomas Nelson of co afsd gent for £200 ... the condition of this obligation is such that if the afsd Jno Brooke shall well & truly observe, perform, fulfill, accomplish & keep all the covenants, grants, articles, clauses & agreements mentioned in one pair of indentures of lease & release [*see above*] then this obligation to be void ... . Wit: Wil Toplis, James Simmons, John Ballard, John Thruston. Ackn 20 Jul 1724 by John Gibbons by virtue of a power of atty from Jno Brooke & admitted to record. Attest: Phi Lightfoot clerk. (Pg 426)

9 Sep 1724. Deed of Lease. Justinian Love of York Parish & Co for 5 shillings leased unto Capt Edward Tabb of same place a 75 a. tr of land bounded by the land now called Thimble Spring, along the Main Road to the Glebe Line & the river ... for the term of one year paying the rent of one pepper corn at the feast of St. Michael the Arch Angel if demanded ... . Wit: John Gibbons, James McKindo, Jones Irwin, Robert Ballard. Ackn 21 Sep 1724 & admitted to record. Attest: Phi Lightfoot clerk. (Pg 427)

10 Sep 1724. Deed of Release. Justinian Love of York Parish & Co for £30 released unto Capt Edward Tabb of same place a 75 a. tr of land ... [*same as above*] ... the sd land being bequeathed to the sd Justinian Love by his father Elias Love decd by his will ... . Wit: John Gibbons, James McKindo, Jones Irwin, Robert Ballard. Ackn 21 Sep 1724 & admitted to record. Attest: Phi Lightfoot clerk. (Pg 428)

10 Sep 1724. Bond. I Justinian Love of Charles Parish, York Co am firmly bound unto Capt Edward Tabb of co afsd for £60 ... the condition of this obligation is such that whereas the afsd Justinian Love hath sold unto the sd Edward Tabb a 75 a. parcel of land by deeds of lease & release [*see above*], now if the sd Edward Tabb shall have, hold, occupy, possess & enjoy the afsd land & premises according to the true intent & meaning thereof then this obligacon to be void ... . Wit: John Gibbons, James McKindo, Jones Irwin, Robert Ballard. Ackn 21 Sep 1724 & admitted to record. Attest: Phi Lightfoot clerk. (Pg 429)

9 Sep 1724. Deed of Lease. James Faison of Charles Parish, York Co for 5 shillings leased to Justinian Love of same place a 75 a. tr of land bounded by

Anthony Armistead, the dam side & by Guess, which sd land being pt/o a tr of land purch by Henry Faison decd from Christopher Garlington decd & fell by inheritance from the afsd Henry Faison decd to his son Henry Faison decd then bequeathed by the sd Henry Faison decd in his will to his son James Fayson party to these deeds ... . Wit: John Gibbons, Jas McKindo, Jones Irwin, Robt Ballard. Ackn 21 Sep 1724 & admitted to record. Attest: Phi Lightfoot clerk. (Pg 429)

10 Sep 1724. Deed of Release. James Faison of Charles Parish, York Co for £30 released to Justinian Love of same place a 75 a. tr of land ... [*same as above*] ... . Wit: John Gibbons, Jas McKindo, Jones Irwin, Robt Ballard. Ackn 21 Sep 1724 & admitted to record. Attest: Phi Lightfoot clerk. (Pg 430)

10 Sep 1724. Bond. Wee Edward Tabb & James Faison of Charles Parish, York Co are firmly bound unto Justinian Love of same co for £60 ... the condition of this obligacon is such that whereas the afsd James Faison hath sold unto the sd Justinian Love a 75 a. tr of land by deeds of lease & release [*see above*], now if the afsd Justinian Love shall have, hold, occupy, possess & enjoy the afsd land & premises according to the true intent & meaning thereof then this obligacon to be void ... . Wit: John Gibbons, Jas McKindo, Jones Irwin, Robt Ballard. Ackn 21 Sep 1724 & admitted to record. Attest: Phi Lightfoot clerk. (Pg 431)

14 Nov 1724. Deed of Release. Between John James of Charles Parish, York Co planter late husband of Temperance one of the daus & devisees of James Foresyth late of same parish decd & Thomas Albritton of same place planter & Agnes his wife the only surviving dau & heir at law of the sd James Foresyth & sister & heir at law to the afsd Temperance of the one part & Thomas Nelson of York Co gent of the other part, whereas the afsd James Foresyth by his will dated 8 Feb 1795 (*sic*) did devise all his land upon the Piney Ridge unto his daus Eleanor & Temperance & their heirs & if either of them should die without issue then the sd land to fall to the survivor & her heirs, & whereas after the death of the sd James the sd Eleanor departed this life without issue & the sd Temperance did intermarry with the afsd John James & by him had issue which sd Temperance & the sd issue of her body afsd are since also dead, & for as much as by the reason of the espousals & issues afsd the sd John James is & stands seized of the land called the Piney Ridge as tenant by the curtesy & the sd Thomas Albritton & Agnes his wife are also seized of the reversion in fee expectant of the determination of the sd tenancy by the curtesy, now this indenture wit that the sd John James, Thomas Albritton & Agnes his wife for 5 shillings paid by Thomas Nelson to the sd John James & for the further sum of £10 to the sd Thomas Albritton & Agnes his wife paid by the sd Thomas Nelson they do grant, release & confirm unto the sd Thomas Nelson all that plantacon &

50 a. tr of land whereof the sd James Foresyth dyed seized in Charles Parish called the Piney Ridge … . Wit: Wil Robertson, Edmund Chisman, John Ballard. Ackn 16 Nov 1714 by John James, Thomas Albritton & Agnes his wife & the sd Agnes being privately examined relinquished her right of dower & admitted to record. Attest: Phi Lightfoot clerk. (Pg 432)

14 Nov 1724. Deed of Lease. John James of Charles Parish, York Co planter late husband of Temperance one of the daus & devisees of James Foresyth late of same parish decd & Thomas Albritton of same place planter & Agnes his wife the only surviving dau & heir at law of the sd James Foresyth & sister & heir at law to the afsd Temperance for 5 shillings leased unto Thomas Nelson of York Co gent a 50 a. tr of land called the Piney Ridge … [*same as above*] … . Wit: Wil Robertson, Edmund Chisman, John Ballard. Ackn 16 Nov 1714 by John James, Thomas Albritton & Agnes his wife & the sd Agnes being privately examined relinquished her right of dower & admitted to record. Attest: Phi Lightfoot clerk. (Pg 433)

21 Sep 1724. Deed. William Ferguson of Charles Parish, York Co blacksmith for £6 sold to Mary Bell of same co widow all that messuage plantacon & 76 a. parcell of land in Charles Parish called the White Ridge & now or late in the tenure & occupacon of Mary Green widow & Wil John a mulatto … . Wit: Francis Hayward, John Gibbons, Wil Robertson. Ackn 21 Dec 1724 by William Ferguson & also appeared Hope the w/o the sd William who being privately examined relinquished her right of dower & admitted to record. Attest: Phi Lightfoot clerk. (Pg 434)

23 Sep 1724. Deed of Lease. Mary Bell of Charles Parish, York Co widow for 5 shillings farm letten unto Elizabeth Tabb of same place widow all that 117 a. tr of land in Charles Parish called the White Ridge lately in the tenure & occupacon of William Ferguson adj land belonging to David Lewis, land of Henry Vendoverick, land that did formerly belong to Mrs. Merry, Thomas Lilburn's line & the Mill Path, which sd land was granted by patent unto Owen Davis & by the sd patent containing 190 a. 76 a. of which land was sold out of the sd patent by the sd Owen Davis the remainder pt/o the sd land containing 117 a. was left by the sd Owen Davis unto his son John Davis & if the sd John Davis should die without issue then he assigned & made over the sd 117 a. of land unto his grandson William Ferguson as per the sd will dated 26 Apr 1705, which sd land was sold by the sd William Ferguson unto the afsd Mary Bell by deed dated 21 Sep 1724 … . Wit: John Gibbons, Edward Wright, Robert Kerby Junr, Wil Toplis. Ackn 21 Dec 1724 & admitted to record. Attest: Phi Lightfoot clerk. (Pg 435)

24 Sep 1724. Deed of Release. Mary Bell of Charles Parish, York Co widow for £30 released unto Elizabeth Tabb of same place widow all that 117 a. tr of land in Charles Parish called the White Ridge ... [*same as above*] ... . Wit: John Gibbons, Edward Wright, Robert Kerby Junr, Wil Toplis. Ackn 21 Dec 1724 & admitted to record. Attest: Phi Lightfoot clerk. (Pg 436)

24 Sep 1724. Bond. I Mary Bell of Charles Parish, York Co widow am firmly bound unto Elizabeth Tabb of same place widow for £60 ... the condition of this obligacon is such that if the afsd Mary Bell shall well & truly observe, perform, fulfill, accomplish & keep all the covenants, grants, articles, clauses, conditions & agreements mentioned in one pair of indentures of lease & release [*see above*] then this obligacon to be void ... . Wit: John Gibbons, Edward Wright, Robert Kirby Junr, Wil Toplis. Ackn 21 Dec 1724 & admitted to record. Attest: Phi Lightfoot clerk. (Pg 437)

9 Oct 1724. Deed. Warren Cary of the City of Bristol merchant & Rebeckah his wife for £150 sold to Philip Lightfoot of York Town, VA gent a messuage & ½ a. of land in York Town which was conveyed to the sd Warren Cary & his heirs by Thomas Chisman & Anne his wife by one indenture dated 21 May 1711 ... . Wit: Lucius Griffith, Joseph Barnes, John Summers, Peregrine Boston, Pates Gravile. Proved 18 Jan 1724 & admitted to record. Attest: Phi Lightfoot clerk. (Pg 438)

15 Dec 1724. Deed of Lease. Thomas Creas of the City of Wmsburgh gardiner & Mary his wife for 5 shillings leased unto Wm Keith & Patrick Ferguson of the sd city all that messuage & dwelling house wherein the sd Thomas Creas & Mary his wife now live & all that lot or ½ a. of land described in the plot of the sd city by the figure 352 being in the sd City of Wmsburgh with all kitchens, stables, outhouses & buildings to the sd messuage & lot of land belonging ... for the term of one year ... . Wit: None. Ackn 18 Jan 1724 by Thomas Creas & Mary his wife & the sd Mary being privately examined freely consented that the houses in the sd deed shall be settled to the uses therein menconed & admitted to record. Attest: Phi Lightfoot clerk. (Pg 439)

16 Dec 1724. Deed of Release. Thomas Creas of the City of Wmsburgh gardiner & Mary his wife for 5 shillings released unto Wm Keith & Patrick Ferguson of the sd city all that messuage & dwelling house wherein the sd Thomas Creas & Mary his wife now live & all that lot or ½ a. of land described in the plot of the sd city by the figure 352 ... [*same as above*] ... forever upon the trust & confidence & to the uses & purposes herein after menconed & declared & to & for no other use, trust or purpose whatsoever, that is to say, in trust & for the only use & behoof of the sd Thomas Creas & Mary his wife during the term of their natural lives & the life of the longest liver of them

without impeachment & after the death of the sd Thomas Creas & the sd Mary
his wife to the use & behoof of Daniel Maupin & Gabriel Maupin sons of the sd
Mary Creas by Gabriel Maupin late her husband decd & of their heirs ... the sd
William Keith & Patrick Ferguson & their survivors shall after the respective
death of the sd Thomas Creas & the sd Mary his wife make sale & dispose of the
sd messuage lot of land & premises & shall be paid ½ thereof to the sd Daniel
Maupin & the other ½ to the sd Gabriel Maupin brother of the sd Daniel Maupin
upon the proviso & condition that at & upon the death of the sd Mary Creas they
the sd Danl Maupin & Gabriel Maupin shall & do release & discharge the
executors & adminrs of the sd Mary Creas of & from all the right, claim &
demand which they shall or may have claim of into or out of a certain legacy of
£55 given & bequeathed to Mary Maupin decd sister of the sd Daniel Maupin &
Gabriel Maupin in & by the will of the sd Gabriel Maupin decd or to any part
thereof or any part or share of the personal estate of the sd Mary Maupin decd ...
. Wit: Francis Hayward, Robert Ballard. Ackn 17 May 1725 by Thomas Creas
& Mary his wife & the sd Mary being privately examined relinquished her right
of dower & admitted to record. Attest: Phi Lightfoot clerk. (Pg 440)

7 May 1725. Deed of Lease. Joseph Stacy of Charles Parish, York Co planter
& Mary his wife for 5 shillings leased unto James Sclater of same place gent all
that 130 a. parcel of land which Simon Stacy father of the sd Joseph Stacy purch
of Robert Sheild Senr & Mary his wife in the Oak Swamp in parish formerly
called New Poquoson Parish but now Charles Parish bounded by the land of
Henry Hayward, land of John Nixon & land of John Eaton, being sold out of the
original patent by Robert Calvert being pt/o 375 a. of land granted by patent to
the sd Robert Calvert in 1687, 300 a. of the sd land being formerly taken up &
patented by Wm Calvert & patented 26 Jan 1663 the other 75 a. taken up by the
sd Robert Calvert ... for the term of one year paying the rent of one ear of Indian
corn at the feast of St. Michael the Arch Angel now next ensuing if demanded
.... Wit: Francis Hayward, Robert Ballard. Ackn 17 May 1725 by Joseph
Stacy & Mary his wife & the sd Mary being privately examined relinquished her
dower & admitted to record. Attest: Phi Lightfoot clerk. (Pg 441)

17 May 1725. Deed of Release. Joseph Stacy of Charles Parish, York Co
planter & Mary his wife for £70 released unto James Sclater of same place gent
all that 130 a. parcel of land ... [same as above] .... Wit: Francis Hayward,
Robert Ballard. Ackn 17 May 1725 by Joseph Stacy & Mary his wife & the sd
Mary being privately examined relinquished her dower & admitted to record.
Attest: Phi Lightfoot clerk. (Pg 442)

17 May 1725. Bond. I Joseph Stacy of Charles Parish, York Co am firmly
bound unto James Sclater of same place for £140 ... the condition of this
obligacon is such that if the afsd Joseph Stacy shall well & truly observe,

perform, fulfill, accomplish & keep all the covenants, grants, articles, clauses & agreements mentioned in one pair of indentures of lease & release [*see above*] then this obligacon to be void ... . Wit: Francis Hayward, Robert Ballard. Ackn 17 May 1725 & admitted to record. Attest: Phi Lightfoot clerk. (Pg 444)

3 Jun 1725. Deed of Lease. Richard Cheshire of Princess Anne Co merchant for 5 shillings leased to Robert Dowsing of York Co bricklayer one lot or ½ a. of ground in the Town of York designed in the plat of the sd town by the figure 59 with all houses & buildings ... during the term of one year paying the rent of one ear of Indian corn at the feast of St. Michael the Arch Angel if demanded ... . Wit: Thos Frayser, Robert Wills, Wil Toplis, Wm Gordon. Ackn 21 Jun 1726 & admitted to record. Attest: Phi Lightfoot clerk. (Pg 444)

4 Jun 1725. Deed of Release. Richard Cheshire of Princess Anne Co merchant for £47:10 released to Robert Dowsing of York Co bricklayer one lot or ½ a. of ground in the Town of York designed in the plat of the sd town by the figure 59 ... [*same as above*] ... . Wit: Thos Frayser, Robert Wills, Wil Toplis, Wm Gordon. Ackn 21 Jun 1726 & admitted to record. Attest: Phi Lightfoot clerk. (Pg 445)

14 Aug 1725. Deed of Gift. Semour Powell of Warwick Parish & Co, VA for natural love & affection have given unto my loving son William Powell of same place when he shall arrive at the age of 21 years all that 182 a. tr of land whereon Thomas Badget now liveth being the lands that I purch of William Major decd in York Parish adj upon the Lodge Land ... & I do also give to my afsd son William Powell when he shall arrive to the age of 21 years one Negro boy named Jack ... . Wit: William Robison, George White, Edm Bird. Ackn 16 Aug 1725 & admitted to record. Attest: Phi Lightfoot clerk. (Pg 446)

18 Mar 1724. Deed. John Brooke of the City of Williamsburgh for £20 sold to Wm Prentis of same city all that messuage or houses standing & being on a lot in the sd city number 51 which house fronts the w being 25' by 16' beside the shedd with the ground which the sd house covers ... . Wit: Lewis Holland, Wm Broadribb, Edward Trindall, Joseph Davenport. Proved 16 Aug 1725 & admitted to record. Attest: Phi Lightfoot clerk. (Pg 446)

11 Aug 1725. Deed of Lease. John Clayton & Wil Robertson feofees or trustees for the land appropriated for building & erecting the City of Wmsburgh for 5 shillings farm letten unto David Menetrie of York Co one lot of ground in the sd City of Wmsburgh & designed in the plot of the sd city by the figure 316 ... for the term of one year paying the yearly rent of one grain of Indian corn on 10 Oct if demanded ... . Wit: None. Ackn 15 Nov 1725 & admitted to record. Attest: Phi Lightfoot clerk. (Pg 447)

108

12 Aug 1725. Deed of Release. John Clayton & Wil Robertson feofees or trustees for the land appropriated for building & erecting the City of Wmsburgh for 15 shillings released unto David Menetrie of York Co one lot of ground in the sd City of Wmsburgh & designed in the plot of the sd city by the figure 316 ... [same as above] ... if the sd David Menetrie shall not within the space of 24 months build & finish upon each lott one good dwelling house then it shall & may be lawfull to & for the sd feofees or trustees into the granted premises & every part thereof to enter & the same to have again as of their former estate to have, hold & enjoy in like manner as they might otherwise have done if these presents had never been made ... . Wit: None. Ackn 15 Nov 1725 & admitted to record. Attest: Phi Lightfoot clerk. (Pg 447)

15 Oct 1725. Deed of Lease. Robert Ballard of York Co carpenter & Jane his wife for 5 shillings farm letten unto Vincent Pearse of the Kingdom of Great Brittain gent all their lot or ½ a. of land in the Town of York designed in the plat of the sd town by the figure 21 ... during the term of one year ... . Wit: Phi Lightfoot, Mathew Jones, Jno Gemmill, Wil Toplis. Ackn 15 Nov 1725 by Robert Ballard & the sd Jane being privately examined relinquished her right of dower & admitted to record. Attest: Phi Lightfoot clerk. (Pg 448)

16 Oct 1725. Deed of Release. Robert Ballard of York Co carpenter & Jane his wife for £160 released unto Vincent Pearse of the Kingdom of Great Brittain gent all their lot or ½ a. of land in the Town of York designed in the plat of the sd town by the figure 21 ... [same as above] ... . Wit: Phi Lightfoot, Mathew Jones, Jno Gemmill, Wil Toplis. Ackn 15 Nov 1725 by Robert Ballard & the sd Jane being privately examined relinquished her right of dower & admitted to record. Attest: Phi Lightfoot clerk. (Pg 449)

16 Oct 1725. Bond. I Robert Ballard of York Co am firmly bound unto Vincent Pearse gent for £320 ... the condition of this obligacon is such that if the afsd Robert Ballard shall well & truly observe, perform, fulfill, accomplish & keep all the covenants, grants, articles, clauses & agreements mentioned in one pair of indentures of lease & release [see above] then this obligacon to be void. Wit: Phi Lightfoot, Mathew Jones, Jno Gemmill, Wil Toplis. Ackn 15 Nov 1725 & admitted to record. Attest: Phi Lightfoot clerk. (Pg 449)

8 Oct 1725. Deed of Lease. James Dowsing of Warwick Co bricklayer for 5 shillings leased unto James McKindo of York Town merchant taylor one lot or ½ a. of ground in the sd Town of York designed in the plat of the sd town by the figure 27 ... for the term of one year paying the rent of one ear of Indian corn at the feast of St. Michael ye Arch Angel if demanded ... . Wit: Wm Gordon, Robt Wills, Jean Wills, Wil Toplis. Ackn 15 Nov 1725 & admitted to record. Attest: Phi Lightfoot clerk. (Pg 450)

9 Oct 1725. Deed of Release. James Dowsing of Warwick Co bricklayer for £35 released unto James McKindo of York Town merchant taylor one lot or ½ a. of ground in the sd Town of York designed in the plat of the sd town by the figure 27 ... [*same as above*] .... Wit: Wm Gordon, Robt Wills, Jean Wills, Wil Toplis. Ackn 15 Nov 1725 & admitted to record. Attest: Phi Lightfoot clerk. (Pg 450)

29 Oct 1725. Bond. I James Dowsing of Warwick Co bricklayer am firmly bound unto James McKindo of York Town for £70 ... the condition of this obligacon is such that if the afsd James Dowsing shall well & truly observe, perform, fulfill, accomplish & keep all the covenants, grants, articles, clauses, conditions & agreements mentioned in one pair of indentures of lease & release [*see above*] then this obligacon to be void .... Wit: Wm Gordon, Robt Wills, Jean Wills, Wil Toplis. Ackn 15 Nov 1725 & admitted to record. Attest: Phi Lightfoot clerk. (Pg 451)

21 Feb 1725/6. Deed of Lease. William Blackston of Charles Parish, York Co for 5 shillings leased unto Simon Hallier of Elizabeth City Co a 100 a. tr of land which is pt/o a greater tr of land called Boar Quarter heretofore sold & conveyed by Ralph Graves of Bruton Parish, York Co to George Baskervyle & afterwards sold by the sd George Baskervyle to Wm Wise of Charles Parish, York Co & afterwards sold by the sd Wm Wise to the afsd Wm Blackston by deeds dated 13 & 14 Mar 1716/7, bounded by John Loyall, sd Baskervyle, land late of Francis Callowhill & land of James Parsons & also 100 a. of marsh ... for the term of one year paying the yearly rent of one ear of Indian corn on the last day of the sd year if demanded .... Wit: James Dixon, James Parsons, Thos Hawkins. Ackn 21 Feb 1725 & admitted to record. Attest: Phi Lightfoot clerk. (Pg 451)

22 Feb 1725. Deed of Release. William Blackston of Charles Parish, York Co for 1,000 lbs of merchantable tobacco released unto Simon Hallier of Elizabeth City Co a 100 a. tr of land & 100 a. of marsh ... [*same as above*] .... Wit: James Dixon, James Parsons, Thos Hawkins. Ackn 21 Feb 1725 & admitted to record. Attest: Phi Lightfoot clerk. (Pg 452)

14 May 1726. Deed. Richd Baker of York Hampton Parish, York Co & Ann his wife for £30 sold to Richd Ambler of same place pt/o their lott or ½ a. of land in the Town of York known in the plot of the sd town by the figure 44 which sd lott was purch by the sd Richd Baker from Wm Andrews & Wm Heron as by the several deeds (dated, viz, Wm Andrews's 25 Sep 1719 & Wm Heron's 14 Nov the same year), which pt/o the sd lott hereby granted contains 8 poles in breadth adj the lott now in possession of the sd Richd Ambler known by the figure 43 & 40' in length .... Wit: John Buckner, Ishmael Moody. Memorandum that 14 May 1726 peaceable & quiet possession livery & seizing

of the within mentioned premises by the sd Richd Baker to the sd Richd Ambler
was given & delivered in presence of us John Buckner, Ishmael Moody &
Charles Cox. Ackn May 1726 by Richard Baker & Ann his wife & the sd Ann
being privately examined relinquished her right of dower & admitted to record.
Attest: Phi Lightfoot clerk. (Pg 453)

14 May 1726. Bond. I Richd Baker of York Hampton Parish, York Co am
firmly bound unto Richd Ambler of same place for £200 ... the condition of this
obligation is such that if the afsd Richard Baker shall well & truly observe,
perform, fullfill, accomplish & keep all the covenants, grants, articles, clauses &
agreements mentioned in one indenture [*see above*] then this obligation to be
void ... . Wit: John Buckner, Ishmael Moody. Ackn 16 May 1726 & admitted
to record. Attest: Phi Lightfoot clerk. (Pg 455)

16 May 1726. Deed. Henry Cary of James City Co gent & Anne his wife &
Locky (Lockey) Myhill of Elizabeth City Co gent & Sarah his wife for £200
sold to Cole Diggs of York Co esqr a 200 a. tr of land in York Hampton Parish
whereof Edward Lockey formerly dyed seized which sd Henry Cary & Locky
Myhill lately recovered (by the judgment of the General Court as heirs at law to
the sd Edward Lockey) of Isaac Collier & Folioh Power ... . Wit: John
Randolph, Joseph Davenport, Miles Cary, Henry Wood, Edwin Thacker, Thos
Corbin, John Stith. Memorandum that upon 16 May---- the sd Henry Cary &
Anne his wife, Locky Myhill & Sarah his wife did deliver full quiet & peaceable
possession & seizing of the land unto the sd Cole Diggs esqr according to the
form & effect of the within indenture, in presence of Wm Smith & Robt Carllis.
Ackn 20 Jun 1726 by Henry Cary & Anne his wife, Locky Myhill & Sarah his
wife & the sd Ann Cary & Sarah Myhill being privately examined relinquished
their right of dower & admitted to record. Attest: Phi Lightfoot clerk. (Pg 456)

10 Dec 1725. Deed of Lease. Robert Cobbs Junr of Bruton Parish, York Co for
5 shillings leased unto John Blair of Wmsburgh merchant two lots of ground in
the City of Wmsburgh designed in the plat of the sd city by the figures 43 & 44
... for the term of one year paying the yearly rent of one grain of Indian corn on
10 Dec if demanded ... . Wit: Pat Ferguson, Thos Crips Junr, Tho Cobbs,
James Wilkinson. Proved 18 Jul 1726 & admitted to record. Attest: Phi
Lightfoot clerk. (Pg 457)

11 Dec 1725. Deed of Release. Robert Cobbs Junr of Bruton Parish, York Co
for £18 released unto John Blair of Wmsburgh merchant two lots of ground in
the City of Wmsburgh designed in the plat of the sd city by the figures 43 & 44
... [*same as above*] ... the sd two lots formerly granted to the sd Robert Cobbs
by the feofees or trustees for the land appropriated for the building & erecting
the City of Wmsburgh by deeds of lease & release dated 14 & 15 Jun 1720 ... .

Wit: Pat Ferguson, Thos Crips Junr, Thos Cobbs, James Wilkinson. Proved 18 Jul 1726 & admitted to record. Attest: Phi Lightfoot clerk. (Pg 458)

14 Aug 1726. Deed of Lease. James Wallace of Elizabeth City Co gent for 5 shillings leased to Robert Dowsing of York Co bricklayer one lot or ½ a. of ground in the sd Town of York being pt/o the Portland known in the plot of the sd town by the figure 78 ... for the term of one year paying the rent of one ear of Indian corn at the feast of St. Michael the Arch Angel if demanded ... . Wit: Wm Gordon, Robert Kirby Junr, John Gomer. Ackn 15 Aug 1726 & admitted to record. Attest: Phi Lightfoot clerk. (Pg 459)

15 Aug 1726. Deed of Release. James Wallace of Elizabeth City Co gent for £20 released to Robert Dowsing of York Co bricklayer one lot or ½ a. of ground in the sd Town of York being pt/o the Portland known in the plot of the sd town by the figure 78 ... [same as above] ... . Wit: Wm Gordon, Robert Kirby Junr, John Gomer. Ackn 15 Aug 1726 & admitted to record. Attest: Phi Lightfoot clerk. (Pg 460)

15 Aug 1726. Bond. I James Wallace of Elizabeth City Co am firmly bound unto Robert Dowsing of York Co bricklayer for £40 ... the condition of this obligation is such that if the afsd James Wallace shall well & truly observe, perform, fulfill, accomplish & keep all the covenants, grants, articles, clauses & agreements mentioned in one pair of indentures of lease & release [see above] then this obligation to be void ... . Wit: Wm Gordon, Robert Kirby Junr, John Gomer. Ackn 15 Aug 1726 & admitted to record. Attest: Phi Lightfoot clerk. (Pg 460)

18 Sep 1726. Deed of Lease. Robert Dowsing & Mary his wife of York Co bricklayer for 5 shillings leased to Joseph Nisbett of same co one lott or ½ a. of ground in the Town of York described in the plot of the sd town by the figure 33 ... during the term of one year paying the rent of one ear of Indian corn at the feast of St. Michael the Arch Angel if demanded ... . Wit: Lewis Holland, Wm Gordon, Jean Wills. Ackn 19 Sep 1726 by Robert Dowsing & Mary his wife & the sd Mary being privately examined relinquished her right of dower & admitted to record. Attest: Phi Lightfoot clerk. (Pg 461)

19 Sep 1726. Deed of Release. Robert Dowsing & Mary his wife of York Co bricklayer for £75 released to Joseph Nisbett of same co one lott or ½ a. of ground in the Town of York described in the plot of the sd town by the figure 33 ... [same as above] ... . Wit: Lewis Holland, Wm Gordon, Jean Wills. Ackn 19 Sep 1726 by Robert Dowsing & Mary his wife & the sd Mary being privately examined relinquished her right of dower & admitted to record. Attest: Phi Lightfoot clerk. (Pg 461)

112

18 Sep 1726. Bond. I Robert Dowsing of York Co bricklayer am firmly bound unto Joseph Nisbett of same co for £150 ... the condition of this obligacon is such that if the afsd Robert Dowsing shall well & truly observe, perform, fulfill, accomplish & keep all the covenants, grants, articles, clauses & agreements mentioned in one pair of indentures of lease & release [see above] then this obligacon to be void ... . Wit: Lewis Holland, Wm Gordon, Jean Wills. Ackn 19 Sep 1726 & admitted to record. Attest: Phi Lightfoot clerk. (Pg 462)

21 Aug 1726. Deed of Lease. Elizabeth Powers of York Town & Co widow for 5 shillings leased unto Richard Ambler of same town gent all her lot or ½ a. of land in the Town of York designed in the plat of the sd town by the figure 45 which sd lot was taken up by Humphry Moody of the trustees & feofees for the Portland of York Town as by deed dated 3 Feb 1706, & by the sd Humphry Moody given & bequeathed by his will unto the sd Elizabeth Powers as by the sd will dated 25 Sep 1707 ... during the term of one year ... . Wit: Wm Gordon, Wil Toplis. Ackn 19 Sep 1726 & admitted to record. Attest: Phi Lightfoot clerk. (Pg 462)

22 Aug 1726. Deed of Release. Elizabeth Powers of York Town & Co widow for £40 released unto Richard Ambler of same town gent all her lot or ½ a. of land in the Town of York designed in the plat of the sd town by the figure 45 ... [same as above] ... . Wit: Wm Gordon, Wil Toplis. Ackn 19 Sep 1726 & admitted to record. Attest: Phi Lightfoot clerk. (Pg 463)

22 Aug 1726. Bond. I Elizabeth Powers of York Town & Co am firmly bound unto Richard Ambler of the sd town gent for £80 ... the condition of this obligacon is such that if the afsd Elizabeth Powers shall well & truly observe, perform, fulfill, accomplish & keep all the covenants, grants, articles, clauses & agreements mentioned in one pair of indentures of lease & release [see above] then this obligacon to be void ... . Wit: Wm Gordon, Wil Toplis. Ackn 19 Sep 1726 & admitted to record. Attest: Phi Lightfoot clerk. (Pg 463)

16 Sep 1726. Deed of Lease. Francis Sharpe of Wmsburgh, York Co planter for 5 shillings leased unto Samuel Cobbs of the City of Wmsburgh, co afsd merchant one lot of ground at Queen Marys Port designed in the plot of the sd Port by the figure 7 ... for the term of one year paying the rent of one grain of Indian corn at the feast of the Annunciation of the Blessed Virgin Mary if demanded ... . Wit: Matw Peirce, John James Flournoy. Ackn 19 Sep 1726 & admitted to record. Attest: Phi Lightfoot clerk. (Pg 464)

17 Sep 1726. Deed of Release. Francis Sharpe of Wmsburgh, York Co planter & Elizabeth his wife for £8 released unto Samuel Cobbs of the City of

Wmsburgh, co afsd merchant one lot of ground at Queen Marys Port designed in the plot of the sd Port by the figure 7 ... [*same as above*] .... Wit: Matw Peirce, John James Flournoy. Ackn by Francis Sharp 19 Sep 1726 & admitted to record. Attest: Phi Lightfoot clerk. (Pg 464)

10 Dec 1726. Deed. Dixon Tyloe of Denbigh Parish, Warwick Co for £8 sold to Thomas Wooton of York Hampton Parish, York Co a tr of land lying on the br of Cheesemans Cr in York Hampton Parish bounded by the land of Edward Caisly & the land now in the possession of John Chapman ... for the full term of 99 years paying the yearly rent of one grain of Indian corn on 12 Dec if demanded ... . Wit: John Chapman, Thos Mallden. Ackn 19 Dec 1726 & admitted to record. Attest: Phi Lightfoot clerk. (Pg 465)

10 Dec 1726. Bond. I Dixon Tyloe of Denbigh Parish, Warwick Co, VA am firmly bound unto Thomas Wooton of Yorkhampton Parish, York Co for £30 ... the condition of this obligation is such that if the afsd Dixon Tyloe shall well & truly observe, perform, fulfill, accomplish & keep all the covenants, grants, articles, clauses & conditions mentioned in an indenture [*see above*] then this obligation to be void ... . Wit: John Chapman, Thos Mallden. Ackn 19 Dec 1726 & admitted to record. Attest: Phi Lightfoot clerk. (Pg 465)

19 Dec 1726. Deed of Gift. Adduston Rogers of York Hampton Parish, York Co for natural love & affection have given to my loving son John Adduston Rogers of same parish a 50 a. tr of land whereon he now liveth bounded by the land whereon Thomas Cox now liveth & the land whereon Robert Wallins now liveth ... . Wit: None. Ackn 19 Dec 1726 & admitted to record. Attest: Phi Lightfoot clerk. (Pg 466)

30 Dec 1726. Deed. Thomas Crutchfeild & Rebecca his wife dau & heir at law to Ralph Bee late of York Co decd for £33 sold to Isaac Bee of same co planter a tr of land & plantation in Bruton Parish which was devised by the will of Robert Bee unto the sd Ralph Bee brother of the sd Isaac & adj to the plantation now of the sd Isaac ... . Wit: Robt Crawley, Lain Jones, Benjamin Echo. Ackn 16 Jan 1726 by Thomas Crutchfeild & Rebecca his wife & the sd Rebecca being privately examined relinquished her right of dower & admitted to record. Attest: Phi Lightfoot clerk. (Pg 466)

20 Dec 1726. Deed. John Taylor of Henrico Co planter & Aris his wife for £30 sold to James Sheilds of the City of Williamsburgh, York Co taylor a 75 a. parcell of land & plantation in Bruton Parish which the sd John Taylor & Aris his wife now hold being bounded by the lands of John Custis, Thomas Layton, James Taylor, sd James Sheilds & Mathew Peirce ... . Wit: Lewis Holland, James Taylor, Mary Wimbish. Ackn 16 Jan 1726 by John Taylor & Aris his

wife & the sd Aris being privately examined relinquished her right of dower & admitted to record. Attest: Phi Lightfoot clerk. (Pg 467)

14 Jan 1726. Deed. James Taylor of James City Co planter for £20 sold to Jas Sheilds of the City of Williamsburgh, York Co taylor all that 50 a. tr of land in Bruton Parish bounded by the dividend late belonging to his brother John Taylor & by him conveyed to the sd James Sheilds, the land of Thomas Layton, the land of Richard Page & the land of the sd James Sheilds ... . Wit: David Menetrie, Jas Sheilds Junr, John Taylor, Joseph Davenport. Memorandum upon 14 Jan 1726 full & absolute possession & seizen of the premises was made & delivered by the sd James Taylor unto the sd James Sheilds in the presence of us John Buffin, James Sheilds Junr, Joseph Davenport & William Taylor. Ackn 16 Jan 1726 by James Taylor & also appeared Mary w/o the sd James Taylor who being privately examined relinquished her right of dower & admitted to record. Attest: Phi Lightfoot clerk. (Pg 468)

16 Jan 1726. Deed. Between Sarah Pegram widow executrix of the will of Daniel Pegram decd of the one part & Lewis Burwell gent of the other part, whereas the sd Daniel was in his life time seized in fee simple of & in one house & lot of ground in Williamsburgh marked in the plat of the sd city with the figure 183 & by his will dated 27 May MDCCXXVI did direct that the same should be sold, now this indenture wit that the sd Sarah Pegram pursuant to the sd will for £10 sold unto the sd Lewis Burwell the sd house & lot ... . Wit: Wil Toplis. Ackn 16 Jan 1726 & admitted to record. Attest: Phi Lightfoot clerk. (Pg 469)

2 Feb 1726. Deed. Elizabeth Brush of the City of Wmsburgh spinster for £80 sold to Thomas Barbar of same city carpenter all her share of the messuage on the n side of the City of Wmsburgh wherein John Brush her father decd lately dwelt, & also those two lotts containing 1 a. of ground marked in the platt of the sd city with the figures 165 & 166 to the sd messuage belonging & held & enjoy'd with the same which sd two lotts were convey'd by John Clayton & William Robertson trustees for the land appropriated for the building & erecting the sd city by their indenture dated 8 Jul 1717 ... . Wit: Stephen Dewey, Richard Pritchard, Tho Walker, Wm Case. Ackn 15 May 1727 & admitted to record. Attest: Phi Lightfoot clerk. (Pg 470)

17 Jul MDCCXXVII. Deed. Humphry Stafford of York Hampton Parish, James City Co planter & Mildred his wife for £40 sold to William Harwood of Warwick Parish & Co gent a lott in York Town adj to the Swan Tavern which sd lot was given unto my wife Mildred by her father in his will & now in the tenure & occupation of Robert Wills of York afsd ... . Wit: None. Ackn 17 Jul 1727 by Humphry Stafford & Mildred his wife & the sd Mildred being privately

examined relinquished her right of dower & admitted to record. Attest: Phi Lightfoot clerk. (Pg 471)

25 Jul 1727. Deed of Lease. William Hansford of St. George Parish, Spotsylvania Co for 5 shillings leased unto Charles Hansford of York Hampton Parish, York Co all that plantation & 100 a. tr of land in York Hampton Parish on the head of Fillgates Cr, the sd land being given to the sd William Hansford by his father Charles Hansford decd by will & is bounded by the land of John Hansford, York Road, the land of William Sledd & the Main Cr ... for the term of one year .... Wit: Richard Ambler, Wm Rogers, John Gibbons. Ackn 21 Aug 1727 & admitted to record. Attest: Phi Lightfoot clerk. (Pg 471)

26 Jul 1727. Deed of Release. William Hansford of St. George Parish, Spotsylvania Co for £50 released unto Charles Hansford of York Hampton Parish, York Co all that plantation & 100 a. tr of land in York Hampton Parish ... [same as above] .... Wit: Richard Ambler, Wm Rogers, John Gibbons. Ackn 21 Aug 1727 & admitted to record. Attest: Phi Lightfoot clerk. (Pg 472)

26 Jul 1727. Bond. I William Hansford of St. George's Parish, Spotsylvania Co am firmly bound unto Charles Hansford of York Hampton Parish, York Co for £200 ... the condition of this obligation is such that whereas the afsd Charles Hansford hath bought & purch of the sd William Hansford a plantation & 100 a. tr of land by indenture of sale [see above], now if the sd William shall well & truly observe, keep & perform all the articles, covenants, grants & agreements mentioned in the sd indentures then this obligation to be void .... Wit: Richard Ambler, William Rogers, John Gibbons. Ackn 21 Aug 1727 by William Stark gent by vertue of a power of atty from William Hansford & admitted to record. Attest: Phi Lightfoot clerk. (Pg 474)

17 Nov 1727. Deed of Lease. Anne Williams (one of the daus & coheirs of John Williams late of York Hampton Parish, York Co planter decd) spinster for 5 shillings leased unto Robert Roberts of same place planter all her 1/3 pt/o 50 a. of land held & enjoyed by the sd Anne Williams in York Hampton Parish, which sd 1/3 is pt/o 50 a. of land purch & bought by John Williams father of the sd Anne late of this co decd of Stephen Fouace of the Kingdom of England clerk by his atty Philip Ludwell of Green Spring in James City Co esqr as by deeds dated 23 & 24 Nov MDCCIX which sd 1/3 pt/o 50 a. of land came & descended to Anne Williams as one of the three daus & coheirs of the sd John Williams decd ... during the term of one year paying the yearly rent of one ear of Indian corn on the last day of the sd year if demanded .... Wit: Wil Toplis. Ackn 20 Nov 1727 & admitted to record. Attest: Phi Lightfoot clerk. (Pg 475)

18 Nov MDCCXXVII. Deed of Release. Anne Williams (one of the daus & coheirs of John Williams late of York Hampton Parish, York Co planter decd) spinster for £12 released unto Robert Roberts of same place planter all her 1/3 pt/o 50 a. of land held & enjoyed by the sd Anne Williams in York Hampton Parish ... [*same as above*] ... . Wit: Wil Toplis. Ackn 20 Nov 1727 & admitted to record. Attest: Phi Lightfoot clerk. (Pg 476)

20 Nov MDCCXXIX. Bond. I Anne Williams of York Hampton Parish, York Co am firmly bound unto Robert Roberts of same place for £24 ... the condition of this obligation is such that if the afsd Anne Williams shall well & truly observe, perform, fullfill, accomplish & keep all the covenants, grants, articles, clauses & agreements mentioned in one pair of indentures of lease & release [*see above*] then this obligation to be void ... . Wit: Wil Toplis. Ackn 20 Nov 1727 & admitted to record. Attest: Phi Lightfoot clerk. (Pg 478)

12 Jan MDCCXXVII. Deed of Lease. Vinkler Cobbs & John Cobbs executors of the will of Robert Cobbs Senr late of York Co decd for 5 shillings leased unto Matthew Pierce of York Co gent the plantation & all the land thereunto belonging which was the plantation & land of the sd Robert Cobbs at the time of his decease & by his sd testament ordered to be sold the same containing 55 a. bounded by the Mill Dam of John Custis esqr, the widow Gibbons Spring Br & the line dividing this land from a dividend which the sd Pierce purch of the sd Cobbs in his lifetime ...during the term of one year paying the rent of one pepper corn at the feast of Christmas next if demanded ... . Wit: Wil Toplis, Peter Condray, Thos Dickson. Ackn 15 Jan 1727 & admitted to record. Attest: Phi Lightfoot clerk. (Pg 478)

13 Jan MDCCXXVII. Deed of Release. Vinkler Cobbs & John Cobbs executors of the will of Robert Cobbs Senr late of York Co decd for £35 released unto Matthew Pierce of York Co gent a plantation & 55 a. tr of land ... [*same as above*] ... . Wit: Thos Dickson, Wil Toplis, Peter Candray. Ackn 15 Jan 1727 & admitted to record. Attest: Phi Lightfoot clerk. (Pg 479)

19 May MDCCXXVIII. Deed of Lease. John Edmunds of Norfolk Co for 5 shillings leased unto Thomas Charles of Warwick Co all that messuage & 112 ½ a. tr of land in York Hampton Parish bounded by John Clarkson & the Poplar Br upon Cheesman's Cr, which sd 112 ½ a. is pt/o 225 a. of land formerly belonging to Thomas Illes & by the sd Thomas Illes will left unto his two daus Katherine & Elizabeth which John Edmunds is son of the sd Katharine Illes afterwards Katherine Edmunds ... for the term of one year ... . Wit: Peter Goodwin, John Goodwin, Anne Goodwin, Richd Bellamee. Ackn 20 May 1728 & admitted to record. Attest: Phi Lightfoot clerk. (Pg 480)

20 May MDCCXXVIII. Deed of Release. John Edmunds of Norfolk Co for
£83 released unto Thomas Charles of Warwick Co all that messuage & 112 ½ a.
tr of land in York Hampton Parish ... [same as above] .... Wit: Peter
Goodwin, John Goodwin, Anne Goodwin, Richd Bellamee. Ackn 20 May 1728
& admitted to record. Attest: Phi Lightfoot clerk. (Pg 481)

11 Jun 1728. Deed of Lease. Christopher DeGraffenried of York Co gent &
Barbara his wife for 5 shillings leased unto John White of the City of
Williamsburgh glazier all that lot of ground on the n side of the Main Street in
the sd City of Williamsburgh & denoted in the tenure & occupation of Joanna
Archer widow & also the dwelling house & outhouses on the sd lott of ground
(excepting out of the sd lott a parcel on the n end thereof to measure 30' on the
length of the lott & of the whole breadth thereof which was heretofore reserved
to Samuel Hyde who formerly possed the same lott) ... for the term of 6 months
paying the rent of one grain of Indian corn on 10 Oct next if demanded .... Wit:
Arch Blair, Wm Comrie, Ban Disbrow. Ackn 17 Jun 1728 by Christopher
DeGraffenriedt & Barbaray his wife & the sd Barbara being privately examin'd
relinquished her right of dower & admitted to record. Attest: Phi Lightfoot
clerk. (Pg 483)

12 Jun 1728. Deed of Release. Christopher DeGraffenried of York Co gent &
Barbara his wife for £115 released unto John White of the City of
Williamsburgh glazier all that lot of ground on the n side of the Main Street in
the sd City of Williamsburgh & denoted in the plan of the sd city by the figure
47 ... [same as above] .... Wit: Arch Blair, Wm Comrie, Ban Disbrow. Ackn
17 Jun 1728 by Christopher DeGraffenriedt & Barbara his wife & the sd Barbara
being privately examin'd relinquished her right of dower & admitted to record.
Attest: Phi Lightfoot clerk. (Pg 483)

15 Jun 1728. Deed of Lease. Samuel Makintosh of Denbe Parish, Warwick Co
planter for 5 shillings leased unto Thomas Roberts of Charles Parish, York Co
planter all that 50 a. tr of land in Charles Parish on the s side of Charles River
adj the land of the sd Thos Roberts ... for the term of one year .... Wit: Plany
Ward, John Hay, Robt Brown. Ackn 15 Jul 1728 by Samll Makintosh & also
appeared Martha w/o the sd Samuel & being privately examined relinquished
her right of dower & admitted to record. Attest: Phi Lightfoot clerk. (Pg 485)

16 Jun 1728. Deed of Release. Samuel Makintosh of Denbe Parish, Warwick
Co planter for £10 released unto Thomas Roberts of Charles Parish, York Co
planter all that 50 a. tr of land in Charles Parish ... [same as above] .... Wit:
Plany Ward, John Hay, Robt Brown. Ackn 15 Jul 1728 by Samll Makintosh &
also appeared Martha w/o the sd Samuel & being privately examined

relinquished her right of dower & admitted to record. Attest: Phi Lightfoot clerk. (Pg 485)

15 Jun 1728. Bond. I Samuel Makintosh of Denby Parish, Warwick Co planter am firmly bound unto Thomas Roberts of Charles Parish, York Co planter for £20 ... the condition of this obligation is such that if the afsd Samuel Makintosh shall well & truly observe, perform, fullfill & keep all the clauses, articles, covenants, grants & agreements mentioned in one indenture of release [*see above*] then this obligation to be void ... . Wit: Plany Ward, John Hay, Robt Brown. Ackn 15 Jul 1728 & admitted to record. Attest: Phi Lightfoot clerk. (Pg 487)

5 Aug 1724. Deed of Mortgage. Edmd Sweeny of Charles Parish, York Co planter for £157:14 sold to Thomas Nelson of York Co merchant two trs of land in Charles Parish one bought of John Northern & Elizabeth his wife containing 100 a. of land as will appear by a release dated 13 Nov 1709 & ackn in York Court 24th the same, the other bought of John Welsh & Elizabeth his wife containing 125 a. of land as will appear by their deed of release dated 17 Jun 1720 & ackn in York Co Court 20 Jun 1720 ... provided that if the sd Edmund Sweeny do or shall well & truly satisfie & pay unto the sd Thos Nelson the full sum of £157:14 at the now dwelling house of the sd Thomas Nelson in the Town of York together with intrest for the same on 5 Aug 1728 then this present indenture shall cease & be voide ... . Wit: Hen Bowcock, James Simons, John Ballard, John Thurston. Proved 18 Nov 1728 & admitted to record. Attest: Phi Lightfoot clerk. (Pg 487)

1 Nov 1728. Deed of Lease. Joseph Wade of James City Co planter & Susanna his wife for 5 shillings leased unto Robert Carter of Lancaster Co esqr a tr of land at Skiminoe which was devised to the sd Joseph Wade by his father Thomas Wade by his will dated 21 Jul 1716 in these words, viz, I give unto my son Joseph Wade 170 a. of land being in York Co at Skiminoe adj the Spring Br, it is called 170 a. more or less is by general estimation supposed to contain about 200 a. & is pt/o a 365 a. tr of land formerly conveyed by Mathew Hubbard & Ellen Huberd by deed of feofment dated 18 Dec 1689 ... for the term of one year paying the rent of one pepper corn upon the feast day of St. Michael the Arch Angel now nest coming if demanded ... . Wit: John Clayton, Samll Cobbs, Lewis Holland, Arthur Dickison, Edwd Ripping, Joseph Davenport. Ackn 18 Nov 1728 by Joseph Wade & Susanna his wife & the sd Susanna being privately examined relinquished her right of dower & admitted to record. Attest: Phi Lightfoot clerk. (Pg 489)

2 Nov 1728. Deed of Lease. Joseph Wade of James City Co planter & Susanna his wife for £120 released unto Robert Carter of Lancaster Co esqr a tr of land at

Skiminoe ... [*same as above*] ... . Wit: John Clayton, Samll Cobbs, Lewis Holland, Arthur Dickison, Edwd Ripping, Joseph Davenport. Ackn 18 Nov 1728 by Joseph Wade & Susanna his wife & the sd Susanna being privately examined relinquished her right of dower & admitted to record. Attest: Phi Lightfoot clerk. (Pg 490)

2 Nov MDCCXXVIII. Bond. Wee Joseph Wade of James City Co planter & Susanna my wife are firmly bound unto Robert Carter of Lancaster Co esqr for £240 ... the condition of this obligation is such that if the afsd Joseph Wade & Susanna his wife shall well & truly observe, perform, fulfill & keep all the covenants, grants, articles, clauses & agreements mentioned in one indenture of release [*see above*] then this obligation to be void ... . Wit: John Clayton, Samll Cobbs, Lewis Holland, Arthur Dickison, Edwd Ripping, Joseph Davenport. Ackn 18 Nov 1728 by Joseph Wade & Susanna his wife & admitted to record. Attest: Phi Lightfoot clerk. (Pg 492)

9 Aug 1728. Deed of Lease. John Clayton & Wm Robertson feofees or trustees for the land appropriated for the building & erecting the City of Williamsburgh for 5 shillings leased unto Hannah Shields of York Co widow one lott of ground in the sd City of Williamsburgh designed in the plot of the sd city by the figure 322 ... for the term of one year paying the yearly rent of one grain of Indian corn on 10 Oct if demanded ... . Wit: None. Ackn 18 Nov 1728 & admitted to record. Attest: Phi Lightfoot clerk. (Pg 493)

10 Aug 1728. Deed of Release. John Clayton & Wm Robertson feofees or trustees for the land appropriated for the building & erecting the City of Williamsburgh for 15 shillings released unto Hannah Shields of York Co widow one lott of ground in the sd City of Williamsburgh designed in the plot of the sd city by the figure 322 ... if the sd Hannah Shields shall not within the space of 24 months build & finish upon each lott one good dwelling house then it shall & may be lawfull to & for the sd feofees or trustees into the granted premises & every part thereof to enter & the same to have again as of their former estate to have, hold & enjoy in like manner as they might otherwise have done if these presents had never been made ... . Wit: None. Ackn 18 Nov 1728 & admitted to record. Attest: Phi Lightfoot clerk. (Pg 493)

15 Nov 1728. Deed of Lease. William Toplis & Lucy his wife of York Co for 5 shillings leased unto Thomas Carry Junr of Warwick Co all that 72 a. tr of land at a place called the Essex Lodge adj Robert Phillipson ... for the term of one year paying the yearly rent of one ear of Indian corn on the last day of the sd year if demanded ... . Wit: Edmund Smith, Matt Lanston, William Harwood. Ackn 18 Nov 1728 by William Toplis & Lucy his wife & the sd Lucy being

privately examined relinquished her right of dower & admitted to record. Attest: Phi Lightfoot clerk. (Pg 494)

16 Nov 1728. Deed of Release. William Toplis & Lucy his wife of York Co for £45:3:3 released unto Thomas Carry Junr of Warwick Co all that 72 a. tr of land at a place called the Essex Lodge ... [same as above] .... Wit: Edmd Smith, Matt Langston, Willm Harwood. Ackn 18 Nov 1728 by William Toplis & Lucy his wife & the sd Lucy being privately examined relinquished her right of dower & admitted to record. Attest: Phi Lightfoot clerk. (Pg 495)

13 Nov 1728. Deed of Lease. Susanna Barbar widow executrix of the will of Thomas Barbar late of York Co decd for 5 shillings leased unto Elizabeth Russell (Russel) of York Co widdow two lotts of ground on the e side of Pallace Street in the City of Wmsburgh next adjacent to the Governours house & are numbered in the plan of the sd city by the figures 165 & 166 being the lotts lately held & possessed by John Brush (father of the sd Susanna) decd & by him the sd John Brush by his will devised in fee equally to & between the sd Thomas Barbar & Elizabeth Brush which the sd Elizabeth Brush hath since sold her ½ thereof unto the sd Thomas Barbar in fee ... for the term of one year paying the rent of one pepper corn upon the feast day of St. Michael the Arch Angel now next coming if demanded .... Wit: Margaret Fry, Richard Booker, Joseph Davenport. Ackn 18 Nov 1728 & admitted to record. Attest: Phi Lightfoot clerk. (Pg 496)

14 Nov 1728. Deed of Release. Susanna Barbar widow executrix of the will of Thomas Barber late of York Co decd for £100 released unto Elizabeth Russell (Russel) of York Co widdow two lotts of ground on the e side of Pallace Street in the City of Wmsburgh ... [same as above] .... Wit: Margaret Fry, Richard Booker, Joseph Davenport. Ackn 18 Nov 1728 & admitted to record. Attest: Phi Lightfoot clerk. (Pg 497)

6 Dec 1728. Deed of Lease. Joseph Montfort of York Co for 5 shillings leased to William Stark of same co all that 25 a. tr of land being pt/o a tr of land purch by the sd Joseph Montfort of Messrs Perry &c & to the sd Joseph Montfort sold & conveyed by John Clayton esqr lawfull atty to the sd Messrs Perry bounded by a swamp a little to the w of the Lodge Bridge, sd Joseph Montfort's land, land of John Read, land of Thomas Vines of York Co & the Mill Pond ... during the term of one year paying the rent of one ear of Indian corn at the feast of St. Michael if demanded .... Wit: Robt Phillipson, Mathew Wills, Ishmael Moody. Ackn 16 Dec 1728 by Joseph Mountfort & also appeared Rose w/o the sd Joseph & being privately examined relinquished her right of dower & admitted to record. Attest: Phi Lightfoot clerk. (Pg 499)

7 Dec 1728. Deed of Release. Joseph Montfort of York Co for £23 released to William Stark of same co all that 25 a. tr of land ... [*same as above*] ... . Wit: Robt Phillipson, Mathew Wills, Ishmael Moody. Ackn 16 Dec 1728 by Joseph Mountfort & also appeared Rose w/o the sd Joseph & being privately examined relinquished her right of dower & admitted to record. Attest: Phi Lightfoot clerk. (Pg 499)

7 Dec 1728. Bond. I Joseph Mountfort of York Co am firmly bound unto William Stark of co afsd for £40 ... the condition of this obligation is such that if the afsd Joseph Mountfort shall well & truly observe, perform, fulfill, accomplish & keep the covenants, grants, articles, clauses & agreements mentioned in one pair of indentures of lease & release [*see above*] then this obligation to be void ... . Wit: Robt Phillipson, Matthew Wills, Ishmael Moody. Ackn 16 Dec 1728 & admitted to record. Attest: Phi Lightfoot clerk. (Pg 501)

7 Jan 1728. Deed. Between John White of the City of Williamsburgh glazier & Margaret his wife of the one part & Richard Packe of same city watchmaker of the other part, whereas the sd John White & Margaret his wife by one indenture of sale dated 17 Jun ---- made between the sd John White of the City of Williamsburgh glazier & Margaret his wife of the one part & John Holloway of same city esqr of the other part for £115 did sell & farm lett unto the sd John Holloway all that lott of ground on the n side of the Main Street in the sd City of Williamsburgh denoted in the plan of the sd city by the figure 47 adj to the lott now in the tenure & occupation of Mrs. Johanna Archer widow & also the dwelling house & outhouses to the sd lott of ground appertaining excepting out of the sd lott a parcel on the n end thereof to measure 30' on the length of the lott & of the whole breath thereof which dividend was heretofore reserved to Samuel Hyde who formerly possessed the sd lott for the term of 500 years, & whereas the sd John Holloway by his assignment dated 15th this present Jan sold & made over unto the sd Richard Packe all the remainder of the sd term of years yet to come unto the sd premises ... now this indenture wit that the sd John White & Margaret his wife for £120 have sold unto the sd Richard Packe all the above specified lott of ground according to the description thereof above set down together with the dwelling house & outhouses ... . Wit: Wm Broadribb, Thomas Claibourne, Joseph Davenport. Ackn 20 Jan 1728 by John White & Margaret his wife & the sd Margaret being privately examined relinquished her right of dower & admitted to record. Attest: Phi Lightfoot clerk. (Pg 501)

20 Jan MDCCXXVIII. Deed. Wilson Cary of Elizabeth City Co gent for £40 sold to Robert Ballard of York Co carpenter all that lott or ½ a. of land being pt/o the land purch & appropriated for the Town & Port of York & described & denoted in the plan of the sd town & port by the figure 13 in the sd Town of

York formerly sold by Thomas Boucher unto Miles Cary of Warwick Co gent father of the sd Wilson Cary by a deed of sale dated XXIII Dec MDCCI ... & more especially of & from the right & title of dower of Mary late relict of the afsd Miles Cary gent decd father of the sd Wilson Cary & of the right & title of dower of Sarah now the w/o the sd Wilson Cary if she should happen to survive him ... . Wit: None. Ackn 20 Jan 1728 by Wilson Cary gent also appeared Sarah w/o the sd Wilson & being privately examined relinquished her right of dower & admitted to record. Attest: Phi Lightfoot clerk. (Pg 503)

20 Jan 1728. Bond. I Wilson Cary of Elizabeth City Co am firmly bound unto Robert Ballard of York Co carpenter for £80 ... the condition of this obligation is such that if the afsd Wilson Cary shall well & truly observe, fulfill, perform & keep all the covenants, articles, clauses & agreements mention in one indenture of sale [see above] then this obligation to be void ... . Wit: None. Ackn 20 Jan 1728 & admitted to record. Attest: Phi Lightfoot clerk. (Pg 504)

20 Jan MDCCXXIII. Deed. Wilson Cary of Elizabeth City Co gent for £100 sold to William Nelson of York Co merchant two lotts or ½ acres of land being pt/o the land purch & appropriated for the Town & Port of York & denoted in the plan of the sd town & port by the figures 12 & 18 lying in the sd Town of York formerly sold & conveyed by the trustees of the sd town land unto Miles Cary of Warwick Co gent father of the sd Wilson Cary by two deeds of sale each dated 4 May ---- ... & more especially of & from the right & title of dower of Mary late relict of the afsd Miles Cary gent decd father of the sd Wilson Cary & of the right & title of dower of Sarah now the w/o the sd Wilson Cary if she shall happen to survive him ... . Wit: None. Ackn 20 Jan 1728 by Wilson Cary gent also appeared Sarah w/o the sd Wilson & being privately examined relinquished her right of dower & admitted to record. Attest: Phi Lightfoot clerk. (Pg 505)

20 Jan 1728. Bond. I Wilson Cary of Elizabeth City Co am firmly bound unto William Nelson of York Co merchant for £200 ... the condition of this obligation is such that if the afsd Wilson Cary shall well & truly observe, fulfill, perform & keep all the covenants, articles, clauses & agreements mention in one indenture of sale [see above] then this obligation to be void ... . Wit: None. Ackn 20 Jan 1728 & admitted to record. Attest: Phi Lightfoot clerk. (Pg 506)

14 Feb 1728. Deed of Lease. Edward Doswell of York Co for 5 shillings leased unto Daniel Moore of York Co a 27 a. tr of land being the sd Edward Doswell's purparty of 109 a. now in the occupation of the sd Danll Moore in the narrows of Old Poquoson River in Charles Parish it being formerly the inheritance of Booth Nutting of parish afsd & descended from the sd Booth Nutting to Elizabeth Doswell sister & coheir of the sd Booth Nutting decd & is the sd Edward Doswell's as son & heir to the sd Elizabeth Doswell decd ... for the term of one

year paying the rent of one grain of Indian corn at the feast of St. Michael the Arch Angel if demanded .... Wit: William Robinson, Jones Irwin. Ackn 17 Feb 1728 & admitted to record. Attest: Phi Lightfoot clerk. (Pg 506)

15 Feb 1728. Deed of Release. Edward Doswell of York Co for £11 released unto Daniel Moore of York Co a 27 a. tr of land ... [same as above] .... Wit: William Robinson, Jones Irwin. Wit to receipt: Jones Irwin, Edward Wright. Ackn 17 Feb 1728 & admitted to record. Attest: Phi Lightfoot clerk. (Pg 507)

14 Feb 1728. Deeds of Lease and release. Agnes Sclater of York Co for 5 shillings leased to Daniel Moore of same co an 85 a. parcel of land being the sd Agnes Sclaughter's purparty of 327 a. of land on the narrows of Old Poquoson in Charles Parish late the inheritance of Richd Sclater decd & descended to her the sd Agnes Sclaughter as one of the daus & coheirs of the sd Richard Sclaughter ... for the term of one year paying the rent of one grain of Indian corn at the feast of St. Michael the Arch Angel if demanded .... Wit: James Dixon, Benit Tompkins. Ackn 17 Feb 1728 & admitted to record. Attest: Phi Lightfoot clerk. (Pg 508, 9)

15 Feb MDCCXXVIII. Deed of Lease. Agnes Sclater of York Co for £80 released to Daniel Moore of same co an 85 a. parcel of land ... [same as above] .... Wit: James Dixon, Benit Tompkins. Ackn 17 Feb 1728 & admitted to record. Attest: Phi Lightfoot clerk. (Pg 509)

13 Mar MDCCXXVIII. Deed of Lease. John Lowry & Jane his wife of Elizabeth City Co, VA for 5 shillings leased to Daniel Moore of York Co a 27 a. parcel of land being the sd John Lowry & Jeane his wife's purparty of 109 a. now in the occupation of the sd Daniel Moore lying on the narrows of Old Poquoson River in Charles Parish it being formerly the inheritance of Booth Nutting of sd parish & descending from the sd Booth Nutting to the sd Jane Lowry now the w/o John Lowry afsd which sd Jane Lowry is sister & coheir to the sd Booth Nutting decd ... during the term of one year paying the rent of one grain of Indian corn at the feast of St. Michael the Arch Angel if demanded .... Wit: John King, Robt Armistead, Samll Smith. Ackn 17 Mar 1728 by John Loury & Jane his wife & the sd Jane being first privately examined relinquished her right of dower & admitted to record. Attest: Phi Lightfoot clerk. (Pg 510)

14 Mar MDCCXXIII. Deed of Release. John Lowry & Jane his wife of Elizabeth City Co, VA for £15 released to Daniel Moore of York Co a 27 a. parcel of land ... [same as above] .... Wit: John King, Robt Armistead, Samll Smith. Ackn 17 Mar 1728 by John Loury & Jane his wife & the sd Jane being first privately examined relinquished her right of dower & admitted to record. Attest: Phi Lightfoot clerk. (Pg 511)

17 Dec 1728. Deed. Samuel Cobbs of the City of Williamsburgh, York Co merchant & Edith his wife for £8 sold to Martha Drewit of same co widow all that lot or parcell of land being at Queen Marys Port designed in the plott of the sd Port by the figure 7 now in the occupation of the sd Martha Drewit & adj to the back pt/o a lott late of Jonathan Deuit now in the possession of the sd Martha Dreuit called The Swan ... which sd lot & premises by indentures of lease & release dated 7 & 8 Oct MDCCIV were by the feofees or trustees for the land appropriated for the building & erecting the City of Williamsburgh granted to Francis Sharp of York Co & by the sd Sharp conveyed to the sd Samuel Cobbs & his heirs ... . Wit: Matt Pierce, Lewis Holland, Jno Francis. Ackn 17 Mar 1728 by Samuel Cobbs & Edith his wife & the sd Edith being privately examined relinquished her right of dower & admitted to record. Attest: Phi Lightfoot clerk. (Pg 512)

12 Feb MDCCXX8. Deed. Between Elizabeth Page of Saint Giles Parish in the fields in Middlesex Co, Great Brittain spinster & Mann Page of Rosewell in Gloster Co, VA esqr of the one part & John Clayton of Williamsburgh, VA esqr on the other part, whereas the sd Elizabeth Page by a certain writing or Letter of Atty under her hand dated 5 Dec MDCCXXVII amongst other things did authorize the sd Mann Page for the use of the sd Elizabeth Page to sell all that tr of land in or near Williamsburgh afsd containing200 a., now this indenture wit that for £280 to the sd Elizabeth Page by the sd John Clayton well & truly paid the sd Elizabeth Page doth release & discharge the sd John Clayton & by these presents by her sd atty hath sold unto the sd John Clayton all that tr of land near Williamsburgh afsd in Bruton Parish containing 200 a. being the tr of land formerly purch by John Page gent decd late father of the sd Elizabeth Page from Mary Whaley late of Williamsburgh widow ... . Wit: None. Ackn 19 May 1729 by Mann Page esqr atty of Elizabeth Page & admitted to record. Attest: Phi Lightfoot clerk. (Pg 513)

16 May 1729. Deed of Lease and release. Daniel Moore & Elizabeth his wife of York Co for 5 shillings leased to Edward Tabb of York Co an 85 a. tr of land being the sd Daniel Moore & Elizabeth his wife purparty of 327 a. now in the occupation of the sd Danl Moore being on the narrows of Old Poquoson River in Charles Parish it being formerly the inheritance of Booth Nutting of sd parish & descending from the sd Booth Nutting to Mary Slater sister & coheir to the sd Booth Nutting decd & so descending to Elizabeth Moore w/o the sd Daniel Moore & dau of the sd Mary Sclater decd ... for the term of one year paying the rent of one grain of Indian corn at the feast of St. Michael the Arch Angel if demanded ... . Wit: R. Hurst, Edwd Wright. Ackn 19 May 1729 by Daniel Moore & Elizabeth his wife & the sd Elizabeth being privately examined relinquished her right of dower & admitted to record. Attest: Phi Lightfoot clerk. {YCDB 515}

16 May MDCCXXIX. Deed of Release. Daniel Moore & Elizabeth his wife of York Co for £90 released to Edward Tabb of York Co an 85 a. tr of land ... [*same as above*] ... . Wit: R. Hurst, Edwd Wright. Ackn 19 May 1729 by Daniel Moore & Elizabeth his wife & the sd Elizabeth being privately examined relinquished her right of dower & admitted to record. Attest: Phi Lightfoot clerk. (Pg 516)

13 Jun MDCCXXIX. Deed of Lease. Robert Armisted & Katherine (Catherin) his wife of York Co for 5 shillings leased to Daniel Moore of York Co a 27 a. parcel of land being the sd Robt Armistead & Katherine his wife purparty of 109 a. of land now in the occupation of the sd Daniel Moore on the narrows of Old Poquoson River in Charles Parish it being formerly the inheritance of Booth Nutting of the sd parish & descending from the sd Booth Nutting to the sd Katherine Armistead now the w/o Robt Armistead which sd Katherine is sister & coheir to the sd Booth Nutting decd ... for the term of one year paying the rent of one grain of Indian corn at the feast of St. Michael the Arch Angel if demanded ... . Wit: Edwd Wright, Adduston Rogers. Ackn 16 Jun 1729 by Robert Armistead & Katherine his wife & the sd Katherine being privately examined relinquished her right of dower & admitted to record. Attest: Phi Lightfoot clerk. (Pg 517)

14 Jun MDCCXXIX. Deed of Release. Robert Armisted & Katherine (Catherin) his wife of York Co for £20 released to Daniel Moore of York Co a 27 a. parcel of land ... [*same as above*] ... . Wit: Edwd Wright, Adduston Rogers. Ackn 16 Jun 1729 by Robert Armistead & Katherine his wife & the sd Katherine being privately examined relinquished her right of dower & admitted to record. Attest: Phi Lightfoot clerk. (Pg 517)

9 Jun MDCCXXIX. Deed of Lease. John Morris of York Co carpenter for 5 shillings leased to John Smith of York Co planter a parcel of land in Bruton Parish on the n side of Queens Cr which James Morrice purch of James Bates in MDCC14 except that part thereof which the sd James Morrice devised to his son James Morrice ...for the term of one year paying the yearly rent of one pepper corn on the last day of the sd year if demanded ... . Wit: Richd Hickman, John Franncies, Gray Skipwith. Ackn 16 Jun 1729 & admitted to record. Attest: Phi Lightfoot clerk. (Pg 518)

10 Jun MDCCXXIX. Deed of Release. John Morris of York Co carpenter for £40 released to John Smith of York Co planter a parcel of land in Bruton Parish on the n side of Queens Cr ... [*same as above*] ... . Wit: Richd Hickman, John Franncies, Gray Skipwith. Ackn 16 Jun 1729 & admitted to record. Attest: Phi Lightfoot clerk. (Pg 519)

9 Jun MDCCXXIX. Deed of Lease. John Smith of York Co planter for 5 shillings leased to Lewis Davis of same co carpenter all that tr of land in Bruton Parish on the n side of Queens Cr which James Morris purch of James Bates in MDCCXIV except that part thereof which the sd James Morris devised to his son James Morris ... during the term of one year paying the yearly rent of one pepper corn on the last day of the sd year only if demanded ... . Wit: R. Hickman, Jno Franncies, Gray Skipwith. Ackn 16 Jun 1729 & admitted to record. Attest: Phi Lightfoot clerk. (Pg 521)

10 Jun MDCCXXIX. Deed of Release. John Smith of York Co planter for £40 released to Lewis Davis of same co carpenter all that tr of land in Bruton Parish ... [same as above] ... . Wit: R. Hickman, Jno Franncies, Gray Skipwith. Ackn 16 Jun 1729 by John Smith & Ann his wife & the sd Ann being privately examined relinquished her right of dower & admitted to record. Attest: Phi Lightfoot clerk. (Pg 521)

4 Jul 1729. Deed of Lease. Mary Lutwidge widow of York Hampton Parish, York Co for 5 shillings leased to Abraham Archer of same place one storehouse or warehouse in York Town upon the bank or shoar of York River abutting on the sd river, upon the storehouse of Thomas Nelson gent & upon the storehouse of Cole Digges esqr ... for the term of one year ... . Wit: Robt Wills, John Trotter, Rd Hurst. Ackn 21 Jul 1729 & admitted to record. Attest: Phi Lightfoot clerk. (Pg 523)

5 Jul 1729. Deed of Release. Mary Lutwidge widow of York Hampton Parish, York Co for £40 released to Abraham Archer of same place one storehouse or warehouse in York Town upon the bank or shoar of York River ... [same as above] ... . Wit: R. Wills, John Trotter, Rd. Hurst. Ackn 21 Jul 1729 & admitted to record. Attest: Phi Lightfoot clerk. (Pg 523)

5 Jul 1729. Bond. I Mary Lutwidge of York Hampton Parish, York Co am firmly bound unto Abraham Archer of same place for £500 ... the condition of this obligation is such that if the afsd Mary Lutwidge shall well & truly observe, perform, fulfill, accomplish & keep all the covenants, grants, articles, clauses, provisos & agreements mentioned in one indenture of release [see above] then this obligation to be void ... . Wit: Robt Wills, Jno Trotter, Richd Hurst. Ackn 21 Jul 1729 & admitted to record. Attest: Phi Lightfoot clerk. (Pg 525)

15 Aug 1729. Deed of Lease. John Clayton of Williamsburgh, VA esqr for 5 shillings leased to Mann Page of Rosewell, Gloster Co, VA esqr all that 200 a. tr of land being near Williamsburgh in Bruton Parish being the tr of land formerly purch by John Page gent decd late father of Elizabeth Page of St. Giels Parish in the fields in Midlesex Co in the Kingdom of Great Britain spinster from Mary

Whaley late of Williamsburgh afsd widdow & by the sd Elizabeth Page & Mann Page as her atty lately conveyed to the sd John Clayton ...for the term of one year paying the yearly rent of one grain of Indian corn at the end of the sd term if demanded .... Wit: None. Ackn 18 Aug 1729 & admitted to record. Attest: Phi Lightfoot clerk. (Pg 525)

16 Aug 1729. Deed of Release. John Clayton of Williamsburgh, VA esqr sold to Mann Page of Rosewell, Gloster Co, VA esqr all that 200 a. tr of land ... [same as above] ... wit that the sd John Clayton doth hereby ackn that his name was used in the sd conveyance by the special nomination & appointment of the sd Mann Page & in trust for him & that the sd £280 paid unto the sd Elizabeth Page for the purch of the sd land & premises were the proper monys of the sd Mann Page & therefore in pursuance of the trust in him the sd John Clayton reposed by the sd Mann Page he hath released & confirmed unto the sd Mann Page the sd tr of land & premises .... Wit: None. Ackn 18 Aug 1729 & admitted to record. (Pg 526)

16 Jun 1729. Deed. Adduston Rogers & Katherine his wife of York Co for £30 sold to Edward Moss planter of the co afsd all their right & title to a piece of land being all the parcel of land that came to the sd Catherine by right of dower by her former husband John Moss lying on the head of Chismans Cr .... Wit: Robt Armistead, Wm Gordon. Ackn 15 Sep 1729 by Adduston Rogers & Catherine his wife (she being first privately examined) & admitted to record. Attest: Phi Lightfoot clerk. (Pg 527)

13 Sep MDCCXXIX. Deed. John James Flournoy of the City of Wmsburgh watchmaker for £160 sold to Joanna Archer of Williamsburgh afsd widow all that messuage or dwelling house wherein the sd John James Flournoy now dwelleth on the s side of Duke of Gloster Street in Williamsburgh & also two lotts of land on which or one of them the sd messuage now standeth & which are described in the plan of the sd city by the figures 16 & 17 & all the houses & outhouses .... Wit: None. Ackn 15 Sep 1729 by John James Flournoy & also appeared Mary w/o the sd John & being first privately examined relinquished her right of dower & admitted to record. Attest: Phi Lightfoot clerk. (Pg 528)

CASE, William, 114
CAUSBY, James, 94
CHAPMAN, Elizabeth, 65; John, 32, 33, 55, 56, 64, 65, 85, 113
CHARLES, Thomas, 116, 117
CHARLES CITY COUNTY, 4, 5, 99
CHARLES PARISH, 1, 3, 4, 7, 9, 10, 14, 17, 18, 19, 23, 26, 27, 28, 31, 32, 36, 37, 44, 45, 54, 55, 59, 60, 64, 65, 72, 75, 76, 77, 78, 79, 84, 85, 90, 91, 92, 95, 96, 102, 103, 104, 105, 106, 109, 117, 118, 122, 123, 124, 125
CHARLES RIVER, 23, 117
CHEESEMANS CREEK, 113
CHEESMAN'S CREEK, 116
CHERMESON, Elizabeth, 2; Joseph, 2
CHERRY ORCHARDS, 16
CHESEAPEAKE BAY, 50
CHESHIRE, Mr., 80; Richard, 51, 56, 107
CHISMAN, Anne, 105; Captain, 1, 7; Edmund, 104; John, 3, 17; Thomas, 17, 55, 56, 75, 91, 105
CHISMAN'S CREEK, 32
CHISMANS CREEK, 55, 127
CHISMANS MILL, 90
CLAIBOURNE, Thomas, 121
CLARK, Elizabeth, 77, 96; Francis, 27; John, 1, 7, 77, 96; Mary, 96; Nicholas, 77, 96; Robert, 21
CLARKE, John, 15, 24
CLARKSON, John, 116
CLATHORP, James, 85
CLAYTON, John, 1, 3, 4, 5, 7, 8, 13, 14, 16, 21, 22, 26, 29, 30, 31, 34, 35, 38, 39, 42, 43, 46, 47, 49, 52, 53, 56, 57, 61, 62, 66, 67, 68, 69, 72, 73, 74, 75, 77, 82, 83, 89, 92, 93, 95, 96, 97, 99, 107, 108, 114, 118, 119, 120, 124, 126, 127

CLIFF, Richard, 72
CLIFTON, Benjamin, 31, 32, 45, 54, 58, 59, 69, 70, 72, 78, 79, 92, 93, 94; Sarah, 70
COBBS, Ambrose, 56, 62; Edith, 68, 124; Edmund, 101; John, 116; Robert, 62, 86, 110, 116; Samuel, 34, 35, 61, 62, 68, 81, 82, 95, 112, 124; Samuell, 118, 119; Thomas, 110, 111; Vinkler, 116
COLACE, Thomas, 62
COLE, William, 76
COLEUE, Thomas, 62, 63
COLLIER, Isaac, 110
COMAN, John, 6; William, 6
COMRIE, William, 117
CONDON, David, 3, 24, 33
CONDRAY, Peter, 116
CONTESSE, Lewis, 76
COOK, John, 4, 6, 7, 12, 13; Mary, 13
COOKE, John, 4; Richard, 48
COOPER, Ann, 67; Elizabeth, 32; Isle, 33; Isles, 32; Lewis, 35; Samuel, 32, 33, 35, 51, 67; Sarah, 35
CORBIN, Gawin, 80; Thomas, 110
CORLEY, Edward, 55
CORRATUCK PRECINCT, 45
COSBY, Widow, 15
COURT HOUSE, 6, 12
COW PATH, 33
COX, Charles, 3, 18, 19, 31, 90, 110; Thomas, 113
COZBY, Charles, 29
CRAIG, William, 72

RAY, Chrismas, 32, 78; Sarah, 78;
   Thomas, 32, 59, 78, 84
READ, Benjamin, 24, 25; Elizabeth,
   24; George, 24; John, 32, 55, 120
READE, Benjamin, 24, 25; Francis,
   24; Robert, 24; Thomas, 41, 42
REDDALL, George, 46
REDWOOD, John, 66
REEDY SWAMP, 101
REY, John Guy, 5
RHODES, John, 94
RICE, John, 86
RICHARDSON, William, 71
RING, Joseph, 45, 46, 51, 52; Mr., 29
RIPPING, Edward, 53, 54, 57, 63,
   118, 119
ROBERTS, Gerard, 54, 55; John, 65;
   Mr., 33; Robert, 94, 115, 116;
   Samuel, 36, 37; Thomas, 23, 32,
   36, 37, 44, 45, 117, 118
ROBERTSON, M., 73; William, 1, 4,
   5, 7, 8, 16, 21, 22, 23, 26, 30, 38,
   39, 42, 46, 47, 49, 52, 53, 57, 61,
   66, 67, 68, 69, 72, 73, 74, 75, 77,
   81, 82, 83, 89, 92, 93, 95, 96, 97,
   98, 99, 101, 104, 107, 108, 114,
   119
ROBINS CREEK, 4
ROBINSON, Anthony, 72; Frances,
   4; John, 4, 72, 76, 91; William,
   123
ROBISON, William, 107
ROCKAHOCK PATH, 10
ROGERS, Adduston, 3, 32, 113, 125,
   127; Catherine, 127; Jane, 15;
   John, 14, 15; John Adduston, 3,
   14, 15, 17, 113; John Addustun,
   88, 89; Katherine, 127; William,
   18, 71, 115
ROSCOW, James, 77
ROSEWELL, 124, 126, 127
ROUVIERE, Claude, 2

ROW, William, 23, 32
ROWAN, Charles, 84; Lidia, 84
RUSSEL, Elizabeth, 120
RUSSELL, Elizabeth, 120
ST. ANDREWS CREEK, 10
ST. GEORGE PARISH, 115
ST. GIELS PARISH, 126
SAINT GILES PARISH, 124
ST. JOHNS PARISH, 11
ST. LEGER, Abraham, 35; Mary, 35;
   Sarah, 35
SANDIFER, Elizabeth, 85; John, 85;
   Thomas, 85
SARJANTON, John, 5, 23; Winifred,
   5, 23
SCHOOL HOUSE, 25
SCIMINO MILL SWAMP, 100
SCIMSHAW, Elizabeth, 2
SCLATER, Agnes, 123; James, 9, 31,
   32, 70, 79, 106; John, 85; Mary,
   31, 32, 70; Richard, 15, 123
SCLAUGHTER, Agnes, 123;
   Richard, 123
SCOTT, Peter, 91
SEBRELL, Anthony, 6; Martha, 62,
   63, 88; Mary, 62; Nicholas, 6;
   Samuel, 62, 63, 88
SELDON, Samuel, 56
SHARP, Francis, 8, 11, 12, 28, 29,
   38, 39, 113, 124
SHARPE, Elizabeth, 112; Francis, 1,
   112
SHEILD, Mary, 106; Robert, 1, 7,
   106
SHEILDS, James, 113, 114
SHELDON, Daniel, 76; Gilbert, 76;
   William, 6, 7, 25, 27, 32, 56, 71
SHELTON, James, 4, 9, 10, 17
SHIELD, James, 28, 43; Robert, 78,
   90
SHIELDS, Hannah, 119; James, 42,
   43, 48, 57

TIMSON, Anna Marie, 43; Captain, 21; John, 39; Mary, 42; Samuel, 39, 42, 48; William, 26, 42, 43
TINDAL, George, 57
TINDALL, George, 57
TINSEY, Elinor, 99
TOBACCO RIDGE, 11
TOBACCO SWAMP, 11
TOMER, John, 1, 7, 9, 10; Thomas, 72
TOMKINS, Samuel, 54; Samuell, 55
TOMPKINS, Benit, 123; Bennit, 78; Samuell, 55
TONIERNOE, Giles, 54
TOPLADY, Isabell, 18
TOPLIS, Lucy, 119, 120; William, 98, 101, 102, 104, 105, 107, 108, 109, 112, 114, 115, 116, 119, 120
TOWN CREEK, 24
TOWNSEND, William, 34
TRINDALL, Edward, 107
TROTTER, John, 51, 65, 88, 89, 92, 126; William, 65, 85
TUNLEY, William, 20
TYLER, Francis, 2, 3, 22, 28, 38, 48, 49, 66, 67, 68, 77, 80, 85, 86; John, 42, 72, 73, 89, 90
TYLOE, Dixon, 113
ULYS CREEK, 94
UNDERHILL, Jane, 48; John, 34, 48
UNDERHILL'S LINE, 62
VAUDERY, Peter, 21
VENDOVERICK, Henry, 104
VINES, Thomas, 120
VIRGINIA, 14, 37, 43, 50, 59, 63, 96
WADE, Ann, 55; Armiger, 4, 76; Edward, 12, 13, 15, 16; Frances, 4; Joseph, 55, 118, 119; Susanna, 118, 119; Thomas, 14, 46, 55, 118; William, 55
WADES SPRING BRANCH, 55
WAGSTAFF, Basil, 40

WALKER, David, 100; Henry, 99; John, 76; Joseph, 13, 19, 45, 46, 48, 51, 52, 62, 64, 69, 70, 76, 88, 93, 94; Thomas, 114
WALLACE, James, 111
WALLINS, Robert, 113
WARBARTON, William, 9
WARD, Plany, 117, 118
WARDE, Thomas, 9
WARNER, Augustine, 41; Elizabeth, 41; Mary, 41; Mildred, 33, 41
WARWICK COUNTY, 6, 7, 12, 34, 36, 64, 75, 77, 79, 80, 86, 90, 91, 108, 109, 113, 116, 117, 118, 119, 120, 122
WARWICK COUNTY, VA, 76, 84, 107
WARWICK PARISH, 107, 114
WASHINGTON, John, 41, 42; Katherine, 41; Lawrence, 41; Mildred, 41
WELCH, Elizabeth, 26, 77, 78, 95, 96; John, 26, 59, 77, 78, 95, 96
WELDON, Benjamin, 28, 80; Samuel, 39, 42, 68; Sarah, 39, 42
WELSH, Elizabeth, 26, 27, 118; John, 26, 27, 118
WESTMORELAND COUNTY, 43
WESTON, Thomas, 33
WESTS CREEK, 13
WHALEY, Mary, 124, 127
WHARTON, Richard, 24, 43; William, 43
WHITE, Frances, 11; George, 107; John, 117, 121; Joseph, 11, 87; Margaret, 121; Ralph, 43
WHITE MARSH, 34
WHITE RIDGE, 79, 104, 105
WHITEHEAD, Thomas, 13
WILD, Daniel, 23
WILKINSON, James, 110, 111
WILLIAMBURGH, 113, 119

Spotsylvania County, Virginia Deed Books, 1722–1734

Spotsylvania County, Virginia Deed Books, 1734–1751

York County, Virginia Deeds, Orders, Wills, Etc., 1698–1700

York County, Virginia Deeds, Orders, Wills, Etc., 1700–1702

York County, Virginia Deeds, Orders, Wills, Etc., 1705–1706

York County, Virginia Deeds, Orders, Wills, Etc., 1714–1716

York County, Virginia Deeds, Orders, Wills, Etc., 1716–1718

York County, Virginia Deeds, Orders, Wills, Etc., 1718–1720

York County, Virginia Deeds, Orders, Wills, Etc., 1728–1732

York County, Virginia Land Records: 1694–1713

York County, Virginia Land Records:1713–1729

York County, Virginia Land Records: 1729–1763

York County, Virginia Land Records: 1763–1777

York County, Virginia Wills, Inventories and Court Orders, 1702–1704

York County, Virginia Wills, Inventories and Court Orders, 1732–1737

York County, Virginia Wills, Inventories and Court Orders, 1737–1740

York County, Virginia Wills, Inventories and Court Orders, 1740–1743

York County, Virginia Wills, Inventories and Court Orders, 1745–1759

www.ingramcontent.com/pod-product-compliance
Lightning Source LLC
Chambersburg PA
CBHW072152270326
41930CB00011B/2401